CONSTANCE MAYNARD'S PASSIONS

Religion, Sexuality, and an English Educational Pioneer, 1849–1935

STUDIES IN GENDER AND HISTORY

General Editors: Franca Iacovetta and Karen Dubinsky

Constance Maynard's Passions

Religion, Sexuality, and an English Educational Pioneer, 1849–1935

PAULINE A. PHIPPS

UNIVERSITY OF TORONTO PRESS
Toronto Buffalo London

Toronto Buffalo London
www.utppublishing.com

ISBN 978-1-4426-5033-6

Library and Archives Canada Cataloguing in Publication

Phipps, Pauline A., 1949–, author
Constance Maynard's passions : religion, sexuality, and an English educational pioneer, 1849–1935 / Pauline A. Phipps.

(Studies in gender and history)
Includes bibliographical references and index.
ISBN 978-1-4426-5033-6 (bound)

1. Maynard, Constance L. (Constance Louisa), 1849–1935. 2. Women educators – Great Britain – Biography. 3. Christian women – Great Britain – Biography. 4. Middle class women – Great Britain – Biography. 5. Women – Education (Higher) – Great Britain. I. Title. II. Series: Studies in gender and history

LA2375.G72P45 2015 370.92 C2015-902236-3

University of Toronto Press acknowledges the financial assistance to its publishing program of the Canada Council for the Arts and the Ontario Arts Council, an agency of the Government of Ontario.

Canada Council for the Arts Conseil des Arts du Canada

Funded by the Government of Canada Financé par le gouvernement du Canada Canada

Contents

Illustrations

Acknowledgments

This book is the product of my twenty-year journey through several institutional archives for the purpose of researching the life of the educational pioneer, Constance Louisa Maynard (1849–1935). Maynard is mostly known for her thirty-one years (1883–1913) as first Mistress of a unique Christian and degree-based college named Westfield (now Queen Mary University of London UK). Before this, however, Maynard was in 1875 among the first women to gain a Tripos from Girton College, Cambridge University; and Kate Perry at Girton College Archives introduced me to key college documents, including writings by pioneering Girton students. Less is known about Maynard's help in establishing (the later renowned) St. Leonards School for Girls in St. Andrews Scotland, in 1876; but archivist Angela Tawes, and former Deputy Head of St. Leonards, Jane Claydon, gave me unlimited access to precious archival photographs and handwritten documentation of St. Leonards early organization. Former archivist, Anselm Nye, and Honorary archivist and historian, Dr. Janet Sondheimer, first introduced me to the vast archival collection of Maynard's numerous publications and unpublished diaries, autobiography, journals, and correspondence at (what was then) Queen Mary and Westfield College, London. Dr. Sondheimer also took me to see the original Westfield College sites in Hampstead, London. In more recent years, Lorraine Screene, current archivist at QMUL, has directed me towards such invaluable materials as Council of Westfield Minutes and many of the archival photographs in this book. In addition, Lorraine Screene and Dr. Thomas Dixon of the Centre for the Emotions at QMUL organized a symposium to celebrate the digitization of Maynard's green book diary and autobiography; and this inspired subsequent conversations about Maynard with Drs. Angharad Nye and Laura Doan, and Helena Whitbread, and others. Closer to home, the Inter-Library Loans Department of the Leddy Library at the University of Windsor, Windsor Ontario, located and made available microfilm copies of Maynard's (then) unpublished diaries and autobiography. Meanwhile, additional archival information in this book has been collected over the years from Royal Holloway College London, Bedford College London, and the University of St. Andrews Library Scotland.

I would like to especially thank Dr. Deborah Gorham, Professor Emerita in the Department of History at Carleton University, Ottawa, who believed in the potential of researching Maynard from the beginning. Other professors and peers who provided support at Carleton University include Drs. Marilyn Barber, Laura Brandon, Frances Cherry, Janice Cavelle, David Dean, Janet Friskney, Jim Opp, Judith Rygiel, and Liz Turcotte. Dr. Martha Vicinus at the University of Michigan, Ann Arbor MI, helped to clarify my developing ideas about Constance Maynard; and, more recently, at the University of Windsor, colleagues in the Department of History have included Drs. Leslie Howsam and Christina Simmons, and in the Leddy Library, Dr. Heidi Jacobs. Editors of journals publishing my related research have included Drs. Matt Keufler and Elsa Richardson.

Finally, the following at the University of Toronto Press have contributed to the formation of this book: editor, Len Husband; general editors of the series, Drs. Franca Iacovetta and Karen Dubinsky; four anonymous peer reviewers; members of the Manuscript Review Committee; associate managing editor, Frances Mundy; and copyeditor, Anne Fullerton. Ontario Graduate Scholarships and Scholarships from Carleton University supported me when I began my research. Financial contributions from Dr. Michael Siu, office of the Vice-President, Research and Innovation, and Dr. Nancy Wright, office of the Dean of the Faculty of Arts, Humanities and Social Sciences, both at the University of Windsor, have subsidized publication of this book. Last, my husband, Alan, has had patience, pride, and love over our many years together. My daughter, Kelly, and son, Greg, also have academic careers that with their unique personalities are sources of pride for me.

CONSTANCE MAYNARD'S PASSIONS

Religion, Sexuality, and an English Educational Pioneer,
1849–1935

Introduction

"Seeking Great Reward from Thee"

In 1885, at age thirty-six, Constance Louisa Maynard wrote a few lines on love: "I am seeking great Reward from Thee, as God should say. So,- straight as a flame, as growing wheat is straight, I *go* to Him. Yes,- Thou *art* more than earthly Love! My choice *is* made!" Forty-three years later she told the reader: "In all subsequent troubles over love, which were many, these lines have helped me to reassure myself that God's love is *far better* than any intimacy formed on earth."[1] The intimacy that Maynard spoke of might surprise us. She had confessed to passionate encounters with her cousin's husband. She had admitted to erotic, possibly sexual liaisons with college women, including her students. Most striking, perhaps, was Maynard's utilization of faith to explain her past same-sex desires because she understood sex as heterosexual.

In this, the unpublished writings of Constance Maynard (1849–1935) provide a significant window into the experiences of a nineteenth-century English educational pioneer. A woman who preserved a religious "green book" diary and a "daily diary" that she wrote in faithfully from late adolescence until her death at eighty-six, her small leather-bound memoirs prove astonishing in their detailed, multifaceted accounts of her public and private life. Her diaries, together with her various journals and publications, engendered Maynard's richly noetic autobiography, which covers periods of her life for which no diaries exist. Still unfinished when she died, Maynard bequeathed it alongside her myriad documents to five close friends, with the request that her life story be completed.[2] Historian Catherine B. Firth complied with Maynard's wish, producing in 1949, under the imprint of British publisher George Allen and Unwin, *Constance Louisa Maynard: Mistress of Westfield College*, the only previously published biography.[3]

Maynard firmly believed that her life was "worth writing because it trace[d] the course of a great national movement, 'the higher education of women.'"[4] She was right. Since Maynard's one extant biography was written over fifty years ago, a reconsideration of this relatively unknown educational pioneer is overdue. Maynard's story provides insight into the development of educational reform for middle-class women,[5] a movement that paved the way for women's future social, economic, and political rights.

Maynard's life is additionally worthy of study for its exploration of how one early educational pioneer "atoned" for her bodily transgressions. To date, little has been written about the impact of faith together with ambition on late-Victorian female-female eroticism, especially on one who embraced suffering as evidence of moral-spiritual purity. This book draws upon the green book, the diary, and the autobiography of Constance Maynard to trace the ways that belief helped her forge a distinct same-sex sexual self-consciousness at a time when women were to be timid, sexually pure, and confined under men to the home. By so doing, this work offers more insights into sexuality in general, while enriching our understanding of one Victorian woman's femininity and sexuality in particular.

To set the stage for Maynard's extraordinary life we must turn to her upbringing. Born in 1849, she was raised in an upper-middle-class family during the relatively stable and prosperous mid-Victorian period. Two generations of Maynard entrepreneurial success overseas had enabled Constance's father, Henry, to invest in South African diamonds. Henry's marriage to Louisa Hillyard, who was of French gentility, further empowered him. As an elite male imperialist, Henry adopted a typically classist, racist, and sexist view of the world, and his views strongly affected his family. Constance believed herself to be "a cut above most" as a privileged member of the "greatest nation on earth." She grew up in a luxurious mansion attended by servants and nurses, with governesses introduced into the household on occasion. In terms of her gender, however, Constance felt unequal. Women were generally deemed both physically and intellectually inferior to men, and consequently had few social, economic, and political rights. Maynard and her three sisters learned the usual "girls' accomplishments" suitable for a life of middle-class domesticity. They were expected to remain in the home, raise children, and be subservient to men. Meanwhile, their two brothers were educated in the Classics to prepare them to run the family business with their father.[6]

0.1 Constance Louisa Maynard aged forty-three, 1892, at Westfield College. Courtesy of Queen Mary University of London Archives/Westfield College/WFD.

The Maynards' social views were consistent with what historians call the Victorian double standard of sexual morality. Constance knew little of sex as a young woman, except that "females were by nature passive, fearful and at times, jealous creatures." Her knowledge – or lack thereof – was quite typical for the times. Women were presumed to be sexually naive, indeed "sexless," in comparison to men's "aggressive nature," which served men well in the competitive public sphere. Victorians believed that love and marriage united the unequal genders, but men were considered more lustful and more entitled to sex from their wives. Not surprisingly, Victorians did not approve of but did tolerate men's sexual dallying and adultery far more than women's.[7]

Although Maynard's upbringing reflected her class, gender, and race, in other ways it was atypical. Religious feeling permeated all aspects of Victorian thought, predominantly through the Protestant Church. Evangelicals, for example, helped to shape the above-mentioned gender and sex ideals, while the all-male Oxbridge specified entry to Anglicans only. However, Maynard's parents' asceticism propagated a faith that owed more to early nineteenth-century notions of Evangelical atonement theology than those Evangelical ideas prominent at the time of her birth and youth. According to atonement-thinking Evangelicals, one was born in sin due to Adam's Fall. Christ's Crucifixion symbolized one's need to resist worldly thought and carnal feeling for personal salvation. This focus on "depraved humanity" contrasted sharply with the incarnational theology that became dominant in mid-century. The Incarnation emphasized that Christ's sacrifice on the cross had *saved* humanity from the Fall. Thus, over a short period of time, Evangelical life-principles based on Biblical Truth and Crucifixiation had significantly modified. The mid-Victorian Christian was to appreciate life – rather than struggle on earth – and rest in his or her (re)union with God through faith.[8]

In many ways, Henry Maynard's entrepreneurial upper-middle-class mindset constituted mid-century Evangelical Anglicanism. But his atonement-like view of human nature as depraved was shaped by his wife's religion, which was extreme. Raised on French Huguenot faith, Louisa Maynard's Puritan-based "fixed life Principle" profoundly impacted how Constance and her siblings were socialized. They could not participate in any typical activities of their class and gender that "aroused the senses," such as dinner parties, dancing, concerts, or the theatre. Most social equals were "shunned" because they were deemed worldly or "not their sort," and so it became virtually impossible for the Maynard daughters to meet suitable men; indeed, only one eventually married. Constance seemed particularly anxious over her mother's emphasis on "the conflict between 'good' [rational-spiritual body] and 'evil' [depraved emotional body]." She wrote at length about the wrong of "self-Approbation" and of her struggle to "sever *that* self-destructive part." Self-seeking, she told the reader, led to "uncontrollable thoughts" about passion and ambition.[9]

It seems incredible that Maynard's repressive upbringing forged her life as an educational pioneer. Yet her parents' strict values are likely what fueled her ambitions and passions. She first heard of the existence of women's colleges when visiting her cousin Fanny Campbell and her husband Lewis in Scotland in 1872. Professor Lewis Campbell, to whom Maynard was sexually attracted, supported the movement for higher learning for women which had emerged in 1848. It was he who told Maynard of educational pioneer Emily Davies' initiation of Hitchin in 1869. Hitchin (renamed Girton in 1873) was the first women's college affiliated with Cambridge University that afforded some middle-class women new career opportunities rather than a life of domesticity.[10]

Maynard's interest in education led her to convince her doubting parents to let her enroll at Hitchin in October, 1872. At twenty-three, she joined those privileged few women who sought new challenges through higher education. It was at Hitchin/Girton that Maynard faced "the battleground between faith and scientific knowledge." Maynard's dilemma was, of course, a phenomenon unique to her era. While Charles Darwin's *On the Origin of Species* (1859) had furthered the idea of white male supremacy, his evolutionary theories also led many, including Maynard herself, to religious doubt. Nevertheless, Maynard clung to her faith, as did most Victorians; after all, society had been raised on the "Truth" of the Bible. The Maynards were among those who feared that "evil" evolutionary thought led to God's displeasure, and ultimately, eternal damnation. Maynard succeeded in Ethics, Logic, and Philosophy at Girton, but embraced the scientific and religious disputes of the times without completely losing her faith. Her studies were notable in other ways. She became the first Girtonian, and indeed among the first Victorians, to attempt and successfully pass the "Mental and Moral Sciences" Tripos examination. Maynard later recognized that her Tripos "was the beginnings of psychology," although Freudian psychoanalysis did not emerge until the early 1900s.[11]

The second conflict that Maynard faced at Girton concerned female friendship. While her peers effused over their love for a friend, the repressed Maynard fretted instead over such "sinful" sentimental feelings. She reconciled this conflict, in part, through the incarnational idea of "God as love" that was taught to her at boarding school. She also learned through college peers that Victorians at large did not view passion between girls or women as unusual. In fact, intimacy between mothers and daughters, between aunts and nieces, and between sisters, cousins, and friends was considered an important part of female development. Female bonds were not only deemed virtuous and a spiritual awakening to God, but a necessary preparation for a girl's "true post" in life, namely marriage and motherhood.[12] It is not surprising that relatively few early college women transgressed norms by seeking career over marriage.

Neither career nor marriage was in Maynard's future after leaving Girton in 1875. Confined to the home, she was not allowed suitors or even female friendships. Yet Girton had fired her intellectual aims and deep emotional longings, as well as her vision of self as Evangelical prophet. Indeed, the idea of "being Chosen" to lead others to salvation helped Maynard pursue her professional goals. The diaries of 1875–80 are striking portrayals of her determination to gain her parents' approval about her "temporary" teaching.[13] From 1876–7 she taught at Cheltenham Ladies' College with former Girtonian and close friend Louisa Lumsden, who was the second love of Maynard's life. Cheltenham was progressive with its emphasis on academic learning over girls' accomplishments, but neither Maynard nor Lumsden were quite satisfied with its aims. In 1877, Lumsden, Maynard, and another ex-Girtonian opened what became the academically-renowned and corporally-spirited St. Leonards School for Girls' in St. Andrews, Scotland. Maynard's devotion to career and to Lumsden led her to refuse marriage to a prominent Scottish minister, Dr. James Robertson, in 1877. She left St. Leonards in 1880 largely because her tumultuous relationship with Lumsden had fallen apart.

Maynard entered the Slade Art School in London in 1880 after returning from St. Andrews, but her interest in higher education remained. She participated in the foundation of a women's college in London named Westfield. In 1882, she became Westfield's first Mistress, a position she held as a single woman for 31 years. Because of her life situation, Maynard's closest bonds were with Westfield women. Her records reveal that she formed particularly strong romantic attachments to students Margaret Graham Brooke and Marion Wakefield, and to fellow teacher Frances Ralf Gray. Each relationship, while intense, failed because of Maynard's faith-based emotional demands. In terms of professional goals, Westfield stood distinct. It was established to prepare genteel Christian women for University of London degrees that, unlike Oxbridge, had been open to women since 1878. By the time Maynard retired in 1913, many Westfield graduates had pioneered women's careers in missionary work, medicine, social work, and teaching, and were involved in fighting for important political reforms like suffrage.

"Records So Startling, Sometimes Painful"

Historians of women have examined how Victorian middle-class values were inscribed on the female body to the extent that women reproduced such values while simultaneously rejecting them. This phenomenon was evident in the cult of domesticity, and women's corresponding demand for independence outside marriage.[14] Considering this, the records of Constance Maynard startle in their profound challenge of domesticity. Maynard described Westfield as her "large family;" yet, she firmly believed that gaining the means to higher education for women "proved to be 'one of the great forces' of the land." Women had "new opportunities to pursue careers and to escape 'the bondage of marriage.'"[15] Some historians argue that Victorian women always had alternatives to domesticity, such as teaching, writing, and engaging in religious work; others posit that Victorians viewed these activities as extensions of domesticity, and that educational reformers did help to change women's lives.[16] This study argues that Constance Maynard's determination to first gain for women the university degree was, in fact, a momentous step in forging equality of education for the sexes, and women's social and economic independence.

Constance Maynard emerges as an even more fascinating historical figure upon examination of how faith shaped her emotional life as a single educational pioneer. Maynard's biographer, Catherine Firth, touched upon certain interconnections. A former Westfield graduate, a dedicated academic, and a close friend, Firth had first-hand knowledge of Maynard and of women's higher education. She detailed how Maynard's upbringing shaped her ambitions even though science stood particularly uneasily beside Maynard's "duty" to God. In fact, Maynard felt compelled to initiate a Girton Prayer Meeting in 1874, and in 1886, a circular "Budget" letter for Westfield graduates. In 1901, she inaugurated a Divinity program at Westfield in an attempt to "evangelize [what she viewed as] an increasingly secular world."[17]

One feature of Firth's biography is its silence about Maynard's interconnection of faith with sexuality, and about Maynard's personal life in general. Writing during an era that did not address matters of sex, Firth found Maynard's emotional "intimate [outpourings] so startling, sometimes painful," that she wished she "could turn away from records which, it seemed, no stranger's eye should read."[18] Historian Martha Vicinus redressed this lack to some degree in a groundbreaking work on romantic friendships among college women that paid some attention to Maynard. Vicinus wrote that college friendships, referred to by both Victorian teachers and pupils as "raves," mostly took the form of pious husband-wife role playing and were vital for pioneers like Maynard. As well as supporting their fight for independence, raves were a means for college women to proclaim their mutual passion even if it was seen – by each other and society – as a romantic friendship sublimated to heterosexual role-playing.[19]

Writing in the 1980s, Vicinus interpreted Maynard as a passive and somewhat naive pioneer who "hid behind a façade of self-effacing Christianity [rather] than admit her power."[20] This may account for Vicnus' exclusion of Maynard in *Intimate Friends: Women Who Loved Women, 1778–1928* (2004), which explores notable women's articulation of same-sex desire through faith.[21] My own reading of Maynard's private writings led me to conclude that she was a powerful woman who was far from passive. Maynard both recognized and expressed her physical feelings for the married Lewis Campbell, and more particularly, for close college friends. In an entry about Westfield student Margaret Brooke, for example, she writes:

> Last week I loved MGB [Margaret Brooke] with *such* thrills of strong excitement that I was taken by surprise. I tried to dismiss them as they seemed as much physical as mental. Yet this week over I gave way. I feel that I have reached such a height of bliss that it can only go downwards after this.[22]

Maynard's enactment of her physical encounters with college women took various forms. Indeed, her description of and self-reference as wife, lover, husband, and mother with loves at Girton, Cheltenham, St. Leonards, and Westfield suggest that raves involved erotic role-playing that was far more fluid – and diverse – than scholars like Vicinus recognize. Furthermore, Maynard's unique role as Mistress of Westfield was as unprecedented and unchallenged as her increasing emotional demands. In 1888, for example, she boldly "claimed [her] motherhood instincts" as a single independent woman in her disastrous decision to adopt an illegitimate six-year-old named Stephanë Rosabianca (Effie).[23] Maynard's longing for passion, and contradictory view of it as sin, had even more serious ramifications for the "ravees" under her control. In addition to what they reveal about the life of an important educational pioneer, Maynard's records challenge the range of activities and meanings normally attributed to Victorian female friendship and gendered power relations.

Maynard's recorded experiences are even more compelling for historians of female sexuality because she lived before and during periods of radical change in sex norms. In general, scholars concede that the diffusion of the science of sexology in the early 1900s influenced social perceptions of intimacy between women. By collating the case histories of their patients, texts by such sexologists as Richard von Krafft-Ebing – and more particularly in relation to Britain, Havelock Ellis – essentially codified "normal" heterosexuality in opposition to same-sex passion and "inversions" like female sadomasochism and incest. Sigmund Freud's subsequent theories about "normal" psychosexual development versus the "thwarted sex instinct" further helped to constitute different-sex eroticism as the dominant sexual norm. Consequently, modern women who desired women increasingly saw themselves as erotically different from heterosexual women, although the term "lesbian" did not come into general English usage until after the 1920s.[24]

As a late-Victorian, Maynard's creative understanding of her same-sex desires was realized through various religious-secularist discourses, from both her own day and the past. Indeed, her ongoing search for same-sex sexual identit(ies) seems remarkable for a woman of her time. Nonetheless, despite her fluid notion of desire, Maynard ultimately believed that life was a test due to Adam's Fall and Christ's Crucifixion. The search for "True Spiritual life," or shun of world, was one for the individual to self-impose. Even so, as noted, such staunch views on the dichotomy of the spiritual and earthly had modified with the onset of incarnational thinking. Mid-century Evangelical thinking integrated the earthly and spiritual through emphasizing redemption through the Cross and the Church. In general, Victorians were far more optimistic about human nature, the pleasures of life, and human progress.[25]

The upper-middle-class Maynards thus suffered a life of contradiction under Louisa Maynard's fixed life Principle. They lived in luxury, they embraced progress, and yet they were socially deprived as "Pilgrims and Strangers." As Constance noted, "I recall Mother's pursuit of 'moral conscience' and ensuing decree that 'the Will must be repressed.'" Louisa was particularly drawn to the sermons of Church of Scotland minister Reverend Edward Irving (1792–1834), who preached "that evil [the flesh, the world, and Satan] had *even* tempted Christ." Irving's fellow clergymen deemed his theology "repressive" and even "heretical" in the late 1820s. He was in fact deposed from the Church for his "denigration of the Deity" – but this view was exactly what attracted Louisa to this faith. She not only denied her children a social life: she raised them to believe that such "moral goodness" as kindliness was "simply not good enough for God. He wanted 'divine goodness.'" Constance recalled her deep confusion as a child when told to "seek 'heavenly goodness' by knowing God through her *mind,* not her emotions."[26] At age nineteen she wrote in her green book:

> All through life pain and sorrow for sin *must* continue. I cannot find a single text of scripture that might impute Satan's omniscience. His darts poison the intellect, producing distrust of God. Others inflame the will, moving it to acts of ambition or passion, which leads us away from the true spiritual life.

She could "only conclude that the 'true spiritual life'" must mean unquestioning "obedience and humility to God." She must fear her human nature for this "was 'evil' speaking."[27]

Throughout her life as an educational pioneer Maynard "sought God's love" through early-Victorian Evangelicalism and conversion. Yet she "never felt God's love," despite her search for true spiritual life. Nor did her bonds with college women last. God never "shew her that 'special someone' with whom [she] could share 'one heart, one faith and one Lord.'" When she mulled over her "failings with love," Maynard decided, "My only wrong was choosing human love over divine love."[28] Though she knew of sexological and psychoanalytical language in later life, she still maintained that her struggles were faith-based. The diaries and autobiography of Constance Maynard attest to how one late-Victorian woman expressed through her faith desire(s) that, at times, appeared to transgress feminine norms as well as Victorian ideas about romantic friendship and sex.

"Dare I Leave in Boldest Ink, all I Really and Truly Think"

Despite Maynard's multiple recordings about her professional, religious, and personal life experiences, as the above quote suggests, her language(s) of desire and sex are difficult to grasp.[29] Her entries on love, while numerous, are sometimes tantalizingly vague, and seem deliberately so, though this is not entirely surprising. Few Victorian women left records behind and most, including Maynard, adopted a typically Victorian propriety about sex at large. The fact is that we know little about the nature of Victorian female friendship during a period in history when women were viewed as submissive, and sex between women as opposed to "passion" was inconceivable. As a result, pioneering historians in the field of female sexuality have taken varied stances on the relationship of these friendships to the history of lesbianism. Carroll Smith-Rosenberg advises scholars to be cognizant of the "sensual and platonic" nuances of these friendship bonds. In contrast, Lillian Faderman argues that Victorians accepted romantic friendships as unproblematic because they were "asexual." Adrienne Rich meanwhile proposes the "lesbian continuum" as interconnecting all forms of female bonds in a common rejection of "compulsory heterosexuality."[30]

Historians (among them, Lisa Moore and Terry Castle) continue to debate these and other overarching paradigms. Also to note is Michel Foucault's well-known and sharp contrast between the premodern governance of sexual "acts" as sinful, and the modern shift towards understanding sexual "actors" through an internalized self-identity. Nonetheless, a postmodernist approach to identity formation has remained crucial to studies on past sexuality. The development of queer theory, inaugurated by Judith Butler and others, further highlighted the tenuous relationship between scripts about sexuality and individual performance. Historians of female sexuality now consider identity formation as one of a series of unstable identifications, such as gender and sex, which individuals mediate through a lifetime of experiences with other discourses.[31] For Maynard that negotiation happened through faith.

Despite these refinements to the history of female sexuality in general and homoeroticism in particular, there is still argument over how to describe – and ascribe – Victorian female bonds. Indeed, inserting the "lesbian" into history has led to stranglehold debates over what constitutes lesbian sexuality. For example, while Leila Rupp rejects the use of the term *lesbian* to convey past female-female eroticism, Vicinus finds it useful.[32] Also in dispute are the activities considered as reflecting lesbian identity or behaviour. Scholars often portray their subjects as having exceptional desire for women, as being masculine-like, or as exhibiting an open resistance to heteronormativity. Less attention has been paid to the conceptualization of female bonds outside this narrow frame. Sexuality, unlike race and gender, is most often seen in terms of identity rather than power. Historical evidence for mother-daughter eroticism, for example, or a hierarchical and power-based eroticism between two women, has been mostly excluded from studies on female sexuality and lesbian history because of its connotations of sexual abuse. Yet these sorts of female relationships were an important part of Maynard's diverse experiences.

To better understand the nuances of Constance Maynard's same-sex relationships, we can turn to the insights of queer theory. Sharon Marcus, Anna Clark, and Julian Carter are among those who have recently reinterpreted Victorian female-female passion – such as that between friends, sisters, and mother-daughter – as a shared femininity rather than asexual, lesbian, or incestuous. This helps us to understand that such forms of intimacy did not destabilize Victorian heteronormativity. In "On Mother-Love: History, Queer Theory, and Nonlesbian Identity" (2005), Carter develops Smith-Rosenberg's work by proposing that girls often adopted the nurturing as well as erotic mother-daughter bond in their same-sex friendships. As Clark usefully explains in "Twilight Moments" (2005), some encounters may have involved "not utterly" prohibited behaviour that went unnoticed by society because of women's "passive" nature. Meanwhile, Marcus' *Between Women: Friendship, Desire, and Marriage in Victorian England* (2007), posits that mainstream femininity not only encouraged women to display their capacities for tenderness, piety, and altruism: the cultural climate also provided women opportunities to flaunt forms of desire and aggression that they could not display with men. Marcus, Clark, and Carter advise scholars to abandon their preconceptions of strict gender and sex divisions in order to recognize that Victorians viewed female bonds as central to heterosexuality and to lives around men. A queer approach to Victorian female friendship reminds us of the fluidity of gender, desire, and sex, but warns us against reifying and projecting current hetero and homosexual identities onto the past.[33]

A similar argument can be made about the fluidity of the relations between sexuality and religion. As John Maynard, Michael Mason, and others have observed, scholars' tendency to separate faith from sex ignores the ways in which Christianity has built upon sexual language. Historians often place sexology at the centre of British Victorian thinking about sex. Yet the drive to intermingle discourses of sex with issues around faith was as central and as distinct to Victorians as it has been in all cultures and ages. Foucault has shown how the Victorian Church articulated sexual practice within the context of Augustinian asceticism. Sex was deemed a site for uncontrolled lust, and a haven for inversion and vice such as prostitution. However, opposing views on sex also existed that alongside a rich mixture of Christian sects, inspired religious discussion on such topics as sexual freedom. The eminent and rather conservative medical writer Dr. William Acton, for example, called for the toleration of prostitution because of men's great physical "needs."[34]

David Hilliard, Frederick Roden, and Patrick O'Malley are among those scholars who propose that aspects of Victorian religion were "culturally queer." Hilliard's groundbreaking study, for example, suggests that men of varying classes found within late nineteenth-century Anglo-Catholicism an opportunity to explore a desire that did not lead to heteronormativity. O'Malley posits that the meaning of Catholicism itself shifted in mid-century and provided some men "building blocks for constructing later minoritized sexual identities." As Roden explains, "The Christian [particularly Catholic] model of liturgy, devotion and biblical literacy" became for some Victorians a vehicle to express their same-sex desire, and helped to shape the broader language of homosexuality at the fin de siècle. To term such longings "aberrant" is to dismiss Victorians' deep connections to their faith, and indeed, the power of spirituality itself.[35]

Maynard's records convey that English Victorian women, too, used and subverted the language of faith for self-empowerment and sexual self-recognition. Yet, surprisingly little scholarship has examined Victorian women's interconnection of faith, ambition, and power with dissident sexualit(ies). Most studies have focused on how Victorian women used faith as a social, economic, or political platform, and lesbian and gay work, in turn, has neglected religious culture in favour of defining sexual identities in "homosexual" arenas.[36] It is only in recent years that scholars have turned to religion in the histories of female sexuality. Callum Brown's excavation of women's carving of "patterns of religiosity" contributed to the history of religion, gender, and female sexuality. Others, such as Sue Morgan, Vicinus, Joy Dixon, Lesley Hall, and Sandra Peacock, have fruitfully analysed how faith shaped women's cultural identity and sexuality.[37]

A queer approach to Constance Maynard's interconnection of faith with her goals and same-sex desires has been very briefly but usefully explored by Sue Morgan, who compared Maynard with Mary Benson, Ellice Hopkins, and Bessie Craigmyle. Morgan assessed that each woman's "particular theological transgressiveness" – in Maynard's case, the language of atonement theology – helped them to articulate their goals and "dissident same-sex subjectivity" within a heteronormative society tolerant of female friendship.[38] Frederick Roden, Ruth Vanita and others' queering of the writing of such well known writers as Christina Rossetti and Eliza Keary similarly reveal the various forms of erotic energy that mid- to late-Victorian women expressed as same-sex love and embraced as religious ecstasy. Roden's characterization of Rossetti as a "queer virgin," for example, posits that Rossetti's "Anglo-Catholic voice" challenged "patriarchal heteronormative culture" by depicting such things as a non-phallic Christ and sexually-charged all-female religious communities.[39]

Further examples of Victorian women's subversion of gender, sex, and faith in relation to Maynard's experiences are found in novelist Susan Warner's *The Wide, Wide World* (1850). Warner's "longing" to emulate the power of "the erotic male evangelist, [who] charmed his congregation," seems reminiscent of Maynard's later self-visualization as an Evangelical prophet. Maynard's faith-based concept of gender and desire as powerful, fluid entities was also evident in the poetry of Mathilde Blind, who much like Warner, Rossetti, and Keary, depicted aggressive gender-neutral figures that enacted same- and opposite-sex desires through faith-based reveries. Meanwhile, Richard Dellamora's work on Radclyffe Hall can be usefully contrasted with Maynard's experiences. While Hall's involvement with psychology in the 1920s helped her to reconcile her marriage, same-sex affairs, and Catholicism, the older Maynard who was raised on Victorian mores, found little comfort in the language of psychology.[40] We can conclude that Victorian women found in religious metaphors and language powerful forms of self-expression that were distinctly different from the next generation of women's understanding of sex and sexual self-identity.

Queering Maynard's atonement allows us a more fluid space to imagine her particular self-identit(ies) as a pious, upper-middle-class Victorian who remained single and dedicated her life to educational reform in the late 1800s. This study will reveal how faith became for Maynard a nuanced means in which to express her new role as an educational pioneer and her passions as a woman. Brought up on early-Victorian Evangelicalism, she came to envision suffering within the context of incarnational-based Evangelicalism; that is, the mid- and late-century celebration of humanity conjoined with but contradicted Maynard's view of humanity as depraved. As a result, in her transgressions as a pioneer and her longing for love, Maynard wavered between accepting and rejecting ambition and passion as God's gifts. She drew from and interconnected various social discourses with the language of her faith to express her same-sex desires as an educational pioneer.

Marcus' queer approach to female bonds is useful in defining the nuances of Maynard's same-sex bonds, although Marcus' fixing of women's identities and their same-sex desires into categories like female friendship and female marriage seems somewhat rigid, if not conceptually problematic. Laura Doan's recent vision of a critical queer historiography that analyzes change over time while facilitating provisional notions of past same-sex behaviours is helpful here. Maynard's different same-sex experiences at different times in her life did not automatically change the meaning of female-female intimacy for Maynard.[41]

Nor did Maynard's same-sex experiences alter her understanding of sex as heterosexual, even though her understanding of same-sex desire did evolve over time. As Roden, Dellamora, and others' propose, new links between Christianity and classicism helped shape what became the broader language of homosexuality in the fin de siècle. Maynard's adoption of a Hellenist-Christian language in the late 1880s does suggest her progression towards some understanding of an identity and practice of same-sex acts as homosexual.[42] However, this study proposes that Maynard's emergent same-sex sexual self-consciousness in the late 1860s and early 1870s forged her sexual identity as an educational leader in more unique ways. Moreover, even as new scientific theories challenged the older Maynard's views on gender, class, race, nation, and eventually sex, faith shielded her against the new ideas about non-normative sex. According to her records, she continued to operate in the very different register of desire/sin/atonement/redemption until the end of her life in 1935. Her understanding of her same-sex sexual self-consciousness through faith was not only about identity: it was also about power.

"The Instinct Toward God"

Maynard first formulated the idea of sexual pleasure and power as God-given at age twenty-three, when she found herself deeply attracted to her cousin's forty-two-year-old husband, Lewis Campbell. Maynard depicted herself as a young naive woman who tried to resist Campbell's ongoing flirtations throughout her three-month stay with the family. She was aware that the esteemed Professor often trifled with his students' emotions, but deemed him worthy and "honorable" because he curbed his "irrepressible yearnings" through "a noble religion of sorts."[43] As chapter 2 argues, their interconnecting narratives around love and religious duty – his was tied to a moral imperative, and hers to a theological relinquishing of worldliness – found form in Maynard's experiences as an educational pioneer.

Chapter 4 highlights Maynard's subsequent submissive role in her personal and professional relationship with Louisa Lumsden at Girton (1873–75), Cheltenham (1876–77), and St. Leonards (1887–80). However, Lumsden's agnosticism, bullying, and volatile leadership in general at St. Leonards left Maynard appalled, and even traumatized. It "was a pain," Maynard wrote, that "reached paralysing intensity."[44] When she found the strength to leave Lumsden, Maynard thereby disavowed Lumsden's method of leadership. She had more willingly participated in Campbell's "game" in 1872, and thus, Maynard enacted her own version of it as Mistress of Westfield.

When Maynard first became Mistress of Westfield in October 1882, she had full intentions of maintaining her position. Chapters 5, 6, and 7 chart Maynard's journey towards what became her highly successful career as Mistress. However, the lonely Maynard soon turned to college women for love. Her green book effused "love" for an early Westfield student, nineteen-year-old Margaret Brooke:

> Last night she [Brooke] came and in an instant I had my arms around her, my love, my darling!... She says I am the greatest treasure that God could have possibly given her. Do I not return it? Her presence brings a strong fascination that *is* partly physical, and draws my love with a force almost painful.[45]

This entry that echoed many others written in the late 1800s and early 1900s strongly suggests the erotic-spiritual component in Maynard's college raves, including the above mentioned role-playing. She spoke fondly of "long kisses on the lips" with Westfield loves "by the firelight" in the privacy of her room. Although Maynard at times questioned "the something not quite right" about her same-sex intimacy, there is no evidence in either diary or autobiography to suggest that Maynard viewed her behaviour as abnormal. She justified her earthly passion as an awakening "to God's love." As Christian Mistress of

Westfield, Maynard believed she had "the right to see human love as His great treasure."[46]

Just as Campbell had toyed with Maynard's sexuality, so Maynard dallied with fellow students' emotions at Girton, and one young student's naivety at St. Leonards. Chapters 3 and 4 examine how Maynard formulated same-sex love as passionate while also being part of a shared suppression in God's name. Chapters 5, 6, and 7 analyse Maynard's further exploration of her longings while Mistress, in particular for fellow teacher Frances Gray and Westfield students Margaret Brooke and Marion Wakefield. As chapter 7 argues, Maynard's response to her passionate encounters with Wakefield was particularly severe. For several years she tried to persuade Wakefield "to bring *every* thought to the obedience of Christ" through stringent fasting and celibacy to "cleanse" their physical interactions.[47] It was also in her atonement that Maynard found understanding for her failings in leadership and love. Chapter 6 analyzes her queer in-persona of the "dejected lover who battled years of [Frances Gray's] whistling heartless winds" through acts of self-abnegation like fasting, physical pain, "mental bondage," and solitude.[48] Indeed, throughout her life, self-denial took on a full meaning for Maynard in the absence of hope for professional or personal satisfaction.

Nonetheless, even though Maynard adopted what we today may call an inappropriate role as an educator, we should examine her behaviour within the context of her culture. As mentioned above, Maynard lived at a time when women were to be sexually innocent and subservient rather than independently minded. Thus it cannot be surprising that she felt conflicted as an educational pioneer. Nor was her profound need to self-punish entirely out of place in the early 1900s. Krafft-Ebing coined the scientific term *female masochism* in 1886. A decade later, British sexologist Havelock Ellis similarly proposed that latent masochism was the "natural sexuality of women" since they were passive and less sexual than men. It was only when "women *sought* intense pain" that it became "perversion." Not surprisingly, any form of active female sadism was conceived by most sexologists as "monstrous" perversion. The links between pain, sex, and femininity were not unique to late-nineteenth and early-twentieth-century culture; the "eroticism of pain" in the late 1700s, for example, shaped female desire in yet other ways.[49] Regardless, we must note that European literature from at least the Middle Ages conveys a long history of individual adoptions of languages for love – whether divine or earthly, ecstatic or painful – in order to explain the erotic-spiritual feeling that swept through one in the presence of a beloved.[50]

As a late-Victorian, Constance Maynard's particular circumstances all worked to inculcate in her a form of reveling in pain as though it were a mark of grace. Faith, suffering, and the exercise of power help to explain Maynard's behaviour in her adult relationships. On one hand, her same-sex bonds involved culturally-prescribed forms of femininity: selflessness, submission, religious duty, and spiritual-erotic feeling. However, since her role as an educational pioneer was unprecedented for a woman of the time, Maynard's faith-based sexual power over students went largely unchallenged. She could assert herself even as she enforced "atoning" on self and others for worldly feeling. Maynard's fear of her earthliness ran deep. The idea of religious despair over God's disfavour of worldly sentiment is a difficult concept to grasp, certainly. Yet Maynard's need to suffer for human love proved excruciating: "I *hate* self-denial!" she exclaimed in 1905. "I would break it if I could!" Even so, as she admitted in her autobiography, "When my attempts at meditation, courage and perseverance did not meet with the response from Heaven which I looked for, I adopted ever more ever more punitive measures."[51] Sadly, Maynard's measures caused lifelong bitterness for herself and the college women who she loved.

As conflicted as Maynard was about her same-sex desires as a late-Victorian educational pioneer, she found little solace in the new theories of sex. Throughout her tenure at Westfield (1882–1913) she consistently advised her young loves to resist human passion in order to seek a moral faith-based consciousness. Ellis may have at the turn of the century called female sadomasochism a monstrous, "bestial" perversion,[52] but Maynard, for her part, never mentioned terms like perversion or sexology at this time. In August 1926, however, ideas taken from psychoanalysis did enter her autobiography: "I suppose *today* psychoanalysts would call my [past] feelings [for women] 'a thwarted sex instinct.' This to me is an extremely disagreeable term. All I know is that 'I had a hunger which needed satisfying' like the need 'for food.'"[53] Scholars debate the impact of psychology over sexology on British society in the 1920s, and so Maynard's awareness of it may not have been the norm. Nonetheless, she continued to situate her past relationships within the context of faith, albeit writing sometimes oddly hybrid statements that included psychological terms: "My craving was not the instinct toward marriage, *surely not*, it was the *instinct toward God*, which can be satisfied with nothing less."[54]

Constance Maynard recognized love and its potential for physicality, but her means of understanding that physicality was through faith. Love was God's gift. Love was God's test of her faith. This complex *fluid* binary existed in a heterosexual relationship (Lewis Campbell) and a same-sex relationship (Louisa Lumsden, Margaret Brooke, Frances Gray, and Marion Wakefield) if earthly love was not consecrated to God. At the same time, Maynard's view of love as God's test culminated in forms of domination over young women in whom she had gained trust and love. As a late-Victorian educational pioneer, Maynard had no means of understanding her lifestyle choice as a cover for her sexual orientation, as it became for many twentieth-century lesbians. Nor would she have perceived her behaviour – or the role that it played in her interaction with students – as we might today. Shortly before her death in 1935, Maynard still asserted, "My *only* wrong was choosing human love over divine love."[55]

"The Truth in Love, Dear"

Censorship versus "truth." Discourse versus experience. Queer scholarship warns the feminist researcher against linking a relationship between truth and linear narrative. Certainly, viewing personal records as a window into a "real" life is as problematic as reifying a unified, transcendent self. This dilemma raises the question of whether scholars may ever claim either to know the truth about past experience from *any* primary text, or to respond to those texts without codifying their own language to mimic them. The answer to both is probably not. Yet, however exaggerated or contradictory, the diaries and autobiography of Constance Maynard present a remarkably in-depth account of one late-Victorian woman's life experiences as an educational pioneer. In this, Maynard's records offer us fascinating aspects of someone's struggles in another period, and that knowledge allows us self-reflection and perhaps the opportunity to know ourselves better. The autobiographical or diary "I," however fugitive, partial, and unreliable, is the privileged textual double of a real person, as well as a self-evident textual construct.[56]

I do not take lightly Maynard's injunction to Catherine Firth: "Speaking (sic) the truth in love, dear, and don't forget the love. What I shared with others must not be hidden."[57] I would like to think that Maynard knew that her eloquent account of her life not only raised new questions about gender and sexuality for her own era, but also for subsequent ones. As such, the following chapters attempt to let

Constance Maynard's voice provide insight into these historical moments. A queer approach to Maynard's voice allows a more fluid interpretation of her pioneering role and desires as neither the antithesis of male-based power, nor a "pure" guide to spiritual and/or heterosexual love. The records of Constance Maynard reveal that faith led her to utilize her culture's norms, her unique academic position, and her erotic desires to express a distinct, embodied femininity as a late-Victorian educational pioneer. Her circumstance illuminates the need to recognize elusive desires and behaviours that did not necessarily create stigmatized identities. Past individuals may not have been fully able or willing to conceptualize their behaviour, particularly if they were devout or lived during an era on the brink of cultural change. As Maynard explained, "It was not that my ambitions or desires were wrong; my transgression was in viewing both as more compelling than God. 'Temptation' is the testing ground where God 'presses' on the very spots of acute feeling."[58]

Chapter One

"Sweetest of Earth's Glories, Love!" 1849–1871

I know what *Love* can be
How it speeds away to get a last Goodnight kiss
How it has ever one more aim to gain or word to write.
Yet God claims the cost most fiercely; and stilling all our cries,
By holding out no other gain or prize
But only, - "I am here, come thou to me."[1]

Above is one of the many sonnets that Constance Maynard composed in the early 1900s to reaffirm her faith: "The knowledge and love of God *is* far better than the Sweetest of earth's glories, Love!"[2] Yet according to all records, faith fired Maynard's worldly feelings. She began her green book diary in 1866 at secondary boarding school "to chart [her] Christian progress," but she soon divulged another aim: "I *long* for some harder flight," she lamented of her education, and she did improve it for future women. By 1871, the green book had "evolved into a record about [Maynard's] soul *and* heart," thus she started her daily diary to note educational and social events.[3] Maynard's autobiography proffered a third narrative about her ambitions and passions as an educational pioneer. In this record, written between 1915 and 1930, Maynard analysed her personal history within the context of nineteenth- and twentieth-century concepts.[4]

Maynard's frankness in revealing her feelings lends poignancy and thus great historical value to her personal accounts, and their variations reveal deep reflection on those feelings. The juxtaposition between diary and green book finds provocative voice in written entries about Maynard's life as Mistress of Westfield College. In her diary, she effused pride in her success: "We stand apart from most other English women's colleges. Westfield students are the *first* to gain the B.A. degree." In sharp contrast, her green book of the time mused over her "failure with [same-sex] 'love,'" a theme that had evolved since her student days at Girton: "God has taken you from me because I have loved you in far… too earthly a fashion. Go, my Love, Go! I relinquish *You* in order for *Him* to speak to my heart."[5]

What seems remarkable about the above green book entry is Maynard's adoption of faith as a means of understanding and resisting her same-sex desire. Her biggest sin, as far as she was concerned, was choosing human love over divine love. Scholars have examined how women's beliefs and roles in communities of faith empowered them to seek important social, economic, and political gains. But little remains written on how the interconnections between religion and ambition shaped female-female desire; especially hierarchical bonds that involved suffering for human love.[6] This chapter draws on the diary, green book, and autobiography of Constance Maynard to examine how her early upbringing forged her role as an educational pioneer, and helped to formulate her sexual self-identity.

Certainly, all writing on Maynard's upbringing portrays it as financially privileged. Her father's ancestors were an example of socially-mobile individuals who sought imperialist ventures in the 1750s. Like his grandfather before him, Henry Maynard (1800–1888) was sent overseas in 1819 to become a wealthy merchant. His discovery of South African diamonds in the 1830s made him a rich man.[7] Henry Maynard was further empowered in 1837 when he married Louisa Hillyard (1806–1871), whose genteel ancestors were members of the landed French aristocracy. They started a family two years after their marriage and over an eleven-year period, Louisa gave birth to eight children. Josephine (Tissy), born in 1839, was followed closely by Henry (Harry), who was born in 1840. The next surviving child was Gabrielle (Gazy), who was born in 1845; Dora (Do) followed quickly in 1846. Constance was born on 19 February 1849. She was described as an attractive child, her large luminous eyes and her "unusual golden brown hair" being her particular crowning glory. George, born in 1850, was considered "delicate" because he suffered from asthma and arthritis.[8]

The 1850s was a relatively good decade in which to raise an upper-middle-class family in England because of political and economic stability and the rise of the general standard of living. It was an era of moral-based consumption, as evident in tax on certain items and the classification of activities like crime and leisure. Maynard's autobiography illuminates how this vibrant period benefitted imperialist entrepreneurs like her father. When she was five years old, the family moved from their rented house in London to a massive estate in Hawkhurst in Kent: "Life was idyllic indeed," Maynard recalled. "Beyond [our mansion] Oakfield lay flower-filled gardens, orchards and ponds, which eventually opened up into the Kent country side." There were frequent comings and goings of family and guests, as well as expensive "holidays to the sea."[9]

However, despite her privileged upbringing, Maynard remembered her infant years as "loveless." In some ways this circumstance was not surprising since upper-middle-class children saw little of their parents. Raised by live-in staff like nurses and governesses, the child's "getting a smack with the rod" was perhaps more common than a kiss. Similar to other elite homes, Oakfield had delineated spaces for its members. Louisa Maynard kept to her drawing rooms while a staffed wing was devoted to a nursery and schoolroom for her children. Constance and her siblings Gazy, Do, and George were raised by a nurse called "Jebb" and at times, their eldest sister Tissy supervised them. This situation apparently was far from ideal. Jebb was "often bad-tempered," Constance recalled, "And we all lived in fear of Tissy's nasty ridicule. There was this tone of contempt, as if we were worthless!" Constance had few memories of any interaction with her father as a young child.[10]

It seems that Louisa Maynard – largely absent from her children's early lives – was "a *huge* presence … from 5 until 13." Certainly this had its advantages: "She instilled [in us] a love of Knowledge," Constance declared, a passion that Constance undertook as an educational pioneer. However, Louisa's presence had an equally negative impact upon her family. As Constance's cousin Mary King recalled of Louisa Maynard's child-raising, in "Reminiscences of the Maynard Family":

> Her most obvious concern was to instill a careful exactness in everything they [children] did, each had to have an answer to what they were doing every hour of the day … Nor was quarrelling allowed in the nursery and school room. At the time I thought this was wonderful, but now I'm not so sure. All actions were controlled so that nothing spontaneous or demonstrative was permitted.[11]

In Constance's view, "Mother's pressure was unceasing" because of her faith. "The merest trifle was examined under the exponent of her fixed life Principle, 'turn from the world.' We were told that sensation dulled the keen edge between right and wrong." No Maynard child could attend the usual social events of their class like parties or plays, or dress fashionably. Since "Mother mocked society," Constance explained, "our friends were mostly poor local villagers, who were 'equal' in God's eyes yet 'unequal' socially." As a result, the Maynard children came across as odd, condescending individuals who, Mary King claimed, "were difficult to be around." For her part, Constance felt awkward around social equals because of her lack of socialization.[12]

As adolescents "our activities were as strictly monitored," Constance asserted in her autobiography. "We girls were told to be humble and obedient." Tracts, fiction, and magazines of the day prescribed such female behaviour while stressing the dignity of domesticity and motherhood. Since Victorian women had few rights, Louisa and her daughters were typically confined to the home with its accompanying gender norms. In terms of education, a governess was only hired on occasion for the girls: "I do not recall one spark of real interest," Constance recalled. "Some reading aloud, perhaps a French verb to repeat...and of arithmetic I remember only one single rule, 'Turn the fraction upside down, and proceed as before.'"[13]

Similarly to other adolescents of their class, the Maynards attended private same-sex boarding schools for their secondary education. Harry and George received an education in the Classics from age ten to eighteen. Constance, like her older sisters before her, entered the genteel setting of Belstead at age fourteen in October 1863 to develop her "female accomplishments." She summed up her Belstead experience under its kindly founder, "Mamie":

> I loved the cheerful "busy-ness" over all sorts of trifling matters. I felt as if all pressure was lifted off me and I could be myself. But Lessons were not Belstead's strong point. Arithmetic was particularly stupid and unexplained. When I earned the title, "First Class" student, Mamie told me to "set an example by keeping up a tidy room and appearance."[14]

Henry Maynard did not consider his daughter's academic talents either. He removed Constance from Belstead shortly before her seventeenth birthday and told her, "You can do well enough at home with three sisters above you who have been educated till they were eighteen." Henry's attitude reflected the times, as did Constance's silent response. She resented her father's actions, yet was expected to be grateful about becoming a "grown-up-daughter-at-home." She remained home for the next seven years under her mother's fixed life Principle.[15]

"Christian Progress"

Constance sought to maintain her "emotional" ties to Belstead through a religious diary. She began her green book in 1866 following Mamie's advice, "write your 'Friend.'" In other words, chart her "Christian progress" towards God: "Mamie says I have a wise and loving Friend in God. She says, 'God will never misunderstand you.'" It is telling, however, that Maynard opened this record with a "new year motto" from her mother: "So foolish was I, and ignorant: I was as a beast before Thee."[16] This seems a stark contrast from Mamie's religiosity and, indeed, a harsh maxim in general for a sixteen-year-old. Yet the words set the tone for this at times self-deprecating record. One is struck by the enormous impact that Louisa Maynard had upon the family. Indeed, even Henry did not interfere with his wife's austere faith-based life Principle. He had proposed to her in 1827, "but she only accepted him when assured of his Christian faith."[17]

Certainly, Louisa's concern was one Victorian's response to the rise in worldliness. Society at large feared the onset of science, evidenced by the increase of church building and attendance following state intervention of welfare and education. Various Christian sects coexisted alongside the largely Protestant faith, and many, including the Maynards, took refuge in Christian-based works that integrated Darwin's "evolutionary cycles" with the "days" of creation.[18] However, the Maynards' belief in atoning for the Fall and Christ's Crucifixion was out of sync with an Evangelicalism that largely reflected the Biblicism of Christian socialist Reverend Frederick Denison Maurice (1805–72). For Maurice, the Incarnation doctrine was the "true biblical guide to life. It showed that the Crucifixion had *redeemed* mankind from original sin." Christians "should celebrate life on earth."[19]

The above suggests how Evangelical-based life principles (Biblical Truth, active conversion, and stress on Christ's sacrifice) can evolve and change over time. Nonetheless, as scholars David Bebbington and Boyd Hilton argue, Evangelicalism largely reflects the prominent ideals of its time. Mid-Victorian Evangelicals tended to embrace the technological and scientific development that had forged British global power. Imperialists particularly took advantage of the Liberalist times. Henry Maynard's economic success coincided with the rise of free trade that shaped ideals around male competiveness and moral righteousness. These modes of thought would slowly erode the power-based conservatism of the gentry.

Constance's records evinced a familial-nationalist pride over social position at home and wealth overseas that mirrored the privileged entrepreneurial thinking of Evangelical Anglicanism. Her father apparently brought home from his South African mine "the biggest diamond" ever found. Meanwhile, visits to see England's "finest on exhibit" seemed as important as attending church on Sunday. The Maynards' interest in nation and science led them (and indeed many Evangelicals) to follow natural theology, or belief in "knowing God" apart from divine revelation through nature and scientific enquiry. Constance and her siblings undertook such amateur scientific pursuits as astronomy, geology, botany, and physiology. It cannot surprise us that the era shaped scientific and incarnational thinking, and the idea of human progress. Many from the middle classes adopted a "Christian humanitarian" outlook towards "Rest in Faith" and the social healing of all.[20]

Given this theological outlook and cultural climate, the Maynards seemed overly fixated on suffering. Constance, for her part, never quite freed herself from it. In 1905 she wrote in her green book, "I still see why I...lecture on the Atonement. It is a *vital* center of religion because it reminds us that we have something to do."[21] Here, we see influences of Constance's upbringing and can measure it against her somewhat cynical autobiographical account:

> I recall a "dreary Sabbath" filled with dull church services ... Lastly, Father [Henry Maynard] would give us a very solemn piece: "Hark, universal Nature shook and groaned. Tis the last Judgment; see the Judge enthroned." It was meant to teach us that due to "the Fall" our hearts were thoroughly bad.[22]

In some ways, the Maynards adopted a typical stance on faith. If a child dared to defy religious dogma he or she defied both the Holy Father and the earthly father. However, since it was Louisa's belief that must be followed, we see the significance of Victorian female pietism: "Mother's obsessive search for the 'Truth,'" Constance wrote, meant that "most work was condemned when tried by the central words of the Bible." Mid-century incarnation-based writing was "naturally dismissed as 'emotional complacency'" when compared to "the Truth." Yet it should be noted that early-nineteenth Evangelicalism had emerged during a period of horrific famine and recurring plagues. Popular texts of the time had included William Paley's *Evidences of Christianity* which, published in 1794, emphasized suffering as a part of God's plan.[23]

Henry Maynard considered Paley's historically-grounded *Evidences* as "among the foundational Truths" because it traced "the ultimate 'benevolence' of mankind" in face of suffering for sin. It was Louisa Maynard's belief, however, that led to the family's divergence from mainstream Evangelicalism. She was convinced that Scottish Reverend Edward Irving "spoke the Truth," even though his *Doctrine of Incarnation* had been '"damned for its portrayal of Christ's 'humanity'" since 1828. Irving's message, based on low Christology, did seem foreboding: "Christ was tempted by evil, so God creates apprehension in the heart of man and forces repentance, by a sort of moral torture, into the bosom of religious despair."[24] As Maurice noted in 1853 of Irving's theology, "What *could* the Incarnation on his [Irving's] hypothesis be *but* the descent into a radically *evil* nature?"[25] Nonetheless, Irving's acceptance of suffering with a kind of gratitude resonated especially with Louisa Maynard's fixed life Principle:

> She [Louisa] told us that feeling "safe" in one's faith or with daily acts of kindness was more dangerous spiritually than a crime filled life … I [Constance] remember I cried bitterly in my little bed. It was not for any particular wrongdoing, but for what looked to me to be so much worse, a general conviction of sinfulness and ignorance and discouragement.[26]

Here, we see evidence of the depth of Constance's religious despair as a girl. As Mary King explained, "She [Louisa] would say, 'No one is *born* good; so *being* good is not *good enough* for God.'"[27] In fact, Constance felt so overwhelmed by her sense of failure that by age seventeen she felt driven to suppress the will. A green book entry in April 1866 conveyed her fear of earthly feeling, for which she now largely blamed Belstead:

> You may feel His presence near in your weakness upon His love, but you may be treating Him like an earthly friend or lover. I believe this state of feeling to be compatible with spiritual life, but it is also very dangerous …

> The over excitement of a natural feeling, was, I think, the greatest danger at Belstead. It can bring us great remorse because it drives us in shame away from God.[28]

Maynard's final thought on the matter was that attaining "'Truth' through the 'divine' body must mean blind obedience and humility to God." After all, she had grown up to fear her human nature as well as suffer for it.[29]

In her autobiography, Maynard criticized her mother's ongoing attempts to sever what she called her "emotional and mental furniture." It is clear that even as a child, however, she was exposed to different ideas about Christianity, some based more on incarnational theology. She remembered her "wonder at a governess's impassions about 'the marvel of grasping the idea of God as love'"; she recalled Mary King having said, "Fly to God for He is never beaten"; but Mamie's Bible lessons on "salvation through the Crucifixion" had the most impact. Maynard explained the notion that "God's pardon felt liberating to an adolescent who believed that sin was the very worst thing that could happen to you."[30]

According to her green book, 1867 was a milestone in eighteen-year-old Maynard's emotional-religious process. As such Belstead-related maxims as "Christ died for me" continued to fill the book, so too did her mother's "Sayings" warn against thoughts of pardon: "The Crucifixion means that *we* must decrease"; and again, "*Happiness* consists in the denial of that self which *Pleasure* gratifies."[31] By March, Maynard faced a crisis of sorts: "I feel torn! 'Desperately' ploughing through Irving to better understand 'Reason.'" Irving's theology frustrated her, and so she turned to works that led her towards incarnational thinking and natural theology. She was drawn to Paley's *Evidences* because it "showed that one could know God, in part, through one's own nature and God's 'Guiding Intelligence.'" In June, she ended her debate thus: "*I* think God means 'Reason' to be satisfied in a great degree in *this* world; it is not simply knowing God, it is knowing the true estimate of *us*!"[32]

Maynard's turn towards theology that emphasized the interconnection between God and human nature was notable. It was through Paley that she came to view her feelings of same-sex desire as God's gift for her work as a Christian educational pioneer. Queer theorists have argued that the sheer sensuality of incarnational theology within mid- to late-Victorian Catholicism made it a powerfully resonant model for the articulation of same-sex sexuality.[33] I suggest that Maynard's merging of early- and mid- to late-Victorian Evangelicalism within her parents' odd mix of faiths (Puritan, Presbyterian-indebted Anglicanism), and natural theology, provided the building blocks for *her* own particular sexual identity. She never quite freed herself from atonement-thinking, but her self-search in 1867 helped her envision a more holistic self.

Maynard's search for "the true estimate" of self in 1867 inflamed an earlier awakening in her life. This pivotal moment occurred in 1863, at age fourteen, as she listened to her mother's criticism of the superficiality of relatives and of worldliness at large:

> Later, when I was reading Isaiah 6, I was really struck by the words, "Whom shall I send, and who will go for us?" This brought to mind the thoughtlessness of some I had seen that summer, and worldliness itself, and I suddenly thought that a real prophet was needed now, as ever it was in Isaiah's time.

Maynard maintained that "from this day on, [she] fully believed that God had singled [her] out to be a prophet. This, I decided, was to be my object in life." Indeed, the idea of doing God's work in this way helped her satisfy her emotional-intellectual cravings and appease her guilt over worldly passion. While her mother cautioned her to *know* God rather than *love* Him, Maynard's belief in her God-given aims took her down another path as an educational pioneer. Her imagined role of prophet provided a fluid space in which to explore the forbidden emotions that she had craved since childhood.[34]

"Self-Fulfillment!"

Maynard's struggle with her "emotional and mental furniture" likely inspired her second diary. On 1 January 1871, five years after starting her green book, she began what she called her daily diary. The diary is a factual account of her social life, and becomes testimony to her lifelong commitment as an educational pioneer. Indeed, through this record of events emerges a powerful woman of great talent and ambition, whose identity was shaped in part by Victorian narratives around nation and science as well as class, gender, and race.

The early diary reveals Maynard's socially isolated young womanhood. She and her sisters had no friends or suitors since they could not attend events typical of their class and gender. Their social lives revolved around entertaining their mother's devout elderly house guests and village charity work, with an emphasis of course on conversion through atonement theology. An entry about "Leading blind [villager] Harriet Boxall to God, to please *Mother*," symbolized Maynard's sense of confinement. "*I* shall teach Harriet *Braille* for self-fulfillment," she wrote.[35] Nonetheless, despite her confined home life, Maynard travelled extensively with her family to picturesque resorts in Europe or to bustling cities in Britain. There were weekly trips to London to shop and visit cathedrals, museums, and galleries, or to see the latest science exhibition. Maynard particularly felt "thrills" when looking at "the electrical experimentation with wire and the first bicycle" at the Crystal Palace in London in 1871. It is noteworthy that she fought to install light bulbs and the telephone at Westfield. She was also among the first women to own a bicycle in the late 1880s.[36]

Maynard's life changed in 1872 when her mother "disappeared" due to chronic asthma: "She could only 'rule' us from her drawing-room," Maynard explained in her autobiography. In her diary, she noted her joy over being allowed to stay in London for two month periods "to take drawing lessons." This unexplained privilege seemed odd, given Louisa's social rules and life Principle. Constance, for her part, fully believed that art gave her "freedom of interpretation." Drawing "an eye square, because it looked square in dark shadows," evoked the multifaceted "layering of 'truth'" – the "interconnection of evidence and experience." Art-making would become an important outlet for Constance in many ways. For example, as Mistress of Westfield, she emphasized to her students the interplay of self-expression (emotion), evidence (reason), and Truth (faith) that she believed "was crucial to one's success in life."[37]

The second important change in Maynard's life was a dramatic shift in her relationship with her father, who sought her company when his wife developed asthma. Henry Maynard was by this time a very wealthy man who held enormous social power. Catherine Firth's allusion to his "reputation for integrity, competiveness, and pleasure in 'moderate opulence'" suggests that Henry adopted Anglican Arnoldian-like ideas about masculinity.[38] Meanwhile, his impetus to provide a schoolroom and Hall for Hawkhurst villagers evinced his paternalist "cultivation" of the "lower orders."[39] It was thus with "great pride" that Constance noted her "father's new-found respect of [*her*] keen mind" when they discussed topics like nature and faith, and of her delight in his pampering: "I liked Boulogne because without my sisters my particular wants were indulged," she asserted in July 1872.[40] Maynard's self-esteem seemed to blossom at this time, which was crucial, given her troubled childhood.

On the more negative side, Constance's closeness to her father inculcated in her a mix of nationalist, class, and faith-based snobbery. This is not entirely surprising, given Henry's faith(s), imperialist ventures, and social views. The more pessimistic, Puritan-like Evangelical literature of the time adopted ideas from scientists like Malthus and Darwin to lament the "moral plague" created by industrial urbanization – irreligious workers, vice, crime and disease at home – and "heathen lands" overseas.[41] When Constance accompanied her father to Scotland in 1871, they were quick to "scorn the 'frivolous wrongdoing' [dancing and drinking] of [their] society" at the new luxurious hotels. But they were even more critical of the lower classes: "Walked down streets of factories with workers; as wretched looking a crowd as *ever* we saw – miserable dissipated looking people for the most part"; and again, in the Lake District, "Came across minors on strike. Want a raise from 18 shillings to 24. Father says 'it's too much' and they will be *starved* into submission!" In fact, Maynard's "disgust" of what her father called the "sloth, disease and immorality" of the British urban poor, and "degenerates worldwide," was a common theme in her diary.[42]

Henry Maynard was vexed when his eldest son Harry "showed an interest in the poor." Yet Harry believed that "immoral degenerates" (as his father called them) were worthy and should be saved. Harry's conversion to the more popular incarnational-based Evangelicalism of the day grieved both parents, but Henry barely tolerated Harry's aid to victims of the cholera outbreak of 1872: "I support Harry," Constance asserted in her diary. "Our parents fail to apply their [faith-based] values to the matters of life."[43] It was through Harry that Constance would experience the revival groups Moody and Sankey, and the Salvation Army, which united all Victorians through the testimony of faith, conversion, and nationalism at large.[44] However, unlike Harry, she retained her father's class and race-based values, which shaped her faith and attitude towards conversion. She noted her "revulsion" for villager Harriet Boxall, and later her "disgust for" her Italian-born adopted daughter Effie; even her middle-class fellow Girtonians "repulsed" her.[45] She encouraged philanthropy as a student at Girton and as Mistress of Westfield, but only in the form of Bible readings. When an ex-Girtonian opened a Settlement House for workers in 1898, she remarked, "No lever is strong enough to reform the drunken man or elevate the coster-monger woman who sells in the streets." Indeed, she never ceased to believe that the working-class "polluted" society.[46]

The most telling entries in the early diary convey Maynard's ambition. In fact, the diary immediately introduces the reader to "the Bill," which was a "work time-table" instituted by Maynard after leaving Belstead in 1866 so that she and her sisters, Gazy and Do, could self-study the Classics of Greek and Latin, and German and History. A "good Bill meant 36 hours per week," Maynard wrote, "but I sometimes reach as high as 43 by getting up early and writing in shorthand to get down more information." Although Maynard may have initiated the Bill to retaliate against leaving Belstead early, neither parent objected. This is somewhat expected, since knowledge and learning was important for many Evangelicals.[47] The Maynards likely recognized that the Bill effectively "monitored" their daughters' activities as well. When Henry added a "school-room" on the west of the house, Constance spent the majority of her time working there. She "kept the Bill" until leaving for Girton in October of 1872.[48]

Maynard's intellectual pursuits seem remarkable given that she assumed her formal education had ended. Nor was she aware of the mid-century developments in educational reform for her gender and class. It was in 1858 that educational pioneer Dorothea Beale had founded Cheltenham, which was among the first girls' schools to advocate measurable goals through education rather than girls' accomplishments.[49] In the early 1870s, while Maynard kept her Bill, a new type of girls' high school emerged in London that followed the ideals of Beale and other educational pioneers like Frances Mary Buss. Maynard later recognized that her training at Girton (1872–5) and subsequent work at Cheltenham (1876–7) and St. Leonards (1877–80) contributed to the movement for educational reform for girls and women. St. Leonards offered a female equivalent to the boys' public boarding schools in its emphasis on the Classics, the sciences, and "male" character-building through such activities as sports. Although most private schools including Belstead retained the early-Victorian model, improvement in girls' education spread throughout the twentieth century.[50]

The founding of University College in London in 1828 had proved a milestone in middle-class men's higher education, despite its lack in Oxbridge's status as an examining body; thus, educational pioneers were keen to gain similar opportunities for women. Elizabeth Jesser Reid's initiation of Bedford in London in 1849 proved a daunting venture, but it was the first women's college to provide university lectures. It was twenty years later that Emily Davies founded Hitchin, which was the first women's college attached to Cambridge. In Davies' view, women could achieve as well as men if they followed the same curriculum. In truth, Hitchin students' training in the Classics and the sciences was poor in comparison to men entering university: "We tend to flounder around," Maynard wrote of her studies at Hitchin in October, 1872. This said, her overall sentiment was one of joy: "It *is* like being afloat a stream that has *real* destination."[51]

In 1873, Hitchin moved to a new building about three miles from Cambridge and was renamed Girton. It was in 1873 that its three pioneers (among them Louisa Lumsden) passed the official exams in the Classics. In 1875, Maynard successfully completed her studies in the new field of Mental and Moral Sciences. Unfortunately, Cambridge did not yet grant degrees to women, and would not do so until 1948. However, the fact that the situation in Oxbridge contrasted with that in London proved crucial to Maynard's role as an educational pioneer. Her diary contends that University College's granting of degrees to women in 1878 inspired her to found Westfield College in October 1882.[52]

"Suffer Her Flesh"

Perhaps to contrast a diary that briefly noted public events, Maynard's green book evolved into a lengthy, faith-based account of fleshy love. Her Belstead experiences in 1863 initiated such self-explorations. In her autobiography, she bitterly noted her mother's curbing of one close friendship:

> I do not think it was a "foolish affection," but it was discouraged by mother ... She was so severe on my friendship with sweet Fan [Fanny Williams], and read my letters and checked them. She would not let me stay with Fan, or even see her for ten years.[53]

Nonetheless, green book depictions of Constance's love for Fan as "genuine," or as "a 'touch of heart,'" seemed consistent with Victorian perceptions of female romantic friendship. Dinah Craik's *A Woman's Thoughts about Women* (1858), for example, advocated passion between women as integral to a young woman's social and spiritual development. Twentieth-century biographers such as George Layard also mentioned it: "She [Lynn Linton] said Adeline Dalrymple caused her 'to become lost in a dream of nameless yearnings.'"[54] The events around Fanny thus suggested Louisa Maynard's repressive stance about intense female friendships, given Victorians' and early-Edwardians' general approval of them. As Firth and Vicinus note, Louisa curtailed the friendship not because Fanny was "worldly" – Fanny was quite pious – but because she feared Constance's deep emotional attachment to Fanny.[55]

Constance's frustration over Fanny lasted several years. In 1871 she lamented, "Was invited [again to Fanny's] and Mother refused for me – I am twenty two so why should I still be refused? Oh, unkind, unkind!"[56] It wasn't until 1873 that Fanny visited and Constance was able to see her again. By this time, Constance was a student at Girton and had explored friendship away from her mother's watchful eye. One wonders if Louisa allowed the pious Fanny to visit because she hoped Fanny might "remind" Constance about "religious duty." Constance did undertake conversionism at Girton, but she found Fanny's plea to "bring into captivity *every* thought to God" abhorrent. She had reread Paley's *Evidences* and concluded that "submission of Will *confined* freedom and happiness ... I was strangely ready to part with her," Constance concluded of Fanny's visit.[57] But they did remain friends until Fanny's death shortly after.

Maynard's second Belstead friendship did not last, yet it is also noteworthy. The green books of 1866–9 poured forth attraction for Virginia Dalrymple, whom Maynard had not seen since Belstead either: "She was the most beautiful girl I had ever seen"; and "I miss seeing her long golden hair and lovely fawn-like eyes."[58] An entry in 1869 following their chance meeting by a train station almost depicted Maynard as a bashful male admirer:

> Walking on the path from the train I heard, "have you forgotten me Consey?" and there was Virginia. I did not know what to say or do. I *knew* I loved her, but I did not know to that minute how much I loved her. I could only hold her hand and look at her, her face pale with a subdued expression. It cannot be but that she has had struggles with herself, and with worldliness all around her and no Christian friend to lean upon. Oh! Is it hard for her too? [59]

They met again by accident on the street in 1880:

> I held her close, so close. Oh! *How* I had longed to see her again! I remember all the times I went back to the train station in the hope that God would show her to me. I never saw her and cried again and again over the disappointment.[60]

It seems that their meetings, hugs, and touches offered the emotionally repressed Constance fluid moments of same-sex desire. Historian Kate Flint characterizes such moments as "queer encounters" in new public spaces that afforded women opportunities to meet and fantasize about each other. Whether on the path or urban street, Constance expressed her longings through gender norms and biblical passages. She "contented" herself by sketching both Virginia's and Fanny's faces from memory and hung the framed images in her bedroom until her death in 1935.[61]

Constance also formulated her passion for friends through scientific discourses and natural theology. For example, electricity became a metaphor for her attraction to a Hawkhurst villager friend named Hetty Lawrence. She had "marveled at Hetty's beauty, faith and wisdom" since 1867, but "Mother *strongly* disapproved of 'sentiment' for an '*unworthy*' [villager]." George could no longer visit Willy Bishop for that reason, and so both pairs "kept quiet about friendship."[62] However, Constance found her new feelings for Hetty troubling: "When I see her, it is as if we both hold the end of electric chains and sparks exchange between us – *I* know then I am holding God"; and again, "She [Hetty] says, 'It seems as if we know each other like sisters!' *I* feel that we do." Considering the sisterly love, spiritual connection, and physical sparks, Constance eventually understood that her feelings were as much based on the physical as the spiritual. Nonetheless, she likened her "sparks" with Hetty to electric energy; she understood the "thrill" of touch as a "natural force" that brought friends closer to "knowing God;" and, most of all, she was drawn to Hetty's nebulous idea of fleshy desire: "I [Hetty] *feel* the dark chains [desire], but I keep a little piece of God unruffled in my heart." True happiness was, after all, the denial of that pleasurable self for God.[63]

Constance's awakening to desire, coupled with her fear of "*failing* God if [she] did not suffer [her] flesh," seems extreme to readers today. Yet for Constance, the idea of "a lifelong crucifixion [wa]s most beautiful."[64] It would, in fact, prompt another extraordinary facet of her sexuality in her need to suffer for it. Her upbringing on Irving had certainly inculcated in her a form of reveling in pain as though it were a mark of grace. As a young girl she had cried bitterly over *feeling* sinful, yet did not understand what sinfulness *was*. As an adolescent, she more actively sought physical and psychological self-punishment to test her faith:

> One day I thought I would pray alone, so I went in between the hazel bushes and knelt down on last year's dead leaves. When I got up I looked

down at my bare knees and I saw that some of the leaves were holly and that they clung on. I thought, "Holly prickles and I did not feel it. Oh, this was *real*, real prayer."

Constance's "proof of faith" was played out in her symbolic crucifixion of her flesh which, she believed, her parents and God expected of her.[65]

Certainly, Constance recognized that her "proof of faith" was in part culturally-based. She might have been raised to believe in the depraved quality of *all* souls before God, but she understood that womanly passivity and selflessness were both expected and interconnected to subordination to men. She read typical literature of the time, such as Mrs Beeton's guides to domesticity, which emphasized that "women's 'qualities' were best suited in the home." Evangelical discourses similarly stressed women's '"natural' piety, humility and subservience [was] a deliverance easily attained if she kept out of life [public sphere]."[66] Constance did not take gender norms "as a matter of course." As she remarked, "It is very strange, this 'going out into life.' George looks forward to his life with Harry with *pleasure*. It is *my* pleasure to look forward to his coming home"; and again, "We met a young man who spoke of his fight with consumption. Father commented that he should have his story printed. Oh if only I were a man I should write it! But I can't, I can't! I must let it rest."[67]

Despite her gender frustrations, Constance claimed that she felt more repressed by her mother's religious life Principle: "I felt it *most* keenly ... Of all us girls, *I* got it the worst." Her description of her adolescence does paint a bleak picture. From age eleven to fourteen (1860–3) she was home alone because George, Gazy, and Dora attended boarding school. "I think of the way I was, reading alone, and writing mostly about religion. I usually felt unhappy, which was always translated into the fact that I should pray more."[68] Upon leaving Belstead (1865) Constance became the youngest daughter-at-home, and thus relatively few duties fell her way. Louisa may well have "aimed to bring all [her children] to an unworldly spirit;" however, Constance helped her mother compile a catechism about "principles of faith," and "revise the Prayer-Book to bring society 'out of the vanity of Time.'" Constance's account of their work between 1869 and 1871 revealed the ever-changing religious climate, and her mother's reaction to it:

Ritual was now in full force and the church fashionably "High." All theological views echoed those from Rome; ... choirs in full robes, long-skirted curates. We looked upon every [religious] innovation as misleading, and

> something to be avoided because it would destroy the soul. In the forefront was the Prayer-Book, which was largely Protestant as where some of the services, especially the Baptismal ... We began with the morning service, and went on. We inserted Scripture wherever possible, since it is the only safe ground. It [the prayer book] never went anywhere, but Mother felt better after writing it.[69]

Interestingly, queer theorist Eve Sedgwick argues that the religious innovations that Louisa Maynard adamantly declared "misleading" and "something to be avoided" offered emotional and aesthetic satisfaction for some late-Victorian males who struggled with feelings of effeminacy or same-sex desire. We could argue that Louisa's choice of Scripture for the Prayer-Book – which likely reflected Irving's ascetic views – was also queer. As David Bebbington notes, Irving's homily, "rely on God alone, rather than visible sustenance [like Ritualism]," had long since been dismissed as ill-suited for conversion.[70]

When we turn to the green book, it seems that Constance's struggle with her "depraved nature" paralleled with gaining her mother's approval. An entry in 1868 was particularly telling: "After all these years of our talks and reading together, I have confidence in Mother's judgment of our separation from the world. She is slow to admit anyone to 'her circle,' and now, she believes *me* to be a Christian!"[71] Constance's turn to Paley's *Evidences* in 1867, and again at Girton in 1873, was undoubtedly a milestone in her emotional-religious process, but Louisa's possibly unhealthy impact upon Constance's life was as evident. An entry in 1869 clearly laid out Irving's schema for salvation – a life principle that Constance attempted to follow and lead loves to follow throughout her life: "We are under *complete* domination of three enemies, the flesh, the world and Satan. Are we helpless? No because God has left us Christ's Atonement, which is enough to employ us." Constance declared that it was through acts of self-denial that the "nature beyond us" would abide in God and transcend the evils that existed apart from God.[72]

We can conclude that within the incarnational-based mid-century Evangelical climate existed forms of extreme Evangelicalism that were conducive to religious despair. Louisa Maynard's Biblicism, ideas of the Crucifixion, and duty towards conversion led her to impose upon her children principles of conduct based upon worldly self-denial. As scholar John Stachniecoski notes, since Victorian girls felt socially inferior to boys, those raised on an ascetic faith could more easily slip into compensatory suffering.[73] When writing in 1925, Constance voiced anger over this aspect of her past: "It makes me angry as well as sad. Mother did me untold mental damage." Her remark of course linked her adolescent experiences with the new scientific "mother-blaming" language. By the mid-1920s, Freudians followed sexologists' to posit that a mother's repression of a daughter could invoke life-long "forms of masochism to obtain love and respect" in the daughter. Nonetheless, Constance concluded of her thoughts, "I see that I was beginning to find who I was through religious and intellectual inspiration." The fact that some late-Victorian scientists viewed female masochism as agency, rather than natural female submission, suggests the nuances of both Victorian femininity and faith.[74]

Constance Maynard's contemplations about her early upbringing remind us that to focus only on what religion *did* to a woman like Maynard is limiting. It fails to acknowledge the myriad ways that faith helped Maynard to achieve professional success and transform educational systems for women that still remain today. Her green book, diary, and autobiography convey that there was within Evangelicalism a powerful leaven conducive to intellectual endeavour and higher learning, as well as spiritual authority. In fact, as Dixon, Morgan, deVries, and others argue, close attention should be paid to the ways in which Victorian women's fight for social, economic, and political reform "interpolated into different religious traditions, each of which provided women with different degrees of room to manoeuvre."[75] Constance Maynard's life reveals how the complexity of the Victorian religious and secularist landscape enriched one individual's experiences in compelling ways.

It is through Maynard's records that we recognize how faith, belief, and practice can function – sometimes simultaneously – as both empowering and oppressive. As we have seen, religion was many things to the young Maynard: a belief; a world view; a mode of conduct; a divine privilege; a consolation; a shelter; a justification; an expression for love. Throughout her tenure as Mistress of Westfield, Maynard consistently spoke of her "special mission to teach girls to learn to love God." Her link of higher learning and religion forged new career opportunities for women as missionaries, medical missionaries, educators, and social workers. At the same time, her understanding of God's reward for her work through "His gift of human love" reinforced her belief in new possibilities for the reinvention of the self. The following chapters convey the ways that Maynard adopted faith with various cultural discourses for powerful expressions of hetero- and same-sex love.[76]

Faith was also for Maynard a nuanced space for resistance. It cannot be surprising that Maynard's upbringing augmented her self-doubt and sense of wrong. After all, her ambitions as an educational pioneer stood at odds with her culture and her faith. She was forced to negotiate her aims within in a largely secularist male-dominated field. As a result, Maynard often blamed her failure in leadership as a personal loss of faith rather than the result of her society's overt sexism. Faith also drove Maynard to try and convert those she loved. Her belief that God's gift of love was also His test of her faith led her to repress those in whom she had gained trust and love. It was a complex mode of conduct that, understood as faith, bordered on pleasure as well as pain and frustration for Maynard: "Am I a Minotaur that I must eat a maiden's heart!" she exclaimed of her behaviour towards one Westfield love.[77] Maynard's records disclose the depths of her own angst as she suffered the loss of love. Her anger, shame, and guilt caused such extreme bouts of depression during her years as Mistress that at times, she actually contemplated suicide.

A queer approach to Maynard's experiences reveals that Maynard's "suffering" was not simply defeatist or a perverse outcome of her familial and cultural experiences. The fact that her resistance of the flesh involved various dominant-submissive role-playing is a case in point. Indeed, Maynard's behaviour suggests the numerous forms of pleasure and power that emanate from suffering for worldly sin – especially when one holds social power over others and also feels responsible for their souls.[78] Moreover, if Maynard's measures of self-denial were occasions for self-indulgence, they were also opportunities for her cathartic healing of public and private wounds. The ensuing chapters shall reveal how faith helped Maynard gain a new sense of empowerment and self-respect in her often lonely and frustrating role. During a period when many women adopted subordinated domestic roles in sometimes loveless marriages, Maynard drew on late-Victorian discourses, and especially faith, to formulate a powerful and vibrant sexual self-consciousness as an educational pioneer.

Maynard's embodied femininity as an educational pioneer was neither submissive, nor naive, nor asexual. Therefore, her private writings challenge the range of activities and meanings normally attributed to Victorian female friendship and "gendered" power relations. Indeed, the records of Constance Maynard teach us that the problem of unfettered power or passion is not so much its existence, but its control. Maynard mused on this fundamental dilemma in 1899: "Confidence alone is pure, sweet, and grave, but rather lacking in force. Passion alone brings tortures and jealousies, but it is strong. Could not the two be united? Here is the danger."[79]

Chapter Two

"Crisis, Restraint and Liberty" 1869–1872

In her account of the year 1872, Constance Maynard described herself as a vibrant young woman who stood on the threshold of life: "At twenty-three, I was noted for my array of well-tested opinions and for my wonderful eyes and smile. This year I got Liberty as few girls in the '70s got it, got it in full measure." She still suffered under her mother's fixed life Principle, "turn from the world," but travels with her father and self-study had given her much more confidence. Of her emotional longings, Maynard wrote, "There is an overwhelming force in every woman's heart. Mine had found no expression at all. Who would discover the wealth of those untroubled depths?"[1] The excavator of Maynard's deep-seated passions was the highly esteemed and enigmatic Professor of Classics, Lewis Campbell, a man twenty years her senior. He opened up to her the world of secular intellect and the intoxicating world of love and desire. In this instance, aspects of Victorian heteronormative masculinity forged the pious Maynard's sense of her sexual self in both limiting and self-empowering ways.

Maynard explained that her initial awakening to (hetero)sexuality was understood through reading romantic poetry and taking "sneak peeks at novels at railway stations." She recalled one experience, at age twelve: "I read about the sensuality 'of the kiss' in Tennyson's 'Fatima' and wondered, 'What does this feel like?' I thought I could make a good guess. I had similar sorts of attractions towards male cousins which felt so exciting at the time." According to other female writers, Maynard's youthful experience was not so atypical. Even though Victorians wrote about and fantasized about sex, most households did not discuss it in detail. In fact, sexual pleasure was considered inherently dangerous for girls and women since they were viewed as passive and fearful by nature.[2]

2.1 Constance Maynard aged thirty-one, c. 1880. Courtesy of Queen Mary University of London Archives/Constance Maynard/WFD.

Throughout her teenage years, however, Maynard keenly felt her "growing need for passion." Her curiosity found form in "shy glances at the nudes at the Royal Academy," but when she dared to "make eyes" at George's friend, "vivid words from Tissy sent [her] away with [her] hands clapped over her ears to howl in the garden." From this mortifying incident the eighteen-year-old Maynard learned that respectable women must not flirt with the opposite sex. Her diary revealed her society's views on young men's flirtations: "Harry *is* good, but he is *known* to 'like a laugh and a pretty girl.'" The Victorian double standard of sexual morality notwithstanding, Louisa Maynard "really fretted" over what she called, "Harry's lapses into 'evil.'" When he moved to London to work for the family firm she arranged numerous family visits "to watch over him." Harry's marriage freed him from his mother's tether, but Constance lamented the daughters' plight: "We had no London season, no parties, and no possibilities of love affairs." While most girls of their class were groomed for marriage, whether consciously or unconsciously, Louisa raised her daughters to be spinsters. Only Dora eventually married, and then not until she was thirty.[3]

In February 1869 of the "eventful year," as Maynard named it in her autobiography, she wrote in her green book, "He who searches my heart sees that I care more about my own imaginations than thinking of God." Her thoughts were based upon the "new year motto" from her mother which, taken from Psalm 37.3.4., warned the Christian that while desire was God-given, "*give* d[id] not mean *grant* the desires of thy heart." The entry ended with Maynard's own thoughts on the matter:

> I think this is *more* satisfactory than fulfilling them. Desire is better answered by having vocation for it *taken away* than by having it granted. Youth has been pleasant, though not satisfactory. The future ought to be far happier because the fluctuation of feeling will decrease as knowledge gets firmer.[4]

At age twenty, when most women of her class "mooned" over friends and imagined heterosexual romance, Maynard tried to resist all human sentiment because God wished it: "I long for excitement of feeling!" she exclaimed. "But I sincerely *hope* that my insane longing will quite pass away." Here we see evidence of how her particular faith shaped her sexuality in young womanhood. She could only conceive of "worldly desire" as an evil. In a sense, longing was to be Maynard's "burden of religious despair." In her autobiography, Maynard voiced deep resentment over her "ignorance in love" as a young woman: "Love and Marriage were such great things. *Must* they be forever hidden away? Were they *never* to be touched on by speech or writing?"[5]

In fact, marriage was to be a topic of conversation not once, but twice that year. Although no one saw the significance at the time, Louisa privately decided that as Tissy was nearly thirty, the age at which she herself had married, "it was time to begin to look around." This decision did not mean that Tissy was allowed to attend social evenings or dances; instead, Henry dutifully brought home two eligible but apparently "dull and impervious" doctors. Because "lynx-eyed Tissy saw through the little ruse de guerre and scouted it rather unmercifully," Constance commented, "There were no more guests of this nature." Such experiences were doubtless bitter for Tissy, but the incident also left a sting for her youngest sister too, as seen in her addendum: "Years later I remember a dinner party where I met a captain Môntan Wilbraham-Taylor, whom I thought was splendid. I can remember thinking, 'Why did *we* never meet a man like this when we were younger?'"[6]

Perhaps Maynard's bitterness over romance also stemmed from the events surrounding her own first marriage proposal later that summer. In mid-July, both she and Gazy visited family friends where Constance met the eldest son, Harry Collisson, who planned to become a clergyman. Although their encounter was brief, Harry asked Constance to marry him. Her green book entry, written a month later, gives an almost lurid account of the first whispers of love with Maynard's emphasis on fleshy sin:

> I became earthly minded, I am ashamed to say. My first feeling was one of pleasure mixed with great trembling, and then an overwhelming feeling that it must not be allowed for an instant ... Oh, the trial of the next few days! He was in the background of every thought, yet with a sense of some irreparable loss.

The thought of intimacy with "*any* human being was wholly insupportable," she concluded, especially with someone "so penniless in comparison to [her] wealth." The green book covered a few more pages about it "all being very distressing," but when Collisson returned to Oakfield to fervently argue his case Maynard "gave him no hope."[7]

Key to the Collisson episode was Maynard's first-hand experience with heterosexual love and its far-ranging emotions: from his ardent desire, her responsive "flush," and her recognition that while it "was pleasant" she was not attracted to him. The event also unveiled for Maynard her own needs. She had used the language of faith to reject Collisson as "wholly insupportable," but her mother's scorn of Collison's "ridiculousness" was another matter. In fact, her anger at her mother led Maynard to realize that to be passionless, as "unworldly" as it was, was out of the question. Her self-questioning was exemplified by the "great and pleasurable impression" that *L' Hotel du Petit St. Jean* had upon her. Guarded as Maynard was about how she came to read this novel, she later confessed that *L' Hotel* "opened [her] up to the world of love – that all sorts of 'inarticulate stirrings' were explained to [her]." It was at this time that she read Paley's *Evidences* which, she claimed, revealed that human nature was connected to God. One wonders at the significance of a green book entry in April 1869, "Only love can do it!"[8]

"My Poetic, Faithless Lover"

It was not until March 1872 that Maynard first experienced the world of love. Indeed, her autobiographical account of the passion between the "Christian woman and her poetic, faithless lover" in *L' Hotel* mirrored that described between herself and Lewis Campbell in her green book. Yet Maynard's autobiography made no connection to this in its oblique, haunting yearnings. It is through the green book that we learn of Campbell's great impact upon Maynard's ambition and passion, and Maynard's recognition of her limited upbringing and position as a Victorian woman in general. Indeed, the green book astonishes in its candid account of her feelings, and provides remarkable insight into this important time in her life.

To set the stage for this key relationship in her life, Maynard explains that she had been invited to Fanny and Lewis Campbell's home by her Aunt Amelia (Fanny's mother) since 1867. Louisa Maynard had refused her sister Amelia because she knew little about the purportedly secularist Lewis, except that he was from impoverished gentility and had "succeeded in life through scholarships" at Oxford. Fanny, who had met Lewis at the Oxford commemoration in 1858, was "considered a good wife" who had been vital to her husband's academic success. At forty-two, Lewis was well respected. He had a number of publications under his belt and held the Greek chair of St. Andrews University for many years.[9]

When Amelia invited Constance to visit in February 1872, she was "suddenly granted permission." Constance noted her surprise, although her parents had "loosened [their] reins" since 1870. Dora had been allowed a month of trial nursing at Queen's Square Hospital in London. Tissy meanwhile was to train at a local Convalescent Home that summer. While Henry and Louisa viewed these activities as extensions of female domestic roles, Dora and Tissy were nevertheless receiving "professional training." Dora entered the profession seriously in 1879.[10] Yet, despite the Maynards' somewhat progressive attitude to women's careers, Louisa had remained strict about visits to worldly family members. Hence Constance was thrilled to set off to St. Andrews in Scotland. She would have been even more astounded had she known that her life would be forever changed on both an emotional and intellectual level.

The green book described in great detail Maynard's pleasure in settling into a "quiet, but delightful routine" in the Campbell's sumptuous home, The Scores. Mornings were always spent with Aunt Amelia but afternoon activities varied. Sometimes she walked with Lewis or attended university lectures. On other afternoons Fanny held "charming afternoon teas" which were equally stimulating. Indeed, it was at these functions that Constance became more aware of women's rights and educational and sanitary reforms, and heard for the first time of the merits of women's higher education. Lewis, she learned, had supported higher learning for women since the emergence of the movement in 1848.[11]

At the same time, etiquette played a part in the Campbells' consideration of Maynard's strict upbringing: "Lewis chose his words carefully while Fanny excused any amusement that mother might condemn," Maynard wrote in her autobiography. "So I missed the county ball, dinners and card-parties, remaining behind with Auntie." Nonetheless, the Campbells frequently entertained, and Maynard wrote "ecstatically about life at St. Andrews" to her family, explaining "all the wonders of University talk."[12] She even gained permission to stay longer, "so long as [she] exercised self-discipline" in her worldly environment. Maynard, however, had already formed her own opinions on that score:

> Secular it is certainly, but the delightful brightness and warmth of intellect seems to me to take off from the thing which oppresses the very spirit of this world. It is only on Sunday that I feel shock as I watch them read novels or have parties and card playing. Perhaps these are not sins but simply the love of them. I have come (perhaps too willing) to believe that the various schools of thought, expression, action and society are up to individual people.[13]

2.2 Lewis Campbell, 1863, Professor of Greek at the University of St. Andrews, Scotland 1863–1892. Courtesy of the University of St. Andrews Library/ ALB-1-102.

Despite her concern for what she saw as their disrespect for the Sabbath, the idea of freedom of thought was clearly innovating for Maynard. She was supposed to suppress worldly intellectual and emotional self-expression. Yet she relished "peoples respect for [her] opinion," even though "such self-seeking was weakness [of faith]." In fact, she "knew that [she] was seizing the opportunity to bring forth a kind of self [she] had recognized before by glimpses."[14]

Maynard's realization of her ambition and the notion of "Liberty" took form upon meeting Isabella Cook, the daughter of a late moral philosophy professor of St. Andrews whom Lewis had greatly admired. Cook mentioned that her older sister Rachel was attending Hitchin College, and that Rachel aimed to be among the first women to sit for the Cambridge Classical Tripos: "Learning about this whole new world [for women] is exactly what I feel I have been waiting for," Maynard wrote in her green book. "I won't disobey my parents, but I will move heaven and earth to get there!"[15]

When Isabella mentioned that Lewis had tutored Rachel in Greek for the Hitchin Entrance Examination, Constance knew that she had his support, and an opportunity. After all, "*Fanny* had encouraged" her to take walks alone with Lewis, and Constance felt comfortable with it due to her companionable relationship with her father. When she "raised 'the Hitchin question'" Lewis, as she expected, "advised [her] to give it serious thought." Constance was "not only taken" by Lewis's support of women's higher education: "I greatly admire his melancholy mind," she confessed. Their afternoon walks had drawn them towards each other's "aspirations and compassions." Meanwhile, the "loveliest part of the evening" was the "sparks" exchanged "when Lewis's eyes 'met [hers]' as he read Plato, Electra, Iliad or Shakespeare while [she], Fanny and Auntie drew or sewed." Implied here, besides Maynard's growing infatuation with Campbell, were gender roles played out in separate spheres. The Scores may have been Fanny's domain, and even a space to discuss feminist issues, but when Lewis was home the women were expected to listen and obey.[16] This form of gender and sex hierarchy was reflected in Maynard's relationship with Campbell over the years.

Underlying Maynard's strong attraction for Campbell was concern over his religious perspective, which she debated at length in her green book: "L [Campbell] thought me very *theological*, so I introduced the inspiration of the Bible ... to prove it had *brightened* my life" and that of millions of others. The theologically-liberal Campbell agreed that the Bible was inspired by God, but said it was one among the many "God-given lights like reason, science, nature and art." He had apparently emphasized his point: "Your [Maynard] religious hero [Edward Irving] may well breathe a lofty spirit of devotion. But there is more greatness in men like Shakespeare who have reached out to a wider audience... and condemned no one." Like many intellectuals of the time, Campbell challenged what he called "religious dogma." He would ask her, "What beliefs *can* one believe? What kind of gratification *can* be pursued?" Is it not "*sin* that debases us, and ties us to the earth?"[17]

Maynard could not dismiss Campbell's position, "What touches us deeply on any side touches our inner self, our spirit," since her self-search in 1869 had led her to envision intellect and passion as God-given pleasure. However, seeking "True Spiritual" life was so embedded in her psyche that she could only argue, "a life with God means that we *must* condemn the world." Campbell delighted in the irony of her liking his society, and would tell her, "God condemns *sin* - the world is in our hearts." Maynard felt intellectually beaten by Campbell, but she disagreed with his assertion that "the Will g[ave] one access to the spirit through *understanding*." In Maynard's view, those "of Will could not receive God," let alone gain any form of "spiritual understanding." Spirit was the intelligence and the immaterial that was independent of corporeal existence. Lewis, she concluded, "ha[d] no religion at all, only a noble code of ethics!" Campbell's "ethics" did, of course, reflect the mid-century idea of the harmony between God and humanity. Nor was his notion of spirit-faith-understanding atypical for the intellectualism of the time.[18]

Their religious differences notwithstanding, Maynard admitted to "a sort of intimacy" between them. It is notable that neither Fanny Campbell nor her Aunt Amelia was mentioned in either diary or green book after mid-February, while her feelings for Lewis became paramount: "He is the centre of the life that I find myself in!" In fact, just like the Christian heroine in *L' Hotel*, Maynard had fallen for her "poetic, faithless lover." When Lewis mentioned that their connection "fit into regions where Fanny had failed," she responded to that knowledge. Certainly, his enactment of the "misunderstood husband" was a ploy to gain her sympathy, but when he spoke about love she "lured him on" by waxing ignorant on the subject. She knew full well that her very "naivety" was part of her attraction to him.

Needless to say, if Campbell had left his wife for Maynard it would have been truly scandalous for the time. Yet their interactions evinced the often contradictory norms that were particular to Victorian masculinity, femininity, heterosexuality, and romantic friendship. Constance would later note that Fanny accepted "Lewis' little 'ways' with amusement." While he flirted with their female friends, or various young male students, she formed a series of separate romantic friendships with women. Fanny's admission to Constance after Lewis' death in

1914, "I always liked women best," was meant to explain and lament her neglect of Lewis in later life. It may also suggest that Fanny and Lewis had separate erotic interests. Constance, for her part, seemed to accept their behaviour. Fanny's confession had also helped to assuage Constance's *own* guilt over Lewis at that time.[19]

In March 1872, such thoughts were far from the young Maynard's mind. She declared herself completely "intoxicated by L's melancholic outpourings" on love and ambition. He assured her that "*nothing* was more worth experiencing," but that his choice of career over love had led to intense regret and disappointment. He further explained that he had found "certain resolutions" to his dilemma. His academic "duty" to his pupils sometimes found form in "deep love. With love," he added, "there always comes to my heart an irrepressible yearning to protect students from pain and evil." Campbell's "irrepressible" longings for students suggested that Victorian male bonds could be as directly ardent as those between women. For her part, Maynard was wise enough to suspect that Campbell's emotive-religious outlet was masked by his role as a lecturer. His position condoned his attraction for "sweet natured pupils" like Herbert, for beautiful prodigies like Rachel Cook, and "was somehow connected with his love for her." She appeared to find Campbell's oblique discourses of power romantically appealing.[20]

When Maynard chose to scold herself for falling in love with Campbell, she adopted the language of her faith: "Love is weakness"; and "Love lets wants out." Yet such claims did not prevent Maynard from expressing her desire for Campbell. In fact, faith became for Maynard a means to both understand and condone her love for a married man: "There is sadness in his [Campbell's] face, and suffering. *This* is what draws my heart to him." She also rejoiced in "intangible, exquisite" moments, like the time they "stayed out to watch the sun dip below the horizon," and had "run down the hill holding hands and laughing."[21] In this, Maynard's description of their liaisons evoked the rituals of heterosexual love, or as Victorian writer Frederick Saunders put it, "assuring the mysterious attraction of heart for heart." Heterosexual relations "should take but one form, [hierarchical] marriage." Of course, Saunders (and society in general) would have been far more outraged by Maynard's flirtations with a married man than by his with her.[22]

There is no evidence to suggest that Maynard engaged in more than heavy flirtation with Campbell, especially when comparing her records of their intimacy in 1880, but her account of her last days at The Scores conveyed the intensity of their desire. Lewis and Fanny attended the county ball and she "counted the hours when he would return":

> When I finally heard the door open I ran into the hall, but Oh! – I was not prepared for such a welcome! – he literally bounded up the shallow hall steps, gave me a kiss on the fore-head, held me by the shoulder, looking at me with a face blazing with joy, while he whispered "home again" under his breath.[23]

Later that night when they were alone "he took her hand and gave it long, long kisses." She "found it bewildering, but nothing more happened, 'thank Heaven.'" On their last night together "Lewis lured me into his study three times," Maynard noted in her green book, adding in her autobiography, another "danger zone … The door of The Scores closed behind me, and it was never, never to be the same again."[24]

Maynard's account of Campbell's behaviour over her three month stay suggests that he took advantage of his power as a male academic and his hold over her. But of note here is Campbell's conflation of passion, ambition, and religion to articulate his role and extramarital passions: love and ambition were bound in his duty as Professor to protect his pupils against evil. He further explained his behaviour to Maynard through positioning love-faith and ambition-faith as powerful opposing binaries. He "acclaimed love," he told her, yet he "condemned its very passion as a degree of [Christian] weakness." Since to be "weak was to be miserable," he said, "one should make the [Christian] character strong" through ambition and self-control. In her green book, Maynard had simply concluded, "I agree with L. Self-control *is* the main ingredient."[25] After all, that was the keyword during her childhood and with the Harry Collisson affair. Nonetheless, Maynard's relationship with Campbell is crucial to understanding her life. She had not only remained a willing participant in his "game" throughout her three-month stay, but would enact versions of it herself when Mistress of Westfield. Her behaviour, whether conscious or not, left life-long scars on those who fell under her spell; and for herself, torment, bitterness, and confusion.

It is then unsurprising that Maynard struggled upon her return home from St. Andrews in 1872. She tried to show an interest in life at Oakfield and keeping her Bill (her timetable for study), but home life paled in comparison to thoughts of Hitchin. And she felt another, deeper loss. She longed for her "sad, poetic lover." For the first time in her life, she "felt a huge distance between [herself] and her family that [she] did not know how to bridge over." She surmised they "thought her unchanged." However, not only did her change feel profound, but she feared it was irrevocable. As a consequence, she spent hours hiding in the garden to ponder her feelings on love and ambition.[26]

In her green book, Maynard implied her guilty pleasure over "the love which Lewis had given [her]." After all, he *was* married, and she was relieved that no one knew of her thoughts. It is also notable that she began calling her green book "My Friend," in whom she now confided about her "secret" love. This starkly differed from her stance during the Harry Collisson episode: "I would like my mother to know about it." While she had felt sinful over liking "feeling desired" by Collisson, she was more troubled by feeling desire for Campbell. Yet "this desire was not better answered by having vocation for it *taken away*" by God.[27]

There is an indication that Campbell had similar feelings. After a couple of "playful and kind letters," one sent "in May spoke of his longing for an absent love." After ending with the words, "I wish I could whisper my private gladness into your ear," he enclosed a sonnet which he claimed he had "written in [her] honour on April 17th":

> Angel, that when like summer dust my heart
> was hot and dry within me, thou dids't not fear
> to whisper comforts in a grief-dulled ear
> and pour thy balm upon a desperate heart.
> Forgive, if, blameless of dissembling art,
> too eagerly I drank when thou was't here
> the proffered benediction from thy clear
> deep eyes, strong pleaders for the holier part.
> Oh! forgive! now that thou art no more near,
> if in my desert soul some trace remain
> of all that thou dids't water with such care.
> My thirst returns. Yet milder doth appear
> the aspect of old familiar pain,
> and happy memories linger in the air.

At the bottom of the sonnet Campbell wrote "I will spare your blushes ... I have not shown it to anyone ... I do not think you'll see any remains of the wants that hollowed the heart in winter time." Implied in Campbell's sonnet was sexual desire set within the context of the religious emotionalism of the era. He was the straying, misunderstood husband, comforted by the "holier" but nonetheless seductive "Angel" with "deep, pleading eyes." He may well have felt desperate about his personal life, but he was toying with her naivety and emotions in his position of power in their relationship.[28] Although Maynard sensed his rebuff, and possibly his dallying by the tone of his letter and sonnet, his promise of a visit to Oakfield later that summer left her filled with excited trepidation and hope.

The "Hitchin Question"

Besides or perhaps because of her ongoing angst over Campbell, Maynard's energy became bound up with what became the "Hitchin question." Indeed, Hitchin may have seemed a way out for her at this time. Her sister Gazy's volunteer teaching at a local dame-school symbolized to Maynard the parting of ways. Gazy was so talented and her goals seemed so low. Nor did she share Gazy's or Dora's enthusiasm for village Bible readings, which they had established while she was at Belstead. Oakfield duties fell more their way than hers, since she was the youngest daughter-at-home, and so she had grown increasingly frustrated over the recent years. Indeed, she felt trapped "like a panther as he walked restlessly up and down in his cage."[29]

Maynard knew she had to secure her parents' support, and then pass the Hitchin Entrance Examination, if she was to pursue her dream. Her diary indicated that she corresponded frequently with Rachel Cook about Hitchin throughout April and early May, but it took until late April for Maynard to raise the topic with her father. Initially, "there was a frowning and, then, 'where's the *use*? What's it for?'" He finally "gave in" as did her mother, on the condition that she would ultimately "return home and live with her sisters." Maynard promised "anything-everything."[30]

In an essay for *The Girton Review* in 1926, Maynard recalled this pivotal time: "There was no subsequent difficulty from my parents. They never balked when I regaled on each promise in the on-flowing tide of life." This was not entirely true. Maynard's diaries reveal her parents' incessant attempts to dissuade her from returning to Hitchin, and from working at Cheltenham and St. Leonards. For each venture, she had to negotiate term by term, promising to return home eventually. She did not see Westfield as "solid" until her father gave his "stamp of approval" after his first visit. Nonetheless, her parents did recognize her talents and her commitment to study: "As controlling as Mother was," Maynard wrote in her autobiography, "she encouraged gleaning in every field. It was exceedingly fragmented knowledge, yet no-one could call it a 'smattering' because it was fired with the most ardent interest."[31]

Maynard faced much opposition from various sources. Her siblings pointed out that she could not possibly pass the Entrance Examination due to her lack of education. The family clergyman condemned Hitchin's Protestant "tone." His admonition, "You will find the intellectual work too engrossing for your own good," reflected that of such scientists as Henry Maudsley, who publically denigrated higher education for women. Maynard was troubled by such remarks: "Is it my duty to stay at home as the others do? If I go to Hitchin, *will* I like it too much?" She knew, of course, that she had to seize this opportunity while it existed. She had proved her passion for learning to herself by her faithful commitment to the Bill since Belstead. Moreover, Dora had just returned from her work at Queen's Square, and Tissy planned to go to Highgate in October.[32]

Preparations for Hitchin's Entrance Examination took a definite turn in early May, after Maynard received "a very formidable" specimen examination paper on mathematics from Rachel Cook. When her parents realized how badly mathematics had been taught at Belstead they quickly arranged for George to coach her in the subject. This seemed core to Maynard's self-being. When she sat the examination in London alongside ten other candidates she at least felt prepared. She wrote three two-hour papers daily over a three-day period, beginning on 19 June: "The exam room is too hot," she complained in her diary. "I feel so anxious and am thankful to pass the days so well." By contemporary standards she seems to have survived a gruelling schedule, so it is not surprising that she returned home feeling a sense of accomplishment. "I enjoyed the challenge of trying to get all my thoughts down," she noted in her green book. Standing at the threshold of the "public sphere," she had also found the "'now or never of the crisis of life' fascinating and inspiriting."[33]

In her autobiography, Maynard declared, "The thought that I was at *last* out on the current of life felt liberating." She would not have been quite as certain of this in 1872 of course. In fact, the diary revealed her fears about failing the examination. Nonetheless, given that middle-class women were usually chaperoned when out in public, "being alone on the streets of London [likely symbolized] the sort of liberty that would now be [hers]."[34] On 27 June Maynard learned that she was "safely in." She did not pass "with great honours," but she was delighted. She received congratulations all round.[35]

Although Maynard's diaries are vague on the matter, it seems that the final stamp of approval for Hitchin lay on Lewis Campbell's shoulders. As noted above, Campbell had promised to visit Oakfield that summer, and Maynard's "anxiety" arose once more when the trip was arranged. Her biggest fear, she claimed, was that her family might "not warm to the man who had drawn her heart to him." Not surprisingly, she voiced her "relief about [her] parents' almost immediate response to L's sympathizing impressible character." Campbell had recommended Hitchin. Harry, also taken with the vibrant Scot, had already accepted an invitation to The Scores for that September. There was also much discussion about Gazy going for an extended visit in 1883.[36]

Maynard's initial conversations with Campbell centred on Hitchin: "He seemed pleased about [her] acceptance," but became "offhand" when she questioned him about his own student experience. He summed it up as "curious," adding, "some parts are painful." Although Maynard dismissed his advice as "more about himself than her," she was ruffled by the "mournful ring of his words," which was far from the encouragement she had expected. When he asked her about life after college she was equally oblique: "I will not discuss the future because I know it is arranged for me [by God]." This green book entry, which was possibly a proposition to Campbell of sorts, implied Maynard's confusion about Campbell and about life after Hitchin. Campbell, admitting to picking up on the latter, told her that from now on he would "be [her] secular conscience." He advised her to broaden her library and rely less on "religious heroes" like Edward Irving, because "real life was earnest and practical."[37]

They discussed their personal relationship the following day, when taking a long walk together alone. Not knowing what to expect, it was a conversation that Maynard had longed for and yet feared, since receiving his sonnet in May:

> He said he "could not speak of his unhappiness all through the winter without compromising others." Then what followed seemed almost like a parting. He thanked me most lovingly for what I had done, saying that "the fresh love which had come to his desolation was just all he wanted," ending with, "but now it is over. I am happy and it will not be the same again."

As to "the sonnet," Maynard concluded of this entry, "when I spoke to him about the first word [Angel], he said it was to mean 'a messenger,' and that is what I *most* want to be!" Campbell had firmly linked his "eager drinking" of the "Angel's balm" to "benediction." The Angel of God had sanctified his "desperate heart."[38] On their last evening together Campbell apparently reiterated his stance: "He cheerfully gave me a long kiss," Maynard wrote, and then "he suggested that keeping life uncomplicated was the best thing; that moments of emergency made one take counsel with one's own, and with the Higher spirit."[39] She did not challenge his "faith-based" decision.

Maynard missed him after he left but claimed that she did "not feel lonely and blank." Nor did she think "that either loving or being loved by Lewis hurt [her]." But neither of them was left unscathed. She struggled not to "fall under him in any way," adding, "He tells me, 'I am quite happy now,' but I feel otherwise." She explained this in her "Friend":

> I know, as the others do not, that his determination to work extremely hard in Greek is to stifle an unspecified love which lives on still passionate and hopeless in his heart. But enough of this! I do not want to write anything better left unsaid, nor is it of use to remember. I love to know his beautiful mind, and am grateful for his affection, and feel that my Master cannot have given it to me for nothing.[40]

Of note here is Maynard's fluid analysis of her feelings and actions within the context of faith. God, she believed, had a reason for giving her the married Campbell. It seems that through religious metaphor, Maynard could avoid further analysis of her own behaviour and that of Campbell's. Nonetheless, her assertion that "Lewis' 'moral code' had curbed his trifling with [her] affection" was an admission that he had, indeed, trifled with her emotions. Moreover, she was angry at his looking at "morality as *apart* from the Saviour." This self-imposed division held him back "from God-given virtues like passion," and from "God's gifts of love" like herself.[41]

Here we also see the beginnings of Maynard's mediation between seduction and resistance. She would adopt faith to help her to resist passion or to explain rejection. Faith also became for Maynard a means in which to condone passionate encounters, particularly if they were mutual. This is not to assume that Maynard would have entered into a physical relationship with Campbell had she the opportunity in 1872. After all, her future same-sex loves allowed Maynard more social freedom to express passion. But the fact that she "never discovered what had made [Campbell] change" is curious in that it never ceased to baffle her.[42]

Writing of this time in 1915, in an age somewhat more liberal towards sex and divorce, an older and wiser Maynard took a more pragmatic, defensive stance on their relationship: "Was it that he felt himself unsympathetically married? That I could give him something he could not otherwise have? ... Fanny was very content but *he* was not. He tried to be, but he was quite lonely in many ways." All in all, "the parting was good," she concluded in her autobiography. "For the next eight years I saw a great deal of him, but it was not the same."[43] Certainly, she grew increasingly disenchanted with him, viewing their professional disagreements and his emotional distance as betrayals of sorts. But their feelings for each other did not entirely cease. She came dangerously close to having an affair with him in 1880, shortly after her four-year relationship with Louisa Lumsden had ended.

Lewis Campbell had a profound effect on Constance Maynard's life, both professionally and emotionally. As she wrote upon his death in 1908:

> He was the only man who came close to me. He directed me towards Girton, and my debt to him is immense ... He also opened me up to the gate of love. We were both very good at self-restraint, but there it was ... At the time I was ashamed to write about it, but I don't mind doing so now.[44]

Love was a degree of weakness, and the weakness of love was irresistible: such was the distinctive desire-resistance dichotomy which bound them. His was driven by the "male" mid-century Evangelical discourse of integrity, self-restraint, duty, and ambition. Hers was set against the earlier-century Evangelical relinquishing of worldliness. This was to become elemental to her future relationships, which were all with women. It was through Campbell that Maynard came to learn that passion, ambition, and one's belief could be interconnected. This led her in a direction which relegated him to the background as an awkward, peripheral figure. He eventually disappeared from view as she traversed farther along her new public path, catching in her arms the women who could share in the contradictions and nuances of her public and private worlds.

Chapter Three

"Caught in the Current" 1872–1875

The recollection of her departure for Hitchin on 14 October 1872 still evoked emotion-filled pride for Maynard in 1915: "Usually *I* stood in the hall as Harry or George turned out into the world, but now it was all for me, for *me*!" During a period when most women did not consider higher education an option, for Maynard it was a reality. Indeed, it would become a tremendous means of opportunity. Although Hitchin had seemed "more like a workhouse" when she had visited in May, she returned home determined to be among the first female pioneers "to take a degree." The symbolic "dead pig" had already gone, and finally her father was to take her to the train station "in honour of the occasion," as he told her. Maynard fully believed that her "famous St. Andrews visit opened [her] up to the idea that life could be different." It was later that she recognized that college "had produced a sense of restraint that became intolerable."[1]

Maynard's retrospection of her college days attests to its immense impact on her life as educational pioneer. Hitchin not only inspired her academic goals and future as an educational innovator, but also led Maynard to explore new forms of religiosity and same-sex passion. Martha Vicinus argues that through college raves women like Maynard found love and academic support. Yet Vicinus' view of raves as largely subliminal and pious husband-wife role-playing seems limited.[2] As this chapter and chapters 4, 5, 6 and 7 argue, Maynard's self-description as wife, lover, husband, and mother to close friends at Girton, Cheltenham, St. Leonards, and Westfield suggests that raves involved interchangeable role-playing far more diverse than Vicinus described.

A queer approach to Maynard's raves best illuminates their nuances and at times, dissidence from mainstream femininity. Julian Carter and others advise us to reinterpret sexuality and dominance between Victorian women as part of a shared mainstream femininity, rather than classify it through our presentist lens of lesbian, incestuous, or sado-masochistic. The idea of overt mother-daughter eroticism may disturb us but we now know it was compatible with Victorian heteronormativity. Maynard's raves reflected prescribed femininity as well as forms of female-female aggression that college women – similar to mainstream women – did not appear to display in relation to men. Yet by virtue of their milieu, raves allowed college women latitudes of self-exploration apart from mainstream femininity. We glean from rave culture the fluidity and instability of identity formation.[3] College women explored and modified various social scripts in their search for self-expression as educational pioneers.

To contextualize raves as malleable forms of identity formation shaped by "the erotic" illuminates the complexity of sexual self-consciousness. Historians Nancy Partner and Diana Fuss are among those who evaluate subjective resistance as more than a reiterative practice. They theorize the erotic as a set of dynamics to argue that women can and do feel the same forms of desire as men.[4] Certainly, Victorians understood gender and sex as differential principles for distributing erotic agency. Men had sexual impulses while women supposedly had virtually none. Nonetheless, Victorian women who conceptualized sex as heterosexual had erotic lives that also included women. In Maynard's case, faith was another means in which to express her erotic self. This chapter explores Maynard's intellectual pursuits and burgeoning same-sex sexual self-consciousness as a pioneering student at Hitchin.

Before turning to Maynard's complex negotiation of rave culture, we should trace the roots from which it stemmed. As noted in chapter 1, women's fight for higher education was inspired by reform in boys and men's education during and after the 1830s. The efforts of Frances Mary Buss and Dorothea Beale in the 1850s were followed by the introduction of girls' examinations in Cambridge in 1860. By the 1870s, the rise of girls' public high schools across the country encouraged academic achievement rather than girls' accomplishments. The founding of University College in London in 1828 had challenged Oxbridge which, to that point, had monopolized university education, with entry limited to genteel male Anglicans only.[5] In 1847, Elizabeth Jesser Reid persuaded University College London professors to give lectures to "young ladies" in her home. Two years later Bedford College was born, which offered a curriculum decidedly progressive for women of the times.[6]

In 1867, educational pioneer Emily Davies made public "the matter of women's higher education" in Cambridge. Why do "men *ever* fight against women?" she asked. "Why can not a woman receive the best education possible? Why not a women's college attached to the highest educational force in the country?" Davies fully believed that women were as intellectually capable as men and that higher education would "improve the occupations of women." In the words of later Girton graduate Constance Jones, "Davies' faith and wisdom, and courage and tenacity," led her to garner £7,000 through speeches and gain support from *The Times*, which helped validate her scheme. When she convinced Cambridge lecturers that female students offered *new* avenues of research, Hitchin opened its doors to six students in October 1869. Located in Hertfordshire it was, as Davies predicted, the first women's college with connections to Cambridge. Lady Margaret and Somerville were established in Oxford in 1879 for similar reasons.[7]

Although Davies insisted that Hitchin was not a "new variety of girls' school," she warned her students not to "advertise themselves" through overt behaviour or even *go* to Cambridge.[8] Davies' views were respected by her six pioneers, among them the gifted Louisa Lumsden, Sarah Woodhead, and Lewis Campbell's protégé Rachel Cook. Of the entire group, Lumsden stood out. The daughter of landed Scottish gentry, she was the oldest student at twenty-eight and had already received higher education at private schools in Belgium and London. Added to this, her captivating looks and enigmatic personality enabled her to exert power. She soon instigated "College rules" typical to men's institutions of higher learning at the time. Students took turns "sitting at the 'High'"; wore formal dress for dinner; and addressed each other through surnames. Lumsden also organized "male" sports like cricket and wrestling, and nightly recreational activities like dancing and charades. When her peers became overwhelmed by course work she initiated a weekly "College Five" to discuss academic problems. She later organized a debating society to encourage students to speak out publicly.[9]

The biggest concern for Hitchin students in October 1869 was passing the Little-go examination, which Davies had introduced as a prerequisite for the Intermediate and Tripos examinations. The Little-go and Intermediate required passing such subjects as English, Latin, Greek, Theology, Philosophy, and Euclid. The Tripos involved studying four subjects related to the area of the Classics or the Natural Sciences in more depth. In Davies' view, gaining a Tripos was proof that women could achieve as well as men if they followed the same curriculum. Her six pioneers were not as assured. They had not only received far less schooling than men in mathematical subjects like Euclid, but had found some "lectures unfathomable. We were *so* dissatisfied," Lumsden noted in her autobiography, *Yellow Leaves*, "that we demanded the 'shunting' of some troublesome lecturers. The Girton Council accused us of taking things too seriously. After all, *we* were only required to pass the *women's* examination." In other words, they could sit the same examinations as men, but they were not yet officially recognized as such for women.

The situation had improved by 1871. Lumsden, Wood, and Cook had passed their Little-go and Intermediate, and the first Natural Sciences Tripos candidates, Frances Dove and Mary Kingsland, showed great potential. However, despite such successes, Davies was informed in 1872 that the Little-go, Intermediate, and Tripos could still not be regarded as official university examinations as they were for men. This decision proved a bitter pill, even more so six years later when University College London opened up degrees to women. Cambridge would not grant women the degree for another seventy years.

In 1872, the pioneers resented Cambridge's decisions regarding their examinations. It was gender biased and their futures seemed bleak. At the same time, they felt desperately ill-equipped to pass their Tripos even after three years of hard work. Of the six pioneers, only Louisa Lumsden, Rachel Cook, and Sarah Woodhead passed their Tripos. As Lumsden noted in her memoirs, "We found the work an almost insuperable barrier. Rachel nearly threw the whole thing up, and I was forced to opt for Classics when I found the Natural Sciences Intermediate too difficult."[10]

This was the situation that Maynard faced when she entered Hitchin, but a cheerful Davies quickly organized her curriculum for her Little-go, scheduled for December 1873, and Maynard's diary soon effused passion for her studies: "Each morning I awake with a *sting* of delight and anticipation!" Meanwhile, the weekly swim at Hitchin's public baths was as "much of an experience" of college life as was "wrestling" in the library. Maynard's autobiography presented an entirely different picture, however: "The pace was inhuman. I was so tired at night that I would often fall asleep with a book in my hand and wake up stiff and cold before stumbling into bed."[11] The problem was partially resolved by the hire of resident lecturers after 1872. However, since the college initially trained its own staff – Louisa Lumsden was hired as Classical lecturer in 1873 and Mary Kingsland as Science and Math lecturer in 1875 – both lecturer and student continued to flounder with the curriculum.

3.1 Groups of early Hitchin students. Left: c. 1870, Louisa Lumsden and Rachel Cook seated with pioneers Emily Townsend, Isabel Gibson, and Anna Lloyd standing behind them. Right: c. 1873, Frances Dove is standing at far right next to Amy Mantle. Courtesy of St. Leonards School Archives, St. Andrews.

"My Sense of 'Right and Wrong'"

Her curriculum problems aside, Maynard underwent a profound transformation at Hitchin. It soon became clear that the "serious" peers, Louisa Lumsden, Rachel Cook, and Sarah Woodhead were "unbelievers," and Maynard herself found the secularist sphere irresistible. While she tried to "seek God *first*, prayer was an interruption." After all, she told her "'Friend' [green book], the pleasure of life here depends a *lot* on one's feelings and study, and both are very attractive for consciousness *aren't* they?"[12] Her diary of 1873 voiced her excitement over Woodhead's, Lumsden's, and Cook's Tripos successes. Indeed, the fact that Woodhead gained the honour of "senior Optime" for Mathematics, and Cook "beat the three best men" in Classics, was a double triumph in face of the verdict that as women, "they were sure to fail." Meanwhile, the celebratory teas and composed Odes sung in a circle with crossed hands set in place college rituals that Maynard would initiate at Westfield.[13]

Nonetheless, Maynard's new-found love of worldliness tormented her. Her anguish over her "misguided priorities" took form in two counter-narratives in her parallel diaries. Green book entries often ran thus: "I have thrown myself into amusements with a fondness I never felt before. I do not *think* this is because my sense of 'right and wrong' has become less sensitive." Her diary voiced concern, "Reading my Bible seems meaningless ... I *speak* of conviction, but I am eluding the Cloister – although I never shrink from thinking of Hitchin as Satan's seat."[14] It seems that similarly to her stay with the Campbells, Maynard faced at Hitchin challenges to her faith. As such historians as Bebbington and Doreen Rosman argue, late-Victorian intellectuals often erroneously deemed "Evangelical types" as intellectually lacking because they uncritically accepted the infallibility of the Bible. Yet higher education was a preoccupation for many Evangelicals, which perhaps explains the Maynards' eventual agreement to Constance's enrolment at Hitchin.[15]

Sunday caused Maynard to feel the most "desolate," particularly in the earlier years. She always attended church, but she "*dreaded* the evening routine with its political discussion or analysis of some new novel. College etiquette required [they] mingle and [she] kept [her] mouth shut." However, "Sunday was the Sabbath and [she] longed to turn the conversation to Christ." It was during a Sunday in November 1872, she claimed, that "the inception of Westfield formed in [her] mind. From this time on, [she] fully believed that God had chosen [her] out of thousands of English girls to hold the most difficult post in the world."[16] As His "prophet," she could justifiably interconnect faith with ambition to spread her Word.

Maynard's idea of vocation gave her the opportunity to explore same-sex passion, set within the context of the college rave. From the outset, she longed to convert those to whom she was physically attracted – who, as it turned out, were her most powerful adversaries. She was intrigued, indeed jealous, of the beautiful Rachel Cook who had caught the eye of Lewis Campbell; and Cook did prove a challenge. After weeks of trying to woo Cook through incessant proselytizing, Maynard received her "first [and fatal] lesson in unbelief." Cook angrily told her, '"You create your *own* beliefs and then act upon them.' I suddenly saw what I had never realized before," Maynard sadly wrote. "Through our desires we build up the very things that *we* want."

Nonetheless, even though she claimed that Cook's "words plagued [her] for the rest of [her] life," Maynard could not escape her mother's maxim: "Deny that self which *Pleasure* gratifies." God only forgave worldly feeling through the individual's sacrifice of it.[17]

Another challenge to Maynard's sense of right and wrong occurred in her second term when she signed up for Elementary Logic. This one act propelled her towards gaining a First Class in her Little-go and Intermediate, which in turn led her to convince her father to let her "have the gold" by sitting the Mental and Moral Sciences Tripos. This new Tripos, ironically dubbed "the study of thinking man," consisted of four groupings of subjects: Physics; History and Philosophy; Logic and Political Economy; and Ethics. Its particular advantage over the Classics and the Natural Sciences Tripos was that it gave women more of an equal opportunity with men since neither had taken the subjects previously. As Maynard explained, "Psychology, then into its infancy, lay at the background. Metaphysics and the History of Philosophy were incorporated into the 'Mental' papers, just as the history of democracy or emigration was considered Political Economy."[18]

Maynard's interest in human behaviour is hardly surprising, given her upbringing on "the search for the criteria of Truth and moral conscience." Her studies in Ethics covered the "morality" taught in the Bible. However, her Tripos also countered her beliefs about the will as "evil," just as Lewis Campbell's concept of human agency had done.[19] She tackled Kant's theology and Butler's "Sermons on Human Nature" with as much zeal as John Stuart Mill's "epoch-making" *System of Logic* (1843). Mill's *System,* which incorporated a Positivist-Darwinist view of "human progress" as shaped "by unknowable 'truth,'" joined Thomas Carlyle's condemnation of materialist thinking as "immoral." Indeed, Mill's hope to reform the world through intellectual proselytizing reinforced Maynard's self-vision as God's prophet. Meanwhile, Coleridge's ideas on "feeling" became, for Maynard, another reason to intertwine religious and human passion rather than resist earthliness.[20]

One advantage of "the gold," for Maynard, was taking Philosophy with the esteemed Cambridge Professor Henry Sidgwick, whose initiation of Newnham, the second women's college in Cambridge, was considered groundbreaking for a man. However, "getting to know" Louisa Lumsden was the supreme event of Maynard's term. In fact, Lumsden became a central figure in her life for over four years. Their relationship not only conveyed the difficulties that pioneers faced, but illuminated Maynard's struggle with her sense of right and wrong.

Maynard both admired and feared the "aloof and noble 'L' who stood at the head of Hitchin" since she had recently been hired to teach Classics. Therefore, at a time when raves were core to college life, Maynard sought her tall fair-haired tutor's attention: "At *last*!" she exclaimed in May 1873. "We found a secluded spot and spoke until L 'confided' in me. She *thought* she believed in God, but found religion overrated." Then "came the *test*" from Lumsden, "Do you believe in Christ or only in God?" She likely anticipated Maynard's answer, "Christ our Lord is God to me." Maynard would later discover "L's deep revulsion" at the Christological idea of a human-like "mediator between God and man" – particularly a Christ who by way of Irving was "tempted by evil [the world, flesh and Satan]." In 1873, the naive Maynard eagerly tried to convert her love, "If God is like the pure light as it comes from the sun, Christ is like the very same light, only refracted by the atmosphere of the earth." Lumsden apparently admired Maynard's creative exampling of "Christ's mistakes" as proof of human depravity, but she remained sceptical.[21]

The end of term saw a marked change in their relationship. While Maynard deliberately sought Lumsden's academic advice, Lumdsen in turn had made it clear that Maynard was her chosen one – her ravee: "I alone, can go to her room at any hour," Maynard wrote, "and now and then, *even* in public, I stroke the lion's mane." The green book implied the growth of their intimacy in its detail of their romantic liaisons and open demonstrations of affection. Maynard's reference to Lumsden as "My fair Madonna," was hopeful, for Lumsden had declared herself agnostic. As Vicinus has noted, the term Madonna also implied a spiritual-erotic-mother component to a Victorian woman's love of an older, purportedly wiser woman. The lines between faith, passion, and higher learning blurred and interconnected in distinct ways in the new college arena.[22]

Maynard knew that Lumsden alongside other Girtonians hotly defended the notion of "progress through the discoveries of natural science," thus she struggled through Darwin's *On the Origin* and *Descent of Man* to impress Lumsden. Darwin's work was not new to Maynard, but it "unsettled" her as much it had in 1871 when her minister had tried to disprove Darwin's evolutionary theories. At that time, she had read the work of Scottish geologist Hugh Miller, who like other Christian scientists of the era, linked his own formulated "evolutionary cycles" about the species with the days of creation. In 1873, Maynard spoke to a Cambridge minister who explained "evolution as a force guided by God's hand to give man the *choice* to discern good over evil." The idea of "knowing God" through nature (natural theology) likely reinforced what she learned in her youth. She concluded, "The moral tone *is* low in the early part of the Bible." Perhaps the "world *is* slowly improving" and will continue until "the Divine becomes victorious."[23]

Nonetheless, Hitchin had changed Maynard's life. Her autobiography described her mindset of June 1873: "I felt I had been 'caught in the current' and was being locked and buffeted this way and that." She waxed enthusiasm over Tissy's work at the Convalescent Home; Dora's ongoing negotiations about a career in nursing; and Gazy's volunteer teaching at the Flimwell village school room. In private, she knew that Hitchin was an escape that her sisters never had. Because of her secularist studies, she no longer viewed religion as a certainty. Nor did she wish to "bring into captivity *every* thought" to God. The love she craved was more earthly-based than Divine:

> I am filled with indescribable longings to do, or be, or feel something different - better, wider, fuller. These seem very unworthy when I think of my Saviour who has stored my life and opened His very heart of love itself. It is *"love"* that I want, not more, nor less. I want a love "that will take me as I am and rather die than leave me" I do know the dear Saviour, but I have *not* love like that.

Rachel Cook would no doubt affirm this, Maynard ended wryly: "So, *now* do you not suppose that your sensations begin and end with yourself?" Even a year earlier when she had fallen for Lewis Campbell, and "had been in a stronger position than now," she could only respond with "an illogical, 'Oh, I *know* it is not so!'"[24]

"Cruelty, 'Chill' of Doubt, and 'Unusual' Loving Dispositions"

Maynard's second and third years at Girton (the name adopted after Hitchin moved to Girton in October 1873) saw the continuation and the utilization of her college experiences. According to her autobiography, she "learned how to weigh evidence, search for the foundation of truths, and see the far-reaching value of principles that became the springs of action." She passed her Little-go and Intermediate with a First Class in December 1873 and June 1874 respectively. She also became a bulwark of faith. Indeed, her initiation of a Girton Bible study group was testament to both her faith and leadership skills. Her room, or "Church that is Girton," became a refuge for students who feared the growth of secularism at college. In terms of love, she also embraced the challenge, and in no short measure. Work, faith, and love, while vital and challenging, created complex nuances in her life by the very virtue of their interconnection and their inconstancy.

The most immediate challenge facing Maynard, in October of 1873, was settling into her dishevelled new surroundings. The inside of Girton was incomplete, while the muddy quagmire outside was a "dumping ground for broken bricks and mortar." Girton's closer proximity to Cambridge also changed its familial atmosphere, which had its advantages. Students could more easily attend university lectures and social events; they could share their unique experience with other female students from Merton and Newnham Halls; they could visit institutes like the Museum of Physiology; and access to all this became easier when the wagonette was made available to all Girtonians for a small fee.[25]

Girton's location also gained it more notice, even though its distance from Cambridge was supposedly a shield from the public sphere. On the positive side, Davies could entice out eminent guest speakers like J.R. Seeley, the author of *Ecce Homo*, and Madam Bodichon and Dr. Elizabeth Garrett-Anderson, who were active in the early movement for women's rights. However, being "on the public map" created new problems. Convention decreed no male visitors in students' rooms, but unfortunately there was no front door, so male undergraduates could enter the building unannounced. Girtonians tolerated this annoyance, sometimes with relish: "We took great amusement in one conversation which went, 'but what is the point of everything?' followed by the housekeeper's prim response, 'it is for educational purposes Sir.'" They also felt irritation, such as the time when they learned how college women had been mocked through cartooning in *Punch* magazine.[26]

Most of Maynard's work with Lumsden ceased in her second year, but she still saw much of her adored tutor and friend. According to Maynard, their intense debates on subjects like poetry or philosophy were as stimulating as ever. However, diary entries revealed new, unhealthy aspects to their relationship that bordered on cruelty. Lumsden expected deference due to her "noble lineage." She also demanded support for her anger over women's social limitations. Her overt gender bending in charades, wrestling, and cricket troubled Davies because it breached both patriarchal and Christian ideals of femininity. Since Lumsden's "longing to be a man was not to be abated by Christianity,"

Maynard rather pointedly noted, they were left to analyse their relationship within the context of culture and their new public arena. Lumsden assumed the "husband" role in their college rave, while Maynard inculcated the stereotypical feminine stance: "The fact that I say 'yes' during our conversations leads me into difficulties," she lamented. "Yes means yes, I understand, as opposed to yes, I agree. I have to be careful about everything I say."[27]

Clearly, Maynard found Lumsden's lordly taunting difficult to bear. Her account of their lectures on Utilitarianist Jeremy Bentham was a case in point: "L [Lumsden] *delights* in the fact that I hate Bentham's 'chilly' disregard of religion. B [Bentham] argues that we only obey out of fear of *earthly* punishment rather than religious conviction!" Her diary of 1873 became filled with Lumsden's criticism at large, which ranged from "L's fury over God's unconcern about senseless tragedy," to her anger over gender inequality.[28] Lumsden, it seems, wanted Maynard to understand her frustrations, but Maynard would only console her through faith: "It is God's plan"; and again: "We must not doubt." In June 1874 Maynard sadly concluded, "L is *all* that I love, yet she pushes away the still dearer Saviour. When I say, '*I* struggle a lot too,' she mistrusts it, *naturally*."[29] When she deflected their difficulties to problems of belief, Maynard recognized that neither would give what the other demanded. Yet she remained under Lumsden's sway.

Maynard experienced female-female domination by virtue of the new college milieu, yet her rave also reflected curious aspects of mainstream femininity. As historian Laura Mayhall notes, Sharon Marcus' "juxtaposition of fashion and dolls" helps illuminate these components of femininity. For example, the *Englishwomen's Domestic Magazine* revealed to Marcus fashion plates of women gazing suggestively at each other, or of young fashionable women seated beside stern faced female elders. Stories written by women about girls who punished "unruly" dolls or were themselves punished complemented the female-female scenario of submission and dominance. In this, and as evident in Maynard's relationship with Lumsden, women's status as subservient, sexual objects for men did not preclude women's desire for and control over each other.[30]

Marcus' analysis of the doll and fashion culture brings to mind early-Victorian Evangelicals' refute of worldliness; a life principle that such mid-Victorian mothers as Louisa Maynard adopted "to bring [*their* children's] 'Will' to humble spirit." Meanwhile, Lumsden's later reference to Maynard as the "school ornament" at St. Leonards was as telling.

Maynard was the pretty object that Lumdsen adored, yet frequently humiliated at the workplace. This illustrates once again how aspects of mainstream femininity and familial upbringing shaped college women's lives. This is not to suggest that Maynard suffered silently under Lumsden's torment. She engaged in "intellectual" competition with Lumsden over such secularist concepts as Utilitarianism. Indeed, Maynard's justification of "L's cruel treatment of [her as] fired by" Lumsden's sense of gentility, gender frustrations, and agnosticism reveals how ideas about gender, class, sex, science, and faith shaped their rave.[31]

In 1874, Maynard found a solace of sorts through Natural Sciences Tripos candidate, the genteel Frances Dove. Dove also loved Lumsden, but by all accounts, her love was unrequited. Her acts of devotion, such as drawing L's curtains or making her fire, had only served to diminish Lumsden's respect for her. As Maynard remarked in her autobiography, "L told me with a kind of disgust, 'of course I thought it was the servants – do you know it has been going on fully *two years*?'" Maynard's opinion "that [Dove] endured L's unkindness because she was 'self-deprecating'" seemed ironic given her own relationship with Lumsden. She liked to compare their relationships through comments like, "Frances accepted L's respect for *me*."[32] But in truth, they were both victim to Lumsden's power-driven cruelty, and disliked each other because of it.

Little did Maynard know that their love for Lumsden would involve all three in a four-year relationship, or that Dove would set the ball in motion when she accepted educational reformer Dorothea Beale's offer of a post at Cheltenham Ladies' College in November of 1874. Maynard would join both Dove and Lumsden at Cheltenham in 1875. All three were then involved in the founding of St. Leonards in St. Andrews in 1877 where Maynard remained for three years, working with Dove under Lumsden as Mistress.

In 1874, Dove proved that there was hope for a career after completing the Cambridge Tripos. Davies was delighted that Beale had offered Dove a salary of £60 with or without the Tripos. She was as amazed when educational pioneer Frances Mary Buss hired another Tripos candidate to teach Classics at her school, the North London Collegiate. Yet such success reflected Davies' unceasing efforts to promote her cause. Earlier that year, she had raised £1,050 for Girton after delivering a speech at Liverpool. Davies' commitment to Girton was also reflected in the lavish "Girton Party," which was established in honour of

University members who supported women's higher education.[33] The Campbells' attendance at the 1874 affair likely inspired their enterprise, St. Leonards.

As Girton's public spirit developed and its enrolment grew, interpersonal relationships became more complex, and this became an important new topic of debate in Maynard's green book. For Maynard, most issues continued to stem from power struggles around faith, science, class, and passion. She explained that while "etiquette stated that freshmen keep their place," her connection with Cook and Lumsden had exempted her from this rule. However, she "felt desolate" now that Cook had left and Lumsden had become so troubling. Moreover, the six new students who enrolled in October 1873 had created a troubling new dynamic. Amy Mantle was typical of the middle-class "school-girl like" generation of students. By comparison, the genteel Malvena Borchhardt and Henrietta Muller threatened Maynard because they were older and more experienced. She resented Lumsden's respect for Borchhardt's "nonreligious, materialist" views. Muller, she thought, was even "more chilly" with her sensually-based ploys "to lead the weaker students."[34]

Maynard had tasted power with Lumsden and she aimed to retain it. Although she did not admit to it in her records, Borchhardt's and Muller's influence likely inspired her "'private' weekly Bible gathering" as a means to block their control. Although she faced Lumsden's "open repugnance" of her Bible study group, Maynard felt empowered by her new role. Her comment, "I can never entice anyone to say more than yes, but they like to come and listen," evoked her wielding of theological knowledge over others. She deliberately reached out to peers of less personal interest but with whom she could impress, through "serious 'conversations'" about faith.[35]

Maynard sincerely believed that her Bible meetings enabled students to "get to know each other in a way otherwise impossible." The support system did indeed seem vital to the young Amy Mantle, "who became hysterical after cramming on Homer." On the other hand, Maynard's adoption of a proselytizer role had its own rewards. Just as she had admired her "noble L," now *she* basked in approbation from peers, but through the space of faith. She was "devoured with kisses" and tender ministries, and was "treated as the 'final appeal' in matters of the soul." As third-year student Mary Kingsland apparently told Maynard, "I found it was no use shewing that I loved you unless I loved your Lord too." Implicit was Louisa Maynard's fixed life Principle in Maynard's advice: "You [Kingsland] must resist human passion through faith." Only through acts of self-denial could one transcend the worldly evil that existed apart from God. Of course, Maynard's beliefs countered the more Christian humanitarianism of the times that had long disused self-denial as an instrument of persuasion.[36]

For "ravees" like Kingsland, human and divine love had become interconnected in an effort to gain an adored one's favour. Since young womanhood, though, Maynard had queried her mother's decree that she guard against sentiment. Now she was being swept down Girton's intellectual stream, and she craved a "full love" – a love God had shown her when He gave her Lewis Campbell. The green book of 1874 revealed her re-examination of passion; in this case, the passion of female friendship. It was at this time that she reread Paley's *Evidences* and gleaned that, "if one took *all* pleasures from God's hands, then it could not hurt them." She felt alienated from Lumsden, and she was not attracted to Kingsland: "It is the pretty Amy [Mantle] who needs to kiss me!" she exclaimed. "Amy's lips bespeak of passionate loving that sends an irresistible appeal to my heart and *all* my reason gives way!"[37]

Maynard's erotic interactions with Mantle covered scores of green book pages from the spring of 1874 until Maynard left Girton in December 1875. Since these entries were more sexually explicit than those about Lumsden, they reveal more about the nature of college raves. For Mantle, at least according to Maynard, their rave was a preparation for marriage, and Mantle did eventually marry. Perhaps for both women their rave was an intense fling of sorts that allowed each to explore physical passion. As Maynard explained, while Lumsden's "agnosticism slowly pushed me away, so the unusual combination of [Mantle's] loving disposition drew me in." Mantle told Maynard that she was not only orphaned at birth, but had lost an adored male cousin, so "that's why she craved love so much." Maynard thus happily mediated the mother-lover-husband role(s) to explore her place in the rave and to lead Mantle to God. Regarding her role-playing, Maynard wrote, "She [Mantle] wants me to say *my* part of the wedding vows"; and "Often I have called her 'baby,' but *this* time, she leaned back full against me, and stretching out her arms, whispered, 'Mother,' come to me!"[38] This illustrates that despite its incestuous connotation, Maynard seemed as comfortable with her mother role as she was with her husband role in her expression of same-sex desire with Mantle.

One might argue that Maynard's role-playing subverted feminine norms. Yet as queer theorist Julian Carter warns, scholars should pay

3.2 Constance Maynard at Girton with fellow members of the Girton Bible meeting, c. 1874. Maynard is seated on the left hand side with her arm around Amy Mantle, who is sitting at her feet with her arm resting on Maynard's lap. Courtesy of Queen Mary University of London Archives/ Westfield College/ WFD.

heed "to the alternative frameworks within which women understood such intimacies." Bonds such as that between mother and daughter involved "tenderness and responsibility" as well as "sexual desire and activity." Scholars Diana Fuss and Nancy Partner explain this mingling of erotic impulses and feminine identity as an effect of cultural norms and arrangements. They propose that the malleability of identity formation makes social constructs not so easily distinguishable from "innate" desire (or what Maynard called "sparks" and "thrills"). For Maynard and other college women, the fluid exchange of husband-wife and mother-daughter emotional-eroticism involved both a unique and shared hierarchical form of a Victorian femininity. Maynard pandered to Mantle's "passionate, intense thirst for love" as Mantle's husband, and was in turn titillated by "her sensual daughter's" frank discussions about her sexual feelings during their passionate encounters.[39]

However, while empowering and highly pleasurable, Maynard's relationship with Mantle soon raised issues around class. Maynard had already suffered under Lumsden's scorn of her friendship with Mary Kingsland, the "common" daughter of a tradesman. However, "L's outrage" upon discovering that Mantle was both common and illegitimate was a "huge blow" for Maynard, both publically and personally. She had assumed that Mantle was her social equal, and "this line of demarcation was too strong to step over. To think I have let her touch me and kiss me!" she angrily exclaimed in her green book. Struggling between her snobbish and faith-based morality, and her interest in Mantle, Maynard could not be honest with Mantle or with herself. She continued to encourage their power-based relationship even after Mantle learned of her "betrayal of their love" in October 1874.[40]

Lumsden's own issues with class resurfaced when she discovered that the "commonplace" but talented Kingsland had been hired to teach Science at Girton in January, 1875. "It is insulting," she raged to Maynard, who for her part, sympathized with Lumsden's class-based views: "Mary will be a *good* influence at college, but the subtle differences in their lives envelop more than the intellectual." In other words, Lumsden also had "superior" taste, judgment, and outlook. Of course, Lumsden's character and upbringing led her to adopt an elitist world view. She continually demanded deference and was openly hostile if she felt herself wronged. Maynard had seen the extent of this in early 1873, after "a mere servant had informed L" that the Girton committee had cancelled her Tripos presentation due to the lack of quorum. An outraged Lumsden had refused to attend the rescheduled ceremony ten days later.[41] Sadly, Lumsden's volatile nature would always create problems in her professional and personal life.

Suffice to say, overwork and lack of support were also causes of Lumsden's short temper. As enrolment grew, so had her responsibilities as tutor, and then as official nurse, since none were hired at this time. Interpersonal relationships further complicated college life. Although Lumsden advised Mantle to drop to a "General Student" because of poor work, she gave in to Maynard's obstinate assertion, "Amy has come here to take the degree and so she will *not* give it up!" Mantle never got past Little-go, while other Girtonians failed it time after time. Like others before and after, they left Girton feeling resentful and disappointed about a system that set them up for disappointment. Their tutors meanwhile felt incompetent and guilty.[42]

Both tutors and students struggled to navigate professionalism within a society that tied women to domesticity. While Kingsland overcame such contradictions, Lumsden could not. She became emotionally unstable and spoke with bitterness about feeling like a mere "cog in the wheel of Davies' great scheme." The situation erupted in February 1875, when Lumsden's sudden threat to resign was taken at face value by Davies. As Maynard explained in her autobiography, "L had clearly made Davies and the committee weary of her anger, and they probably wanted to be rid of her. L did officially resign, much to *my* relief. I shrank from her fixed face!" However, at the time Maynard effused misery over the event: "L has shaped Girton's ideals for over five years. We have differed, opinion-wise, but I know that I will miss her terribly."[43] While Maynard's entries about Mantle were erotic, they always lacked the intensity of her tortuous, passion-filled narrations about Lumsden. Maynard's relationship with Lumsden would take a hiatus for a year.

"My 'Little Flock'"

It is notable that the summer of 1875 marked an end to Lumsden's connection with Girton and a big change for Maynard. She had taken to what her cousin Mary King called "red-hot Evangelizing" in her second year, but when she and Harry attended the sermon of popular evangelists Moody and Sankey in June, Maynard was inspired: "I was so overwhelmed by the many that 'stood to be saved,' that I returned to Girton longing over the souls of others." Certainly, Maynard's religious intentions were good and would be recognized as such. Nonetheless, her longing for Evangelical piety had affinity with what Argersinger and other scholars call "the ravishing male Victorian evangelist;" a dashing, compelling preacher who believed himself "agent of God's Word." Nor was Maynard the only Victorian woman to imagine this form of male power. American novelist Susan Warner, for example, depicted a fictional female character who watched in "envious admiration as John, a much loved minister," imposed his will on others without sacrificing "their affection or respect." In fact, Warner's range of female selves in *Wide, Wide World* verged on the aggressive rather than the submissive.[44] Maynard's evangelizing at Girton, and particularly at Westfield, would be viewed by some students as disgusting, and by others as vile and sinister. Meanwhile, other students suffered greatly under Maynard's longing to save their souls. Gender, it seems, played a role in Victorian definitions and tolerance of Evangelical "male" faith-sex-power.

Nonetheless, in October 1875 Maynard clearly recognized her new-found power as senior student at Girton – "the observed one by all." Indeed, Girton's somewhat diminutive Mistress, A.F. Bernard, served Maynard's needs very well. She consulted Maynard on college matters; she gave Maynard control of sports for the twenty-two students now enrolled at Girton; and, most importantly, she did not interfere with Maynard's burgeoning Bible study group. As Maynard exclaimed, "It is *my* room, known as 'the Church that is Girton,' that is now the refuge for the weary. I can follow my plans without having to consult anyone!"[45]

Not surprisingly, as Maynard's religious-based power grew at Girton, she found herself increasingly under attack. As leader of one "camp," Maynard was respected for her academic and athletic talents and her position as "senior student." She was afforded privileges such as dining out, and now fondly referred to some tutors as "friends" in her green book. But she was also known as an odd disciple of sorts, and as such was much scorned by the '"Free-thought' camp" led by the more radical Malvena Borchhardt and Henrietta Muller. As far as Borchhardt and Muller were concerned, literal belief in the Bible was illogical because it was patriarchal, dogmatic, and not scientifically based. Biblicism must thus be rejected in full if women were to gain rights alongside men. Maynard deeply resented what she called their "corrupt power at Girton" because she herself struggled with religious doubt. Yet one peer's comment, "those who don't like you, *don't*," implied the growing opposition towards Maynard's coercive, ego-based proselytizing.[46]

The core of the issue for Maynard was evinced by her stances in her green book and autobiography. In May 1875 she noted, "the college is divided right in two [by faith] and I feel sad because it is all my doing." In her autobiography, she took a more defensive stance: "I knew my clique was of a peculiarly objectionable sort, but I knew that I could not go back." The free-thoughts' scorn of her little flock's proselytizing had forced her to retaliate against such "tainted control. I informed my tutors that we were absconding from the debates because of 'controversial' topics like, 'is flirting wrong?' or 'should truth and beauty be aimed at in fiction and in art?'"[47]

The free-thought group took revenge for what they viewed as Maynard's "deficiency of public spirit" by mocking religion during an end-of-term game of Consequences. It must be noted that Muller's scorn of "the flames of hell" reflected the doctrinal decline, in general, towards preaching on everlasting retribution. Nonetheless, freethinkers did create diversity within the women's movement, and beyond, by opposing any reconciliation of women's rights with "patriarchal" scriptural teachings. Muller herself was drawn to theosophy because it made no gender distinctions.[48] Maynard declared Muller's behaviour "sacrilegious," yet she felt torn. While her autobiography hotly justified her faith-based position, her green book voiced the humiliation she felt at the time. She admired the "brilliance" of the free-thought members, and felt deeply "ashamed" of being associated with the so-called "ignorant students." While faith may have provided for her an erotic milieu, it had created impossible demands in an environment that embraced science, in which *she* had embraced science. In truth, she could no longer distinguish between science, faith, love, friend, or foe.[49]

The stress from Maynard's strife at Girton took its toll. Her diary particularly outlined her struggle under Philosophy Professor Henry Sidgwick, who told her, "You are not sufficiently independent of thought, and should not be disappointed if you get a Second in your Tripos." In her autobiography, Maynard asserted that "Sidgwick's negative observations dampened [her] resolve to become the first Girtonian to win a 'First Class.'" Her diary meanwhile revealed that she had fallen behind on her studies since May 1875, and that gaining a Second was the result of this distraction.[50] Nonetheless, she coped well with her Tripos in late November, despite "c[oming] unstuck" on three of her twelve papers written over six consecutive days: "I fought off hysterics," Maynard recalled, "which others like Louisa [Lumsden] and Frances [Dove] had exhausted themselves in doing." Since hysteria was viewed as the result of "emotional 'subforce' over the will," and would later be linked to "female madness," Maynard likely saw her battle as triumphant on both secular and religious levels.[51]

Unfortunately, Maynard's conflicts at Girton created a dissatisfaction within her that conceivably led to unrealistic goals. She believed herself incapable of *any* first-class work simply because she never mastered Philosophy. Yet Girton did not see a first class until 1880, when Constance Jones gained such distinction in her Mental and Moral Sciences Tripos.[52] One has to assume, given Girton's success rate at large, that methods of preparation for degrees had vastly improved by then.

In terms of duty to faith, conversion remained important to Maynard. She would organize the "Five Meeting," in which such friends as Mary Kingsland were instructed to pray at 5:00 p.m. each Sunday. This small informal gathering was the beginnings of the famous Girton Prayer Meeting (G.P.M.) that Maynard began in 1876. For over twenty years, she attended the yearly "Old Students" (O.S.) meetings at Girton in order to promote the G.P.M. and ensure that its elected "Chaplain" was fulfilling her important obligations. G.P.M. members, old and new, automatically became members of "The Budget," a package of circular letters introduced by Maynard in 1887 as a means of keeping Westfield graduates "True." The G.P.M. meanwhile flourished until 1897, at which point it merged with what became the Students' Christian Movement (S.C.M.) under the direction of Robert Wilder.[53]

Maynard remained as equally torn by her "duty to faith. I cared for the cause more than the individuals themselves," she confessed in her autobiography. Certainly, she now faced the paradox of belief in face of her liberal arts education. She also obliquely admitted that her hunger for power had driven her both to woo and condemn fellow Girtonians in the name of faith. The lens of class prejudice meanwhile had prevented her from seeing her "shoppy peers" as social equals. None challenged her intellectually or "suited [her] taste" as Lumsden had done.[54] Nonetheless, college had afforded Maynard the opportunity to test her leadership skills and to learn from her mistakes. For example, as Mistress of Westfield, she emphasized to her students their need to keep strictly to the curriculum required for a particular honour's degree. She had also gained the strength to wage her battles as a Victorian educational pioneer.

Girton was the milieu in which Maynard further explored her sensual nature. Of interest is Maynard's adoption of Irving's theological interpretation of the Atonement for her own sexual-dominant power. Shortly before her Tripos in September 1875, she noted:

> I have *taken out all feeling*, all that makes Religion so lovable. I come to Thee with *bare intellect*, knowing that I am but a half-creature without Thee, useless, miserable, incomplete, and knowing that in Thee is just that which satisfies my being. I mean to go on at it, leaving absolutely everything else to Thee.[55]

Similar to the girl who had knelt to pray upon holly leaves, the older Maynard felt compelled to prove her faith. Rationalism had made her doubt. Love had filled her with earthly desire. She began to toy with her "sweet Amy [Mantle]," just as Campbell had dallied with her own emotions. After a year of erotic lover-husband-mother role-playing with Mantle, Maynard told her, "You are of weak [social] character. You must resist the human flame and view love as a part of God's plan." According to Maynard, an angry Mantle objected to turning her "heart from [Maynard] to the Saviour. I love you too much to do that," she complained. Maynard changed her mind, but she treated Mantle like a plaything. On their last night together she "finally gave in to Amy's pleas," and Amy's release of passion was apparently desperate-like: "She [Mantle] gave me all (I suppose) that one mortal *can* give away to another, and holding her close, I knew I *should* give her up to the keeping of my Lord."[56]

In her autobiography, written in 1919, Maynard told the reader, "I felt *discomfort* over Amy. I told her, 'I can not respond to the private side that seems to give you satisfaction.'" Of course, when Maynard wrote these words, ideas about sexuality were in flux. It was ten years later that she stated more clearly her abhorrence of Freud-like ideas on "Repression" and the "thwarted sex instinct."[57] Nonetheless, always caught up in her need to "seek Him first," Maynard expressed passion within the context of faith rather than gender or sexuality until the end of her life. "Friendship," she summed in her green book review of 1876, "should be based on mutual admiration and passion as well as the bonds of 'one Lord, one faith, one baptism.'"[58]

Chapter Four

"An Unhappy Marriage" 1876–1880

When writing of her four-year relationship with Louisa Lumsden in her autobiography in 1916, Maynard noted, "It seems obvious to me that I was cut out to be always second in command ... Truly I did try to be a perfect wife to Louisa."[1] Certainly, passion left her victim to Lumsden's intense mood swings at Cheltenham (1876) and at St. Leonards (1877–80). However, ambition also caused the failure of their relationship. Maynard no more wished to be "wife" to Lumsden than she did to distinguished Scottish minister Dr. James Robertson, who proposed marriage in 1877. Leadership and longing: this particular binary between ambition and passion engulfed yet liberated Maynard from what she called her "thoroughly unhappy marriage" to Lumsden.[2]

Any examination into Maynard's bond with Lumsden – and disastrous fallout from it – is not complete without outlining the events that led to it. We learn that Maynard had not seen Lumsden since "L's stormy exit" from Girton in 1875 to her home in Scotland. When Maynard left Girton in November 1875, she herself had "to account for the stipulations" to which she had agreed. "First, [she] would not teach, and, second, [she] would come back and live at home 'as though nothing had happened.'"[3] As an early pioneer, Maynard's plight was not atypical of some other peers. Amy Mantle, for example, returned home until she married. Others, however, such as Rachel Cook and Sarah Woodhead, pursued careers before and after marriage, and later joined numbers of ex-Girtonians in the fight for women's rights like suffrage.[4]

Maynard recalled her mindset in 1875 before entering her marriage with Lumsden: she "felt helpless about [her] fate as daughter-at-home"; Harry's business ineptitude was threatening familial bankruptcy; and she learned that her mother's asthma- and digestive-related conditions were fatal.[5] Yet Maynard had thought about escaping her fate while still at Girton. In July 1874 she visited Cheltenham because Frances Dove taught there and "wanted to snag" her. Founder Mary Beale did offer Maynard a post in history, but Maynard feared to "counter [her] family's wishes." That same summer she had visited the Manchester High School where ex-Girtonians Elizabeth Welsh and Sarah Woodhead taught under Headmistress Day. Maynard once again "demurred" when offered a teaching post.[6]

After leaving Girton in 1875, however, Maynard was determined to pursue a career. She attended the first Old Student (O.S.) meeting at Girton in March 1876 in order to promote herself as a candidate for Lumsden's replacement. Bernard, however, was set on Elizabeth Welsh. She told Maynard: "You are not considered satisfactory [because of] your religious agenda." Maynard found some comfort in her newly formed Girton Prayer Meeting (G.P.M.), which symbolized her powerful role at Girton, but she still felt "disgruntled and out of tune."[7] It seems she now felt that secular-based ambition undermined religious motivation.

In July 1876, Maynard persuaded her father to pay for "hydropathical treatment" in Perth, Scotland for her brother George who suffered with arthritis in his knee. She had accompanied George for treatment in Mannedorf in 1874, but her interest this time was driven by self-motivation. She knew that Louisa Lumsden had just accepted a post at Cheltenham, and if they travelled to Perth she could visit Lumsden who lived in Aaron on the west coast of Scotland. It was an opportunity not to be missed.[8]

Lumsden had "approved" of Louisa Maynard's gentility when the latter had visited Girton in 1874, and in turn, Maynard approved of the refined genteel ambience in which Lumsden had been raised. Their talks "were often painful as [Maynard] had to bridge the abyss between them." Nonetheless, tolerating Lumsden's criticism of her proselytizing at Girton gained Maynard the reward she sought, an invitation from Lumsden to join her at Cheltenham. When "L expressed the thought of having [Maynard] as her 'wife'" Maynard had misgivings, of course, because it conjured up images of their bittersweet college rave at Girton. Yet as Maynard concluded in her lengthy green book entry: "Oh! To know her, *is* to love her! *Anything* else is impossible." Lumsden had used faith as metaphor to convince the adoring Maynard, "'you [Maynard] *must* see that I'm *not* irreligious or materialist in thinking."[9]

It is unclear whether some kind of plot regarding Cheltenham was hatched when Maynard was at Glenbogie. It seems likely, however, given some unexplained commentary in both diaries: "Oh! *when* will it all end"; Mary Kingsland's recorded remark, "deep down inside you are dissatisfied, almost wretched"; and in early October, "the answer," in a letter from Frances Dove "imploring [her] to go to Cheltenham to help Louisa out of kindness as a true friend." Clever words indeed. Maynard anticipated her parents' consent given the conditions. As a genteel woman, she would "help [Lumsden] to correct Latin until Christmas." However, she knew her parents' new-found support of Dora's nursing was ammunition for her own future ambitions.[10]

"My Entrance into a Fool's Paradise"

Maynard went to Cheltenham on 13 October 1876; four years to the day after she had entered Hitchin. Thus began her four-year "marital" relationship with Lumsden, or as Maynard later described it in her autobiography, "My entrance into a Fool's Paradise, a paradise I would fall into a thousand times over in the wooing and winning before an unhappy marriage."[11]

Initially, life with Lumsden as "her chief love and duty" was blissful. Duty largely involved correcting elementary Latin, but Beale soon offered Maynard a small salary to teach arithmetic and Latin. Love, however, was remarkable: "I delight in wifehood!" Maynard exclaimed. "I think *always* and *only* of L. I *love* our love!" Flowers, billet-doux, and countless caresses and kisses marked her courtship and marriage to Lumsden. The green book portrayed Lumsden as a woman also in love: "She will often gaze into my eyes and say, 'It is beyond my wildest dreams to have you all to myself. I am truly happy because my work, my home and my wife are all good.'"[12]

Deviant as Maynard's reference to her marriage to Lumsden may appear, it was not entirely surprising for the times. A queer approach to this college friendship helps illuminate its particular emotional-erotic configuration(s) and larger social acceptability. In general, historians debate how to characterize Victorian female couples who modelled their relationships on middle-class marriage. Sharon Marcus and others claim that Victorians' view of female marriage as a variation of heterosexual marriage "alerts us to crucial differences" between Victorian mores and modern concepts of the "asocial, deviant" lesbian couple. Meanwhile, Laura Mayhall is among those who observe that Victorian

LOUISA INNES LUMSDEN

Headmistress 1877

4.1 Louisa Lumsden, aged thirty-six, 1877. Courtesy of St. Leonards School Archives, St. Andrews.

marriage was a heterosexual institution organized around economic functions and biological reproduction. She questions as to whether scholars should infer that female marriage was normative. While this is a valid point, we nonetheless ascertain through queer theory the malleability of mainstream femininity, and the nuances of female-female relations.[13]

As we have seen, college women's fluid interchange of husband-wife and mother-daughter role-playing (sometimes in a single relationship) both subverted and reflected gender and sex norms. In this instance, Maynard adopted the terms "perfect wife," "marriage," "wooing," and "living as one" to describe her bond with Lumsden. Given our understanding that identity formation is shaped by the erotic, I am not convinced that these words were simply private metaphors. I would suggest, rather, that they reveal the complexity of sexual self-consciousness. As Vicinus notes, some women adopted male clothing in what was "a visible sartorial representation" of their marriage and identit(ies). Since few Victorians knew about sexological inversion, and most associated sodomy with "wrong" (mostly male-male) sexual acts, female couples would not be treated as aberrant. According to Maynard's green book and autobiography, neither she, Lumsden, nor any of their friends and family viewed their marriage as abnormal. It was in this representation of commitment that both women found intense, physical passion.[14]

Part of the culture of a committed female bond was the couple's public declaration of "undying love and fidelity to each other." When Lumsden wanted to end Dove's "pressing affection for her [Maynard] quickly stepped in to sort things out." Even after listening to Dove's painful, "Oh! My love for her is killing me," she coldly informed Dove, "You are no longer welcome at our home." Maynard had seen this event as a victory of sorts. Dove could no longer intrude on "their perfect world." Yet Maynard had her own troubles with Lumsden because she felt forced to choose love over belief. Shortly after her arrival in October, Maynard "had proposed that they read the Bible every night." Lumsden firmly declined, using fatigue as an excuse. Maynard had hoped this would change, but it did not. In fact, her persistent proselytizing created tension between them: "It is the same disagreements of past, which usually leads to my crying bitterly when alone in my bedroom at night."[15]

Similar to her experience at the Campbell's and at Girton, Maynard's anxiety was largely provoked by her own religious doubt. Indeed, her

4.2 Constance Maynard, aged thirty-seven, 1887. Courtesy of Queen Mary University of London Archives/ Westfield College/ WFD.

pleasure, pain, and anger over Lumsden, agnosticism, and faith seemed conjoined: "Many said that the Old Testament was constructed by the human mind; that much of the Bible was not true. In truth, *I* [Maynard] thought this until 1880." Maynard's reaction was not surprising given the cultural climate. Although Victorians were not irreligious, it was an era of new thinking about scientific knowledge and evidence, and Bible Criticism was on the rise.[16] Maynard claimed that she "desperately *needed* Ls Christian awakening" in order to maintain her own:

> How does the dawn rise? How does the night begin? Is it not with thee, my friend? I watch, I wait, I pray, but no light gladdens my eyes ... Oh! My friend with deep, violent heart, is there not something of change? Not a confession of weakness? Not the longing for a Christian life with its endeavours?

She concluded, "One of three things will happen: we will part, we will live together with no common aims, or we will live together as one - with one heart, one faith and one Lord." She fervently hoped it would be the last.[17]

Maynard had more than one cause for concern about living with Lumsden "as one." She was upset by Lumsden's agnosticism at home, and she also felt conflict at the workplace. Maynard explained that she had initially been content to "serve under L and Frances," and to "lay down [her] very life [for] two of the best teachers in England!" But feeling intellectually unequal to them vexed her: "L tells me that my Logic lectures are confusing"; and again, "Beale says, 'You have no control in the classroom.' Dove says the same thing." Nonetheless, Maynard fully believed that an educator should inspire learning from within rather than enforce it. She fumed over the thought that both friend and superior considered her teaching methods "ineffective."[18]

Clearly, Maynard's ambitions were as high as Lumsden's and Dove's. This was particularly evident in counter narratives in her records about an event in November. In her autobiography, Maynard described a letter sent from Fanny Campbell regarding the founding of a girls' school at St. Andrews: "She [Fanny] said, '*if* the school was to exist, it was to be very good; 12 staff, all well paid, and well built.'" Campbell wanted both Maynard and Lumsden to become founding teachers. Maynard added, "Of *course* L had *no* doubt because of the number of Scottish girls at Cheltenham, but she made it clear that she wanted the Principalship." The account ended with Maynard's concern about entering a secular institution, followed by her addendum, "I am surprised that this 'great event' of the term is not recorded in either of my diaries."[19]

However, Maynard did comment about the event in both green book and diary. While her diary entry was scant, her upset over Campbell's and the committees' "handing" Lumsden the Principalship was evident: "L may see her 'wildest dreams' as 'fulfilled'! But *I* feel bitterly disappointed not to have got the position." It must have been galling to think that she was simply expected to help Lumsden as she was doing at Cheltenham. Maynard's green book evinced her overall misgivings: "What is the meaning of Girton, my love of L, and my faith? Should I walk away?" Of course, "any thought of going home again, was unendurable," Maynard recalled in her autobiography. "St. Andrews gave me thrills of happiness by comparison, even though I sensed my parents' disapproval; it was too far from Kent; I would receive a salary [£150]; and L would make it a secular school."[20] Here, once again, we see evidence of Maynard's struggle with ambition, passion, and faith, as played out in her different records.

Maynard tried to exert power to resolve her religious dilemma. She knew that the committee "would not take L apart from [her]." She would only agree to teach at St. Leonards School, as it was to be named, if religious instruction was "placed in [her] hands and [she] could teach from the Bible." Lumsden responded violently to Maynard's request since she suspected that Maynard would preach the Atonement: "The girls shall *not* be made anxious about their souls!" Maynard "agreed to teach from the 'secular' text" that Lumsden recommended for sake of St. Leonards' academic success.[21]

Lumsden's reaction, of course, reflected a shift from terror as an instrument of religious persuasion. Indeed, her goals for St. Leonards were clearly socio-political-economic based. In *Yellow Leaves*, she explained, "The Scottish universities were closed to women. My intent was to change this...by undertaking a crusade against the so-called finishing schools."[22] Certainly, the inauguration of girls' public high schools across the country had encouraged academic achievement rather than girls' accomplishments. Lumsden, however, wanted a female "'Rugby' of the movement. The thought came to me that the work Arnold had done for boys at Rugby ought to be done for girls." In other words, girls should study the Classics and sciences, and learn "character-building" through activities like sports.[23]

To further secure her aims for St. Leonards, Lumsden invited the talented Frances Dove to join them. Maynard was particularly upset over this manoeuvre. She knew Dove would accept because she adored Lumsden and would view this as a romantic opportunity. Moreover, the fact that Dove would teach "upper level science while [Maynard] 'was designated' elementary geography and arithmetic" suggested that Lumsden thought Dove the "more intellectually capable." Lumsden clipped Maynard's wings even further by inviting Cheltenham teacher Kate Kinnear to teach upper level Scripture. Caught in a situation that threatened compromise on professional as well as religious and romantic levels, Maynard assured the reader that she "must support a venture with all shares taken." She set off with Lumsden and Dove for Scotland in April as planned, to look over the "Schoolhouse" and to meet society.[24]

Although Maynard's diary waxed enthusiasm about St. Leonards after her trip, the green book continued to convey her concerns. She was irritated by Fanny Campbell, who completely taken with Lumsden, "designated any dirty spade work [Maynard's] way." Her parents now knew about her religious-based conflicts and asked, "*Why* must you go? What is so urgent?"[25] Her sister Dora got to the heart of the situation: "It is obvious that you are 'very much smitten' with Miss. L, and it is so very like 'marrying unbelief' that it can be dangerous ground." Dora knew of her sister's deep romantic attachment to Lumsden, as evidenced in her reference to "marriage," but her concern seemed over Lumsden's agnosticism. Religious issues aside, life with Lumsden had become emotionally trying for Maynard. She was not only exhausted by comforting the capricious L over "serious difficulties," such as Beale's

4.3 The founders of St. Leonards, c. 1890s. Fanny and Lewis Campbell are featured at bottom of photograph. Courtesy of St. Leonards School Archives, St. Andrews.

leadership, but most of their conversations ended in argument, which also left Maynard feeling intellectually beaten.[26]

A further clearly troubling problem for Maynard was Lumsden's insistence that they share a bed when they moved lodgings in November 1876. Maynard did not discuss this particular conflict with Dora or any other family member, at least according to her diaries. One assumes that Lumsden wanted more intimacy, although she does not speak of this in *Yellow Leaves*. Firth's brief coverage on Cheltenham also omitted this important detail. In fact, Firth asserted that "the drudgery of elementary marking" caused Maynard's largest frustration.[27]

It was not unusual for sisters, cousins, and friends to share beds with each other. Indeed, Victorian women enjoyed such physical closeness. However, her sharing Lumsden's bed had made Maynard extraordinarily tense: "It has exacerbated our religious differences!" she exclaimed in June 1877. "*And* I feel like I'm never off duty!" Maynard sought Dove's advice, but unfortunately she not only repeated their conversation to Lumsden, but emphasized her own misgivings about Maynard's religious teaching at St. Leonards. Dove's final blow was to assert, "Her [Maynard's] friendship with Amy [Mantle] far surpassed her present intimacy with you [Lumsden]." It remains unclear as to who said what, and who did what, but each woman knew who had the position of power. The "tears" over love and "lack of religious conviction," as conveyed in the green book, revealed Maynard's fragile subservience under Lumsden.[28]

What seems clear in the above is Maynard's, Lumsden's, and Dove's intermingling of faith, passion, and ambition to air their particular grievances. Lumsden and Dove seemed to share a concern over Maynard's faith, and notably, an understanding of same-sex passion. However, Maynard's "stress over" faith and passion drove her to consult her family physician: "I blamed overwork for my tiredness," she wrote. "I could not admit that L was draining the life from me." Maynard intimated that her exhaustion bordered on what Victorians called neurasthenia; a "respectable" middle-class disease – as opposed to insanity or hysteria – often used as a catchall for conditions from fatigue to anxiety. Maynard's doctor told her that "fatigue ha[d] spread throughout [her] whole constitution." He advised her to "not over exert [her]self." [29]

Nonetheless, although Maynard claimed that her fatigue had resulted from Lumsden's domineering ways, the green book of 1877 is worth closer investigation. Entries written in May and June intimate a third, sexually-based conflict that Maynard faced when sharing Lumsden's bed. A passage on 3 June runs thus:

> I cannot respond to her [Louisa's] ongoing endearment, "now I am satisfied, now I am quite happy." The nearer she expresses the full grandeur of her woman's nature, the more I feel dissatisfaction. I lie awake for hours without strength for prayer in a dumb conflict of feeling.[30]

In her review of 1877, Maynard remarked, "If I touch L, even the *least bit*, I am kept awake, as by an electric thrill, all through the short summer night, catching only the slightest snatches of sleep til the red sunlight lays in streaks on the wall."[31]

Maynard's scientific word(s) of desire reflected those written since 1867 about adolescent friends and Campbell. She experienced "electric thrills" when accidently touching Lumsden, which lingered like "red streaks" of passion "on the wall." Meanwhile, their queer bed allowed Lumsden to "express the full grandeur of her woman's nature" to her doubting wife. Did Maynard think this physically-based desire wrong in 1877? Did the entry imply her tension after a lover's quarrel? Did she resist Lumsden emotionally because Lumsden frequently bullied her? Or pushed "God away"? It seems likely that it was a combination of all. Although Maynard viewed her marriage to Lumsden as akin to close friendship, her reference to marriage implied a sexual element to their relationship as well, for marriage was not viewed by Victorians as an asexual term. Maynard struggled to voice her emotional struggles and religious doubt: "L's physical power over me is *so* intense and *so* painful! I think she could keep me awake til I die of it." Nonetheless, her same-sex sexual self-consciousness was implicit in her secularist-religious language(s).[32]

When writing of this conflict in her autobiography, Maynard claimed that her "struggle was caused by L's overpowering personality. L wanted to destroy [her] faltering faith."[33] She added, "But my decision about my future never wavered because the single argument of my heart was L":

> She [L], in a voice, which, to me, was unending music, sometimes read Scottish love ballads to me in an evening. There were tales of maidens who risked life and reputation to follow their lords in a page's dress; and there were others who held fast to their loves through dire transformations. As she read I felt that was the way I laboured for her, and was content to do it.[34]

Maynard's adaptation of the heterosexual Scottish love ballad is interesting here. She creatively culled fragmented, cultural materials to explain her past feelings for Lumsden. Although Havelock Ellis had by this time (1918) codified the manifestations of inversion and perversion, from same-sex desire to female masochism and sadism, these labels still did not exist as coherent social constructions. Indeed, in all records, Maynard was as comfortable with describing her "wifely role" as she was with subverting gender.[35] When Lumsden took it upon herself to abandon Cheltenham Maynard followed her manly lord. She disliked "leaving the staff to toil through a fortnight longer," but no guides to professional practices existed in women's colleges at the time.[36] In September 1877, she journeyed to St. Andrews in great hope with the second of her poetic, worldly lovers.

"The 'Futility of Life without Love' and Respect"

Maynard's first year at St. Leonards, which opened in a large house on Queen Street in St. Andrews,[37] was tinged by problems similar to those at Cheltenham. She was proud to oversee art and gymnastics for the entire school. However, she resented teaching elementary geography and arithmetic and using "scripturally-based story books of a secular character" because Lumsden wished it. In short, while it was difficult enough to take her "lower position" behind Dove and Lumsden, love exacerbated her feelings of pain, anger, jealousy, and inferiority. Nonetheless, she was caught up in the new venture as much as her fellow staff "who all were pleasant enough," although none were mentioned at length over these years. The Campbells did not really feature in her diaries either. She rarely mentioned Lewis Campbell within a sexual context.[38]

Lumsden began with what became the "calling over" of the forty-four students, including eleven boarders, who wrote examination papers in order to be "classified." This was difficult in the early years with students' differing attainments, and their ages ranging from about ten to eighteen. The "settling in," which involved planning lessons, walks, games, and drills, was also difficult: "We struggled to appear organized even though we weren't," Maynard noted in her diary. By the end of October a routine had been established. They rose at 6:30 a.m. for breakfast, followed by hymns at 7:30 a.m. Classes for all students began at 9:00 a.m., and after a lunch break between 12:00 p.m. and 1:00 p.m., ended at 3:30 p.m. Boarders had tea at 5:30 p.m. and supper at 8:30 p.m.[39]

Maynard lived in what she called "the Schoolhouse" with Lumsden, Dove, and Scripture teacher Kate Kinnear. As Head Mistress, Lumsden oversaw the eleven House-girls or boarders. This would be the arrangement until enrolment grew and boarding houses were established nearby that they would each oversee. One assumes that the living space, together with Lumsden's new position, modified her former domestic arrangement with Maynard, since they now slept separately. They still had their "stolen moments, like their nightly goodnight kiss," but Maynard claimed that she "felt healthier now that [they] were more apart." In an equally odd green book entry Maynard noted Lumsden's calling her a "school ornament":

> L tells me that she cannot do without me, yet I am nothing; an item on display. It is Frances who is everything to L. She superintends the work in every department. I don't begrudge Frances this because she has invested herself in the school in a way that I have not, and so she deserves the reward.[40]

In Maynard's view, "L vastly underappreciated" Dove. She explained, "I have less responsibility yet *I'm* allowed 'privileges,' like staying overnight at The Scores [Campbell's]." Yet she felt deeply humiliated by Lumsden's view of herself, and in turn resented Dove's position and talents. Moreover, entries about Dove's "jarring presence in the Schoolhouse" suggested that their competitiveness at work was exacerbated by their bitter rivalry over Lumsden at home. Maynard surely felt underappreciated as the school ornament; a pretty object or a plaything made to be visually admired, controlled, and punished by Lumsden.[41]

Somewhat troubled by her professional and personal milieu, Maynard's self-contemplation was also shaped by two events outside St. Leonards: the death of her mother, and Dr. James Robertson's courtship. The green book explained how she had first met the Scottish minister at the Campbells' in April 1877. She had liked him, but had been surprised by his proposal of marriage in a letter which ended: "You make me thrill with alternative passion and respect. You are my ideal!" It was clear that Robertson's focus was on her benefit as *his* wife, not her pursuit of a career. Added to that, she was not attracted to him. She quickly sent a reply stating, "I respect you, but...I cannot say that I return your affection." Robertson responded by saying that her reply "was very much what he would have guessed."[42]

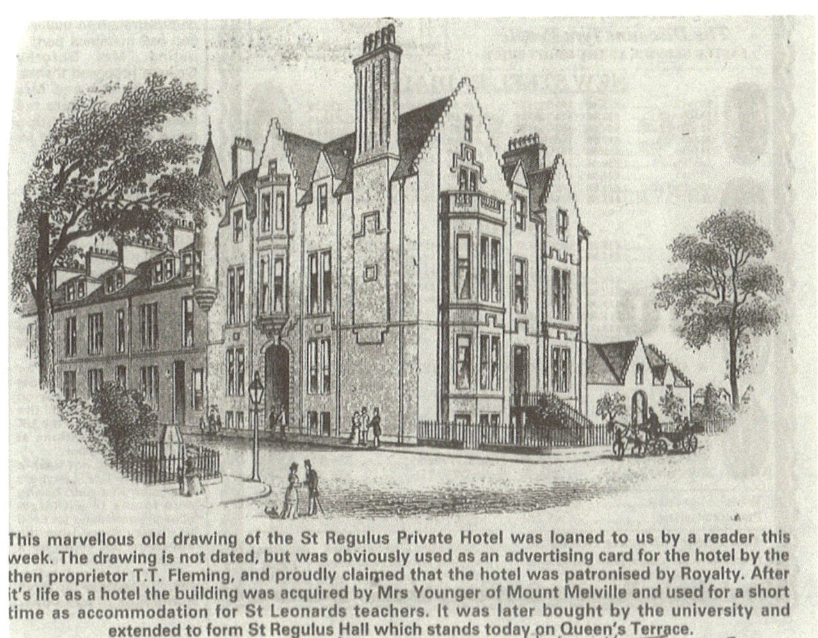
This marvellous old drawing of the St Regulus Private Hotel was loaned to us by a reader this week. The drawing is not dated, but was obviously used as an advertising card for the hotel by the then proprietor T.T. Fleming, and proudly claimed that the hotel was patronised by Royalty. After it's life as a hotel the building was acquired by Mrs Younger of Mount Melville and used for a short time as accommodation for St Leonards teachers. It was later bought by the university and extended to form St Regulus Hall which stands today on Queen's Terrace.

Before use as a hotel, it was leased by the School Council of 'St Andrews School for Girls' & was their home in 1877-82.

4.4 The Schoolhouse, Queen Street, known as St. Andrews School for Girls, where Constance Maynard, Louisa Lumsden, and Frances Dove lived with the boarders until enrolment increased and more Houses could be bought. Courtesy of St. Leonards School Archives, St. Andrews.

When Maynard told her family about the incident her mother "drew drab pictures of poverty in a manse and of an unsuitable life in general," but her father and sisters advised her to consider Robertson's offer. Lumsden, of course, had the most impact upon Maynard's decision. Her outburst about her "pain and suffering" made clear to Maynard that Lumsden feared losing "the woman she loved." Yet the fact that Maynard did not discourage Robertson is telling. It implied Maynard's own uncertainty as well as the powerful discourses around domesticity.[43] Indeed, she sought to maintain Robertson's romantic interest through letters for the next two years.

During the autumn of 1877 Maynard was primarily concerned about her mother, who was close to death. In January 1878 she was

4.5 Frances Dove House Group, 3 and 4 Queen's Terrace, c. 1880. This first boarding house, adjacent to the Schoolhouse, was acquired in 1879 after an increase in enrolment. Dove was the first teacher to be given a House, which upset Maynard. Dove is seated fourth from the right, in the second row, next to two older women to the right and a student in a white hat to the left. Courtesy of St. Leonards School Archives, St. Andrews.

summoned home to face a traumatic yet oddly uplifting milieu. On some days Louisa Maynard's keen foresight surprised all of her daughters: she encouraged Dora to continue nursing; she supported Gazy's decision to counsel soldiers in a nursing home; and she gave Constance permission to pursue a teaching career if she so chose.[44] After three weeks of painful struggle Louisa died on 27 February and was buried on 2 March:

> Her wish was to be carried ... by her six man servants ... along the church path in a little hand hearse – like the poor; and to be followed by the family

> and then all of the servants. We assembled in the churchyard to sing "the strife is o'er" around the open grave. The day ended with us all weeping at home.[45]

Louisa Maynard left behind as a legacy her fixed life Principle, which remained planted deep within her youngest daughter's consciousness. Watching her mother suffer had also led Maynard to ponder "the 'futility of life without love.' It is nothing, *nothing*, except the most empty of miserable forms!" she exclaimed in her green book.[46] Henceforth, she would follow her heart, whether in passion or in aim, whatever the consequences.

Maynard sought to follow her new-found resolve upon returning to St. Leonards. Robertson had planned a visit to St. Andrews supposedly to preach, and she agreed to meet him. She noted that their conversation, as usual, revolved around his feelings: "I had to say, 'I truly sympathize with you but I cannot accept you.'" She added, "Let him speak and look as *L* does and I would be his forever." Maynard believed that her "contemplation of this" forced her to choose career over marriage. Yet her parting words to Robertson, "I'm not saying that I can *never* love you," would have left him with an entirely different impression.[47]

When Lumsden invited Maynard to her home in Arran during the Easter of 1878, she joyously accepted. This trip is of note because it facilitated some frank discussion on the nature of their relationship:

> We spend hours together during the day … L loves to hear me speak on subjects like geology – of which *she* knows nothing. But I like the nights better when we fold so close! Ah! Such times are sweetness beyond words. I feel she feels it too. In several ways we do not suit, but I am so happy![48]

Maynard's green book evinced her delight in their renewed intimacy, and her hope that she could finally convince L to share "one faith and one Lord." But the agnostic Lumsden refused to view their love as a spiritual awakening: "I do *not* wish to analyse my feelings. I *will* say that I only wish that I was a man."[49] Lumsden had voiced anger over her gender constraints and her longing to be man at Girton in 1873. In 1878, she still viewed such constraints within the construct of Victorian heteronormativity, since the term lesbian did not yet exist. Her nod to her "maleness" thus probably had more to do with masculinity than biology, although Lumsden possibly alluded to what we may call transgender here. It seems clear that on some level both women understood their desire as same-sex, and that they gained some self-definition from subverting gender-based norms.[50] For her part, Maynard prayed that Arran promised a future relationship of intimate bliss and equality, set within a perfect balance of aim and faith. In fact, Arran marked the height of their relationship, and thus the beginning of its decline.

Maynard loved Lumsden, but her tendency to accede to L left her frustrated about her self-effacing role. Her teaching methods compounded her problems. She explained, "L praises my rapport with the girls, and then says, 'Yet Frances and I fear you have made yourself essentially one of them. You do not have enough control in your classes.'" For her part, Maynard did not wish to "stand on high" in the classroom like Lumsden and Dove did. She preferred to "reach down to students to give them help of a step or two."[51] Each woman eventually formulated a disciplinary technique, although Lumsden remained too volatile and Maynard too reluctant to use authority openly.

Despite these professional differences, St. Leonards' enrolment steadily grew under Lumsden's, Maynard's, and Dove's capable and creative hands. Conceived as model societies, schools like St. Leonards moved beyond familial metaphors towards analogues that emphasized "loyalty and public spirit" through character-building. Girls were introduced to corporate life through playing sports and regular examinations. From forms one to six they took classes in English, Latin, mathematics, Greek, French, German, history, geography, gymnastics, Scripture, art, and needlework. As educator Sara Burstall explained in 1930, "You [society] must realize that the [female] teacher is 'an expert professional' and is entitled therefore to the deference shown to the skilled professional opinion of the doctor, lawyer or architect."[52]

Of course, "expert professionals" were in place by the 1870s. Even at this stage of the history of St. Leonards, a few students were being prepared for universities. By October 1878, the Schoolhouse had already undergone powerful new modifications under Dove's adept administration. From the allocation of space to rules and duties, each member of the St. Leonards staff knew her role from teaching and playground supervision to overseeing "K," the room allocated as the girls' sitting-room for nightly cocoa parties. When examining Maynard's diary, one gets an impression of her growing capabilities in her professional life. By 1879, she was assigned upper level physics, geography, and geology. Her upbringing on science was evident in her teaching. Students took long walks to find mica, shale, and granite, and engaged in various scientific projects, such as "the making of crystals" from various compounds. By the time she left St. Leonards, Maynard could look back with pride on some of the end-of-term exam papers written by her geography students.[53]

Maynard's love of sports and art furthered St. Leonards' development as a professional institution. Her gymnastics classes were successful because of Maynard's own athletic ability. Only "a small strip of land" was available for athletics, but as Lumden pointed out, rarely any girls' schools even "*had* a playground in 1870s." Maynard's students soon donned an official gym uniform – a blue tunic to the knee with knickerbockers underneath – and were introduced to extracurricular activities like rackets, tennis, and cricket. Bathing in the North Sea also came under Maynard's charge, which was a crucial responsibility given the rough seas. Maynard's appropriation of "male" competitive sports helped transform attitudes towards women's capabilities. She set in place St. Leonards' first athletic sports day in July 1879: a "little tent was set up in the playground for ices and cakes, and at 3 p.m., the entire school watched races, high jump, long jump, and bar exercises."[54]

Maynard's artistic talent perhaps gained her the most attention. Indeed, her diary revealed the success of her "aim to teach liberty within" in her art classes. In 1877 she noted, "Inspired the gifted Ethel who has, in turn, helped raise the level of the whole class." Maynard was able to introduce techniques like "painting in Chinese white on blue linen" and still life. By 1878, her students studied "perspective" through field trips to sketch cathedral ruins or landscapes. They drew "shapes as they s[aw] them," just as Maynard had learned from her drawing lessons in London in 1871. By 1879, she drew alongside her advanced students and demonstrated the figure in clay. Her end-of-term exhibition that year gained her the recognition that she craved. She hung over seventy pencil drawings including her own. Pleased that the reception was well attended, she was even more thrilled by society's commendation of her talent as both artist and educator.[55]

When schedule changes freed up her afternoons Maynard attended university lectures. While she continued her love/hate interest in secular subjects like Utilitarianism, she kept updated on the latest writing and approaches to teaching subjects like geography. Another advantage of St. Andrews was the accessibility of individuals like Arch Forbes, who spoke about the Zulu War. Much to Maynard's delight, "the girls came back in raptures about military ardour and patriotism." Oddly enough, she initiated St. Leonards first school play, Shakespeare's *Twelfth Night*: "I am as intoxicated with drama as *anyone*!" she exclaimed in her diary. "What is to be done if one cannot go near pleasure without feeling its spell?" Social evenings also took on new meaning. She noted dinners she attended alongside her anticipation of "bigger events," such as St. Leonards yearly Ball: "I love to join in the dancing and other activities of these noisy happy evenings."[56]

"A Little Quiet Outlet"

Maynard's pleasant account of college life in her diary contradicted that of her green book, which alluded to her underlying pain. Lumsden's off-and-on criticism of her teaching approach, with vague accusations about her "carelessness," such as "letting the fires go out," left Maynard in frequent tears. She grew to dread "L's set look of disapproval," which was often accompanied by Lumsden's ongoing denigration of her for days. Indeed, in Maynard's view, Lumsden's attitude in general was abysmal. For example, during a diphtheria outbreak in March 1879, Lumsden had apparently "stayed in bed and left [her] sick staff to cope alone. When she finally came down she did nothing but scream and yell, and declare [her staff] both 'inadequate' and 'foolish.'"[57]

Maynard had struggled between staying and leaving St. Leonards since 1878. She knew she was unhappy because of Lumsden's cruelty towards her and volatility towards others in general. In her review of 1878, she noted her misgivings: "I turn thirty next year, almost middle-aged! Life seems so uncertain." Dora's sudden plans to marry a missionary named Frank Moilliet in April 1879 had disquieted her as much as Gazy's question, "Can you *really* survive if you choose career over marriage [to Robertson]?" Maynard could justify her work to her family, but she would not admit Lumsden's power over her: "I don't feel about *anybody* else the way I feel about her, yet my love accompanies a fear of her that at times reaches a sort of paralysing intensity."[58]

Maynard claimed that her "great capacity for loving L" drove her to battle this emotional kaleidoscope throughout 1879. Yet Lumsden, it seems, had developed a personal life beyond her. In a cryptic entry in October 1878, Maynard confessed, "I *finally* told L about my loneliness." She added, "L suggested that I invite two or three girls to my room in the evenings. Their bright faces *are* enough." Maynard's autobiographical account of 1878, written in 1919, suggested otherwise:

> My heart was lonely and hungry beyond words. Louisa had really failed me. There was not one on the Staff to whom I was attracted, and a whole

4.6 St. Leonards House Group, 2 Queen's Terrace, 1881. The group photograph, which once again typifies the early boarding houses acquired by the Council, indicates the student age range from ten to eighteen. Courtesy of St. Leonards School Archives, St. Andrews.

> mass of my affection seemed to be unused. It was here that I thought I found a little quiet outlet of which I need tell no one. As Edward Irving said, "Unless we obey instantly in every way, we never get those minute insights which turn our life from grey uniformity into an *inexpressible* sweetness."[59]

This curious justification, steeped in religious metaphor, conveyed Maynard's perhaps "twilight moment" in her adaptation of Irving's theology to explain why she had turned to one-on-one interactions with students to meet her spiritual-emotional needs. Her thoughts and ensuing behaviour were not yet "utterly" prohibited by society, but her actions as a pioneering female educator would not go entirely unnoticed either.[60]

The first girl Maynard "fell in love with" was eighteen-year-old Katherine Milligan, who entered St. Leonards in October 1877 when Maynard admitted her "loneliness" to Lumsden. Maynard's records implied their mild flirtations that, one assumes, echoed college raves. However, Maynard confessed that her love for sixteen-year-old Mary Guthrie Tait, who enrolled in April 1878, was "not quite as wholesome." She described Tait as intelligent, athletic, musical, and beautiful: "I felt 'that twinge' when she was in the room." She added, "But my innocent feelings for her soon changed." Maynard did not elaborate on this in her autobiography, beyond implications of a sexual tension between them: "I loved that 16 year old [Tait], and I foolishly showed it." Green book entries meanwhile described Tait as a seductress of sorts, who used faith as an excuse to visit Maynard alone at night. Maynard's admission that she, in turn, "responded in full to [Tait's] need to find God," suggested that the more sexually experienced Maynard also encouraged their clandestine meetings.[61]

Initially, Maynard felt a guilty pleasure about her "little quiet outlet. I *wonder* what *L* would say about all this?" she asked in her green book. She possibly enjoyed her secret revenge. She also felt uneasy, and struggled to determine the parameters of her role as an educator. Maynard's dilemma was evident in her comparison of her relationships with Tait and Katherine Milligan: "My affection never harmed *Katherine* as I never saw *her* alone." Maynard tried to limit her meetings with Tait: "I asked her [Tait] 'to reflect on the Atonement, rather than discuss it, and then we could meet.'" Tait apparently disliked the "horrible imaginations that this conjured up." Tait's fear was perhaps not surprising, given it was no longer widely used as an instrument of Evangelical conversion. Tait demanded even more time with Maynard, which the latter "felt obligated to provide." Maynard's longings had clearly created a situation which threatened dire consequences.[62]

In hindsight, Maynard admitted to her weakness: "My poor starving heart fastened upon her advances," she wrote, "and there was 'excitement' that was bad for both sides." It seems that Maynard became entangled in an erotic seduction-resistance of sorts, just as she had with

Amy Mantle at Girton. She was drawn to Tait's sensuality, but must resist earthly feeling. The green book of early 1879 voiced Maynard's ongoing "thrill, yet concern, over Mary's deep sadness and frustration" which, while vague, suggested Tait's struggle to repress desire. When it became clear that Maynard's interlinking of longing and belief led her to justify self-denial, Tait reacted violently. She threw tantrums at home, became defiant at school, and even threatened suicide. Her final retaliation was to show indifference and even contempt for Maynard. She surrounded herself with a circle of "flippant and insubordinate" friends who taunted Maynard in class, leaving the latter to "spend many a night in [her] little room in a rage."[63]

In her autobiography, Maynard lamented, "*Mary* was the one who conquered, not I." Yet both women suffered in this complex struggle around sex. By July 1879 the situation was so intolerable that Maynard was forced to tell Lumsden about Tait: "I softened things," she confessed in her green book, "but L was still distressed. I vowed that I would never repeat my mistake." It seems that Lumsden and Tait each saw something "wrong" in Maynard's conduct as an educator.[64] The power-based relationship that Maynard had found herself in with Lumsden, and more particularly Campbell, would influence her behaviour towards future favourite students as well. In the extreme, Maynard's power over and longing for these young women led to their emotional breakdowns, as in the case of Mary Tait, and future Westfield students Margaret Brooke and Marion Wakefield.

Maynard's struggle with leadership and longing at St. Leonards was, in the end, resolved through disputes with "L over faith." In March 1879, she wrote: "L complains about my Scripture class. She says, 'I don't like students being told to keep green books. They promote a form of weak and sentimental religion.'" There was no further mention of the topic other than, "We have discussed it since and L has been kind." Perhaps Lumsden feared Maynard had introduced the green book to encourage students to write about their "Spiritual" journey or shun of worldliness for Divine love. In any event, teaching Scripture became the dominant topic of concern in Maynard's green book. As it turned out she had good cause. In June, Lumsden began to "needle" her about "sitting in on her classes," which convinced Maynard that "the time of 'trial and sifting' had come. I pictured the possible scenario, that L would call me a weak sermonizer and would take the whole thing over herself. This, I knew, would be intolerable."[65]

In hindsight – and the emphasis *is* on hindsight – Lumsden's concerns "seemed reasonable" to Maynard. "Ever since the Mary Tait affair, I had felt awkward about teaching the seniors Scripture anyway," she confessed in her autobiography. "I felt such dislike from some that I wanted to be out of the Schoolhouse."[66] She thus acknowledged her mistreatment of Tait, and her great discomfort in recognizing that others were judging her behaviour as well as her religious views.

At the time, at least according to the green book, she focused on her problems with Lumsden: "Intense loneliness over the full state of my position returned to me in full force," she lamented. Not only did she feel like a rejected lover, but Lumsden had never seen "her school ornament" as a professional equal either. Lumsden's accusation, "You leave Frances with too much school work," only deepened Maynard's wound. Dove had "been given the first House" that year. She tried to forgive Lumsden's "betrayals" in love and work, and what she saw as Lumsden's guilt over Dove's capability (projected through anger at her). It was only later that she understood the trials of leadership and love, and how it felt when a subordinate effectively ran one's school.[67]

When Lumsden did seize Scripture she released Maynard from the vicious emotional cycle to which she had been tethered. She refused to discuss her decision with Maynard, whose outrage in her green book, "This is what *I* came to St. Leonards *for*!" told all. By December 1879 it was clear to Maynard that her time of trial and sifting was up: "How can I be happy when the love of my life has failed me? She has had the power to torture me and she has done it!" Strong words indeed. Perhaps Maynard's thoughts about leaving Lumsden impelled her towards deliberate, insensitive decisions during the early months of 1880. After dallying with Robertson for over two years, she had no qualms about requesting that he stop all contact with her. In some ways, this was difficult. He did offer an avenue of escape, but his lament "that everything at Whittingham had been purchased with...a view to her taste," implied another controlling relationship that was different, yet similar.[68]

Lumsden's threat to resign in May led Maynard to reconsider remaining at St. Leonards. However, when she learned that the Council had offered Dove the Head Mistress-ship if Lumsden left, and then had smoothed things over with Lumsden, her position on St. Leonards' hierarchical ladder seemed clear. She formally resigned at the end of June, although she had no definite future prospects. As Maynard bid farewell "to many tearful faces" she could not help but feel "a huge release" from her emotional quagmire. Nonetheless, her last moments with Lumsden were painful: "She burst into tears, saying 'How will I go on here when the joy of my life is leaving?'" Later, when alone, Maynard recalled, "I cried as if my own heart was breaking. Oh! My darling! I would have given my very life for thee!"[69] At the end of her life she still pondered their relationship:

> I can not say I understand the matter today, but I *can* say that she never had the same ascendency again ... In the past, especially at Cheltenham, I would say "O Lord Bless us both. I don't want You if she is left out, for she is worth more than I am;" but then I ceased praying for her, thinking, "she had her chance."[70]

Maynard claimed that she never regretted her decision, and Lumsden did appear to "be swept" from her life. According to Maynard, Lumsden left St. Andrews in 1882 after the Council became weary of her tirades and asked her to resign. Dove took over as Head Mistress, remaining at St. Leonards until she became the first Principal of Wycombe Abbey School in 1896. Lumsden moved to London upon leaving St. Leonards, shortly after Maynard became Mistress of Westfield. When Lumsden hinted about teaching at Westfield, thoughts of their history led Maynard to quickly refuse her.[71]

Little is mentioned of Lumsden again until she became Principal of the hostel for female students at St. Andrews in 1889, and where she remained until retiring in 1898. After 1910, Lumsden was a regular guest speaker at Westfield until Maynard herself retired in 1913. It is not clear whether they spoke about their relationship, but according to the diaries, they did discuss their religious differences and Lumsden's failings at St. Leonards. In 1916, at age eighty-five, Lumsden was made Dame, as was Dove in 1918. Maynard's adverse reaction to both implies the continuation of jealousies among these early pioneers.[72]

Life with Lumsden had taught Maynard the futility of remaining in an unhappy marriage. Never again, she vowed, would she concede to a lover over ambition and faith: "I am sick of concealment. I long for a world where I can stand with an open friend and battle face-to-face with an open enemy." The enemy Maynard wanted to battle was not simply secularism. Her search for her "true self" became an important site for exploring the relationship between faith, sexuality, and science. It was only in hindsight that she recognized that St. Andrews had

JANE FRANCES DOVE
Headmistress 1882

4.7 Frances Dove, dated 1882. According to the archivist at St. Leonards, Dove changed rather dramatically in that she went prematurely white. By 1882, seven more boarding houses had been opened that gradually became the property of the Council. St. Andrews School for Girls eventually moved from the town of St. Andrews to what was formally St. Leonards College, a property that was closer to and had originally belonged to the University of St. Andrews. The exact date of the move is not known, but it was during 1883. Courtesy of St. Leonards School Archives, St. Andrews.

4.8 Frances Dove House group, 1896, Dove seated in the second row, fourth from the left, wearing all black. This photograph was taken outside St. Leonards House in the new St. Leonards campus, where the school moved in 1883. This may have been Dove's "going away" photograph, as she left that year to found Wycombe Abbey. Courtesy of St. Leonards School Archives, St. Andrews.

prepared her for her life's work, to fight for women's rights "to the London B.A. degree."[73] Little did she know that the emotions surrounding leadership and longing that had tied her to Lumsden would set the stage for her future primary relationships.

Chapter Five

"A Man or a Woman?" 1880–1883

In May 1879, during the height of her quandary at St. Leonards, Maynard recalled two dreams to convey the nature of her struggles. The first dream "recurred throughout 1872," the year she had fallen in love with Campbell: "I lived alone as a penniless artist. One day, I met a girl who remained with me for many days. She gently received the love of Christ, and when she was with me, she was the beauty and love of my life." This dream had perplexed Maynard, but she now thought it symbolized her love for Lumsden: "She was my Magdalene, taking all I gave without an idea of the cost to me." Maynard's depiction of Lumsden as a religious-sexual temptress was curious here, for Lumdsen was Maynard's "Madonna" at Girton. Lumsden as Magdalene did, however, "epitomize [Maynard's] complex struggle under L" at St. Leonards.[1]

Maynard's second dream "lasted throughout 1876" and was "even more intangible." This was the year that she worked at Cheltenham, but this dream was not only about Lumsden:

> All I remember is the glory of standing together with someone in unbroken love. Was my friend a man or a woman? I cannot tell. There was a perfect understanding of love to let me to think it was a woman, yet at times there was a sense of being protected, and admired, that made me think it was a man.[2]

Maynard's dilemma here was more over power than gender, sex, or faith. She sensed that the close friends in her dreams, namely Louisa Lumsden and Lewis Campbell, were "above [her] in everything." Her "true dream," she now realized, was to find someone with whom she could share ambition, passion, and faith on an equal basis.[3]

This powerful moment in Maynard's life happened shortly after her exit from St. Leonards in 1880. Her resolve to her life situation fascinates in its revelations about one late-Victorian woman's (re)fashion of the self; an exploration reflected in Maynard's fluid interchange of cultural discourses with the language of her faith and her erotic imaginations. Maynard's self-search involved her attempts to dismantle gender, sex, and class, which only reaffirmed for Maynard her social position in society. She thus determined to establish what became known as Westfield College in 1882. As first Mistress of Westfield, Maynard continued to understand sex as heterosexual, and same-sex intimacy as a part of feminine norms. Nonetheless, her expression of same-sex desire in her new college milieu had and would remain what we might call queer. Maynard's intellectual and religious pursuits as Mistress interwove with her explorations of her sexual self as a single educational pioneer.[4] As she travelled down her path towards self-realization, the world, the flesh, and faith became a challenge in distinct, new ways.

The first event notable for its impact upon Maynard's journey was her rekindled passion for Lewis Campbell in the summer of 1880. In her autobiography, she dismissed "the 'strange passing incident.' I have a bare mention of it." Yet her green book covered it in detail, and raises interesting questions about Victorian sexuality. Certainly, she had felt "less drawn" to Campbell in recent years because of her love for Lumsden. Moreover, he had "disappointed" her time and again with his "helpless advice" about her secularist struggles at Girton and St. Leonards. Yet the fact that he was "far above any other man that [she] knew" indicated that Robertson likely seemed poor by comparison.[5] Nor is it surprising that Maynard's passion for Campbell sparked when she and her sister Gazy accompanied the Campbells to Rome after she left St. Leonards. After all, hurt and confused by Lumsden, she was more vulnerable to his attentions and possibly, on a subconscious level, strove to purge Lumsden from her thoughts.

Maynard's green book implied that she initially avoided Campbell, which was not surprising given their history and the societal norms regarding sex. However, the record then suggested that she not only relaxed her position, but exploited the sultry, heated atmosphere of Rome. The fact that she "let his hand steal secretly into [hers] even when Gazy and Fanny were present" seemed blatantly disloyal towards Fanny.[6]

There was also evidence that they sought time together alone. One green book entry described the intensity of one clandestine heterosexual encounter: "I lay beneath his caresses all panting as he gently stroked my face and arm." By the end of their stay the sexual tension between them was at a peak. When released from a "passionate kiss in the twilight" Maynard withdrew, despite feeling "intense rapture. When I saw his face," she explained, "there was love there, still, and blazing." They seem to have discussed entering a sexual relationship, with Maynard adding for emphasis, "I said, 'Lewis, I have let you take a position that no man has ever or can have. You must be aware of this.'" Campbell apparently told her that *he* had "crossed a line" and suggested that they continue only as "friends." He assured her that he would "never repeat his actions; and [he] promised [once again] to go back [to Fanny] and be loyal."[7]

There is no indication of what Maynard really expected from Campbell in her green book. Perhaps her remark concerning his unique position in her life as a man indicated her sexual preference for women. Yet it seems curious that she had never referred to "panting" or "blazing love" in her sexual plays with Amy Mantle and Mary Tait. Nor did she employ this language to describe her love for Lumsden. Do we assume that Maynard's more sexually explicit accounts about Campbell meant that she viewed sex as heterosexually-based? Did she consider her intimacy with women as "passion," rather than sexual? It remains unclear, but it seems possible. If we queer Maynard's same-sex friendships, to this point, we recognize that Maynard did not appear to hold our contemporary opposition between hetero-and lesbian sexuality, or classify mother-daughter eroticism as incest. As Julian Carter notes, we can respect Smith-Rosenberg's ground-breaking view that Victorian heteronormativity did not preclude strong and various forms of passionate bonds between women.[8] Nonetheless, while Maynard's friendships may have been based upon feminine norms, they were forged in the new college arena. This milieu afforded college women a more fluid space for female-female power struggles and competition.

Maynard's confession about Campbell, "I am saved from a love that might wreck my whole life," seemed equally curious.[9] In fact, this green book entry was perhaps more astounding given her cultural milieu. While the double standard of sexual morality condoned men's dallying, the definition of respectable womanhood was firmly linked to ideas about morality, innocence, and female piety. Whether or not driven by her pain over Lumsden, Maynard's defiance of femininity did indicate her passion for Campbell. Had he been willing, she may have entered into a sexual relationship with him and ruined her reputation and hope of career: "I am yet allowed to go a little near it," she concluded of this compelling entry, "and experience a faint shadow of what such a life might be, so now a long shadow remains."[10]

According to Maynard's records, Campbell slipped from her life at this point. Possibly her sense of feeling "jilted" by him a second time turned her once again towards career. She moved to London while he remained at St. Andrews. When closing this formative chapter on her life, Maynard summed her love for both Campbell and Lumsden "as dark abysses [faith] of differences and misunderstandings." Here, Maynard referred to their religious disagreements. Lumsden was "agnostic and Campbell materialist in thinking." Faith was also linked to erotic power. Her love for "strong-minded individuals," she surmised, left her "vulnerable to their emotional control over [her], and yet this still drew [her] to them."[11] One wonders if Maynard now thought herself drawn to those who facilitated her pleasure in suffering. Had she reconsidered her need to atone *for God*? It remains unclear. We can conclude that faith was a complex issue for Maynard. It was a way of seeing that contrasted other forms of late-Victorian Evangelicalism, and also stood in conflict with the changing cultural climate. Nonetheless, faith became for Maynard a means in which to express her passions as a woman, her goals as a reformer, and her aims to evangelize what she viewed as an increasingly secularist world.

Interestingly – although she made no connection herself – Maynard followed the whims of her first dream, which forged her professional and faith-based aims. She enrolled at the Slade School of Art in London which, although short-lived and disappointing, impelled her reflection of desire within the urban space of Rescue.[12] Her diaries do not dwell on these experiences, but they convey her fascination for prostitutes and unwed mothers staying at lock hospitals or Mission houses respectively. Maynard claimed to be "doing God's work" in her attempts at conversion, yet surely these "fallen women" symbolized her own recent sexual struggles. She was shaken when a "girl in a tattered coat" rejected her attempts with, "don't *you* touch me, you!" Possibly it conjured up memories of Mary Tait, or Maynard's own (sexual) reaction to female-female touching. Perhaps Maynard was shocked to feel desire in what Victorians called "the panoply of shame," since female vagrants were considered *sex* delinquents rather than destitute. It is also possible that she viewed her behaviour with Campbell as "dirtier" than the girl's, if the girl was a victim of unwanted male sex.[13]

Maynard felt the most comfortable speaking with prostitutes, who historian Judith Walkowitz suggests, were seen "to embody the animal passions that the...'angel in the house' had suppressed." Were these fallen women, one wonders, another means by which Maynard could imagine same-sex passion? Or were they a form of moral measure? After all, Maynard did not regard her marriage to Lumsden as a savage state of licence like prostitution was. Maynard "gave up" rescue work on the grounds of her gaining "a Bad reputation." Whether or not her tensions were around class or sexuality, Maynard's views about respectability were not shared by other upper-class Christian women. As such scholars as Seth Koven argue, rescue work may have influenced the moral imagination and desires of the many elite women engaged in it, but none appeared to fear for their reputation. Of course, Maynard would have "fallen" herself, had she become Campbell's mistress, despite her class and faith.[14]

"The Inception of Westfield"

It seems that Maynard's re-examination of her past through various cultural explorations reinforced her commitment to doing "True God's work" as an educational pioneer. The newly formed Salvation Army (S.A.) played a part in Maynard's cause: "It exhibits a new type of spiritual life through the spirit of Moody and Sankey," Maynard exclaimed. "I even bought an SA bonnet to walk down the streets!" More importantly, the S.A. inspired her initiation of a G.P.M. (Girton Prayer Meeting) "Ring" letter. While she applauded a social-nationalist religious organization that supported gender equality – as evident in women's roles as S.A. Officers – the S.A. only served to reinforce her elitist, visionary aims. The S.A. may wish "to rehabilitate workers," she wrote, "but I think that society should conquer the poor and wicked." Her goals were clear. Her Ring would prove a vital network for the future Westfield.[15]

As mentioned earlier, Maynard claimed that "the inception of Westfield formed in [her] mind" at Girton in 1872. "From this time on," she wrote, "I fully believed that God had chosen me out of thousands of English girls to hold the most difficult post in the world." This was indeed a powerful claim, and it was in 1881 that Maynard realized the possibility of such an achievement. She had met Caroline Cavendish, who had recently founded the Christian Women's Education Union.

The C.W.E.U. aimed to promote Christian education worldwide, and this inspired Maynard to establish a Christian college in London to begin this important work. She persuaded Cavendish to hold a conference in January 1881 to garner support. Twenty-five attended, including wealthy members of the G.P.M., and the prominent headmistress of Highbury, Fanny Metcalfe. Following Cavendish's plea that "a Christian college *could* be academic," Maynard "emphasized that London degrees were the only degrees (except medical) legally opened to women in England." It was thus "resolved that a Christian college was needed in London to prepare students over eighteen for such degrees." With this in mind, Maynard joined Cavendish and Metcalfe in the search for a venue.[16]

Maynard energetically promoted her idea of a women's college in London throughout 1881. She delivered over eighty speeches at venues from the London School of Medicine to industrial girls' schools in the Midlands. In September of that year, she wrote a paper to be presented at the C.W.E.U. conference in 1882, afterwards printed as *The Cultivation of the Intellect.* The paper developed the arguments raised at the earlier C.W.E.U. conference, insisting that literature, science, *and* religion should be a part of women's knowledge:

> Already we lament the secularising tendency of so many of the best (intellectually speaking) of these schools, and already Christian parents shrink from them ... The common belief that women do not need cultivation is erroneous ... We meet women...whose ideas have been awakened, who, in short, have been and *are* "cultivated" ... Attention must be given to places of instruction for girls - in whose hands the future of the womanhood of England lies.[17]

Cultivation of the Intellect was well received at the C.W.E.U. conference in January 1882, together with presentations on topics such as the plight of workhouse children. It was here that Maynard met Mary Petrie, who facilitated Maynard's meeting of Ann Dudin Brown, an elderly genteel spinster. As Maynard recalled of this pivotal event on 8 February 1882, "I had no idea that she had £20,000 to contribute towards establishing a college on a Christian basis."[18]

Dudin Brown invited Maynard to a meeting with prominent devout Evangelicals Col. Martin Petrie, the Rev. James Fleming, Dr. Thomas Boultbee, and Dr. William Barlow, to discuss the proposed college. This event provided Maynard the opportunity to persuade them against a missionary college: "Your College *must* reach Christians of course, but London's granting of degrees to women on *equal* terms with men will distinguish your College [from those at Oxbridge]." While not offered the position of Mistress at this time, Maynard nonetheless prepared an in-depth proposal on the running of a college for ten students. Boultbee suggested that they formalize matters by going public and instituting both a Council and a "scheme" to add more funds to Dudin Brown's £10,000 investment.[19]

The first meeting about the college held on 3 April 1882 included well connected leaders of the educational community like Sir William Muir, F.A. Denny, and Lord Shaftesbury. A Council was formed consisting of Dudin Brown, Boultbee, Barlow, Fleming, Petrie, and Fanny Metcalfe, while Maynard was voted in as Honorary Secretary. However, Fleming, Boultbee, Denny, and Shaftsbury then voiced concern about "public condemnation" of the venture. Maynard noted Shaftesbury's insistence that "genteel women should not receive *too* much education because the saddest part of his work was with fallen refined ladies."[20]

The Council had cause for concern because society had opposed the movement for women's higher education since its onset in the 1840s. This was evident, for example, when Jesser Reid had founded Bedford in London in 1949 to provide women new access to university lectures. W.R. Greg was among those social critics who warned of "redundant" middle-class spinsters with feverish brains. Meanwhile, Sarah Stickney Ellis' advice books reminded "restless daughters that charity began at home" rather than the public sphere. Further attacks were launched in the 1870s by such eminent physicians as Henry Maudsley, who stipulated that while men may "benefit from a university education," women's higher learning "disrupted the…female organization" and left women "deranged." Indeed, women's new entrance into higher education correlated to "the rise in female hysteria." Of course, not all women diagnosed with hysteria were involved in higher learning. Nor did men escape emotional breakdowns from university education and professionalism. Hysteria was "female" because ideas about "women's weak physiology" and "irrationality" dated back to Greek times. Victorians viewed women as the inferior gender due to their bodily "susceptibility" to fear, anxiety, and self-doubt.[21]

It seems that these ongoing debates about women's bodies, roles, and rights influenced Shaftesbury and other Council members. Maynard claimed that she persuaded Shaftesbury "from speaking out" against the college through stressing her religious motivations: "I said, 'we are on the same side, and are as determined to heal some of the miseries of the world.'" Shaftsbury's advice, "real enthusiasm can accomplish *anything*!" proved self-confirming. Personally reassured, her unrelenting letters of plea to her Council were rewarded. On 8 May 1882 she was offered the position of Mistress of a college which was to be both religiously and academically based.[22]

Maynard began her role as Mistress by presenting a detailed list of her duties to the Council. This list included overseeing all college matters, and arranging lectures at both college and the University of London. She felt the first of many "murmurs of difference" from Council member Fanny Metcalfe, who questioned her staunch Evangelical approach.[23] Nonetheless, her list was cordially accepted as was her college prospectus that echoed the recommendations forged at the C.W.E.U. conferences. The Council only wished to advertise in the Evangelical journal *The Record*, so Maynard sent numerous copies of the college prospectus to friends, relatives, and educators, including the Campbells, Lumsden, and Davies. Of the three, only Davies responded.

Other educational leaders openly harangued Maynard for her "outmoded Evangelicalism." For example, when she attended the yearly Girton committee:

> Lady Stanley bent across the table and said, "Surely, you have no right to be here? You are a traitor in the army." Before I could reply she added, "Are you not all very, very pious?" Again I hesitated, and she went on, "Well, you say so in your paper [*Cultivation*]. You must be so very, very, Evangelical!...Ah, well, there you can sit and all be pious together."[24]

In Stanley's view, Maynard's Evangelical college reinforced Victorian views of piety as a feminine domestic trait. Since female piety challenged male heathenness, Westfield threatened Girton's "male" educational model through its "traitorous" proclamation of "proper" female higher learning. While Stanley criticized Maynard's religious stance as an educational reformer, Maynard had used faith to counter Shaftsbury's misgivings about higher learning for women. We could dismiss Maynard as a conservative non-feminist, based upon Stanley's point of view. Yet it seems clear that Maynard was motivated by religious faith and spirituality, as well as by her commitment to female independence through higher learning.[25]

Opposition, support, or personal endeavour aside, Maynard knew that she must secure a building, students, and staff if the venture was to be launched. The Council wished to open the College that October, which was an astonishing date for such an enterprise, and they were quite opinionated on certain matters. Maynard was angry when the Council decided to hire only one resident lecturer (trained in London or Cambridge). She quickly outmanoeuvred them by securing former Cheltenham student Kate Tristram. Tristram was "young" and lacked the Matriculation, but her Christian background, intelligence, and "pliable nature" made her the best candidate.[26]

After securing Tristram, Maynard began her search for a college site. The Council had emphasized that she seek "the country house." Westfield would be "a moral [feminine] hearth" that would "yet emulate the [masculine] order and energy of a true corporate life." The Council's stipulations were not atypical. Hitchin (formerly known as Benson house) was leased from "a country gentleman." The "task proved arduous," Maynard wrote, "but I finally discovered two semi-detached, three-storey terraced houses" for rent in the rural village Hampstead, which had access to London by train. The Council signed a seven-year lease and "The College for Ladies at Westfield" became a reality. The final name, Westfield College, was chosen in 1887.[27]

On 10 September 1882, Maynard moved into Westfield for her fifth and – as she rightly predicted – "last start in life!" A week later the five candidates, Frances Synge, Margaret Graham Brooke, Emily Thompson, Annie Tristram, and Alicia Bleby arrived for the Entrance Examination. They were expected "to demonstrate general knowledge" of Scripture History, English History, Geography, English Grammar, and Arithmetic; translate a passage in Greek, Latin, German, or French; and pass either elementary Algebra or Geometry. The Council determined that Westfield's Entrance Examination "be of a lower standard than 'The Matriculation Examination'" – the official prerequisite for the Intermediate and London B.A. degree. This decision, alongside the fact that the students were mostly friends of Maynard's, was also predictable. Middle-class boys were prepared for The Matriculation (or equivalent at Oxbridge) at secondary schools, but girls, at best, held a certificate from the newly established Oxbridge Local Examinations. A final difficulty was that the University of London was purely an examining body at this time, and its degrees were deemed inferior to Oxbridge.[28]

It is understandable, then, that Maynard noted the "insurmountable burden" she felt in her "sense of not being allowed to make mistakes" by Westfield Council, the metaphorical public. Yet despite such deep-seated feelings of insecurity, she never wavered from her "true calling."

Perhaps the fact that her first term proved self-fulfilling helped in this respect, even though she suffered through smoky chimneys, leaky windows, and "the multitude of confusing bills which passed through her hands." Kate Tristram was proving "to be the perfect second-in-command; and [her] five genteel students, who were all clergymen's daughters, respected [her] values and were eager to learn."[29]

Maynard's first task was to prepare her students for The London Matriculation by "working up" the subjects that they had sat for the Entrance Examination. This meant, for example, developing the principles and practice of Arithmetic and Euclid. Students also learned such subjects as Natural Philosophy (Physics), Chemistry, and Botany for the first time. Success at The London Matriculation level would distinguish between those Westfield students able to take the B.A. degree and "General students." The degree program was expected to take three years to complete,[30] and would be Westfield's particular academic standard for many years.

Although all students had passed Westfield's Entrance Examination, their educational levels differed dramatically. Similarly to most genteel girls, Synge, Brooke, and Tristram had received education in girls' accomplishments. Bleby and Thompson had fared better with private tuition. Maynard, Tristram, and "Visiting Lecturers" – who were largely female Oxbridge graduates – taught introductory Classics, English, History, Logic, Political Economy, Physical Geography, and Arithmetic. Students were introduced to "the ethical systems" of such key thinkers as Aristotle, Kant, Bentham, and Mill. Meanwhile, male tutors were called on for help with the Physical sciences and Mathematics. But Bleby was so "far advanced" that she was escorted to University College London to take Physics and Chemistry lab work. By November, a teaching routine had been established that served the needs of individual students and a small college building up its academic work and reputation. Understandably, the program was somewhat piecemeal, and Maynard faced many "futile expeditions" to the University searching out suitable lectures for students.[31]

The four new students in the Lent term and two in the May term brought the total for the year to eleven. This pattern or something close to it was repeated year by year until the 1890s, when the Council and society in general was more supportive of women's higher education. In the early days, students rarely stayed for the full course. Many parents thought one year was "a sufficient education" for their daughter. Thus the search for recruits was an ongoing preoccupation and worry for Maynard and the Council. Indeed, the admission of students who failed Westfield's Entrance Examination typified the situation until suitably qualified entrants increased. Maynard's trials with a "nervous invalid" revealed how some saw college as a means to rid a difficult daughter. In this instance, Emily Buxton's needs slowed down study for the entire college. Of the original five, only Alicia Bleby and Emily Thompson took their degrees. Even so, in light of the ideas about women's education, the majority of students who left with only Matriculation in hand in the early 1880s should not be seen as failures.[32]

Two big hurdles for Maynard in 1882 were gaining final approval from both her father and Westfield Council. Her father had indicated his support in a donation of £1,000, but she still feared that he may wish her home. Rather, as she remarked after his visit in November: "His appreciation of the whole enterprise cleared my last shadow of doubt." The Council members were equally supportive. They approved her lecture arrangement and oddly hybrid college rules: "I [Maynard] told them that I encourage corporate behaviour. They must use surnames and refrain from kissing in public. But I emphasized that permission was needed to travel alone, and that all male visitors were considered 'guests' of the Mistress." The Council also agreed to Maynard's request to disallow such worldliness as dancing and parties, even though such activities were not banned at Bedford, Girton, Newnham, or at women's colleges in general. Maynard, of course, viewed these "external restrictions" at Westfield as God's mission. She would "guard" her students against worldliness. However, her external restrictions would, in the end, justify her "internal" passion as Mistress.[33]

In October 1882, Maynard's overall satisfaction was influenced by Divinity, the closest Church of England parish to Westfield. In fact, sermons about "walking alone through the bad streets with the Lord Jesus" reinforced her duty as Christian Mistress. For example, she promoted Westfield graduates to the Church Missionary Society as it had begun to appoint qualified women as missionaries. Maynard's first Bible class, in turn, emphasized the "True guide to a holy life" through Irving's "Parable of the Sower":

> The same seed falls on the ground, but the difference is the reception it meets with. [M]uch of the good seed scattered is wasted if hearts were already occupied [with worldliness] because it only "patters" on the outside. God's Word on an open, unprejudiced heart, brings rich fruit. Let the inner life be in greater proportion to the outer life.[34]

The Sower became Westfield's "motto" and the honeysuckle, Westfield's emblem, because its spiritual-like scent "was something beyond this world." The motto and emblem set in place Maynard's aims for Westfield, "Christ in Education"; in other words, Westfield would be known for its strong combination of Christian theology with "thorough intellectual" learning. At times, her thoughts on "The Sower" were interwoven with secularist discourses. She would adopt Kant's "famous categorical imperative, 'I ought, I can, I will,'" to emphasize that the "inner moral standard be in greater proportion to the outer life."[35]

"A Personally-Conducted Pie"

It seems that contentment in both spiritual and academic life could not satisfy Maynard's day-to-day cravings for human affection. Ever aware of her painful mistakes at Girton and St. Leonards, she was determined "to keep [her] place among her staff and students. After all," she added, "deference' needs to be demonstrated towards me publicly given my role." Nonetheless, she found handling responsibility alone as Mistress (and secretary and housekeeper) both overwhelming and isolating. It was difficult to hear Kate Tristram's "happy laughter" in the evenings. Thus, when the students instituted "informal evening talks with [her]" she happily encouraged them. Indeed, their quiet "assembling outside [her] door" soon metamorphosed into an erotic "personally-conducted Pie." As she gathered them "around [her] armchair in the firelight each night, and kissed each on the forehead, [she] fe[lt] that [she was] in the right place at last." She had no regrets about "the strong bond of affection" that she had with them.[36]

Clearly, Maynard struggled with her new public role. Like many educational pioneers of her time, adopting cool assertiveness likely felt at odds with prescribed femininity, particularly within Westfield's familial-like setting. However, her need for maternal-like rituals was interconnected with another, more powerful desire. In a striking entry written on 16 October, she wrote, "It is certain *attributes* that I seek. It is not so much a matter of *whom*!"[37] Since her life from this point was devoted to Westfield, Maynard turned to peers or students to satisfy her needs. Consequently, her passion, ambition, and faith grew troubling for her in distinct, new ways.

Maynard relied on Kate Tristram as a young colleague, and was fond of her, but she was not attracted to her. Throughout much of the 1882/1883 school year she saw Westfield student Margaret Graham

Brooke (MGB) as "the choice of [her] life." Drawn to the pretty, industrious, pious nineteen-year-old from the outset, the green book was soon filled with entries about love. One entry, "Oh Lord! Keep me steady," implied Maynard's surprise at the intensity of her own feelings. She was apparently even more "awe-struck" when,

> during a Pie discussion on worldliness, this seemingly sweet and demure girl ... leaned hard against me in the dark and whispered, "but Oh! *With love,* I shall never want such things. You fit right down into every corner til no part is empty and hungry - Oh! *How* I want you!"[38]

Maynard's "thrill" over Brooke's passionate outburst was dampened by fear: "I felt *ill* with the responsibility," she explained, owing "to my age, values and role. I had to have a 'straight out' talk with her that night to explain our need for self-control. We agreed that a denial such as this was part of our nature, and a sort of satisfaction to another part [faith]."[39]

Here we see the enactment of Maynard's resistance of human desire that she had encouraged with fellow Girton student Amy Mantle, and St. Leonards student Mary Tait. But as Mistress of Westfield, Maynard particularly wrestled with leadership, religious duty, and physical longing. Brooke, like Mantle and Tait, struggled under Maynard's erotic overtures and atonement-based restrictions about passion: "She declares herself out of control whenever I touch her!" Maynard exclaimed two days after their talk. "I speak of having loved across *that* terrible chasm with L. We pray to keep our hearts...sheltered in His hand."[40]

It remains unclear as to exactly what Maynard told Brooke about Lumsden, but as indicated above, their relationship clearly reflected Maynard's experiences at Girton and St. Leonards. In this instance, however, Maynard held great power over her love. Also evident was Maynard's inability or unwillingness to repress her passion. In March, she confessed, "In public we are controlled and respectful in our manner toward each other." Their nights together alone, apparently, were entirely different:

> She knows my step and stands with outstretched arms as I enter with the almost painful longing expression that love must bring when it comes in force ... She says her world was empty before she met me; that she had often fallen in love before but *that* was hollow and worthless. She says I am her great treasure.[41]

5.1 Early Westfield College group at Marsfield Gardens, 1885. Maynard, aged thirty-six, is centre of the second row. Kate Tristram is to the left and Margaret Brooke is sitting at Maynard's feet in a pale grey dress. Maynard's future love, Frances Gray, is seated to the right with a book on her lap. Anne Richardson is standing behind Gray wearing a hat. Courtesy of Queen Mary University of London Archives/Westfield College/WFD.

Maynard's desire was also "drawn with a force that [was] almost painful." She teasingly acceded to Brookes's subversion of her gender: "I become her [Brooke's] most reverent husband. She is my joy! What need I write of her when I have these visits each night? 'My hearts-dearest,' she says, 'I am all, *all* yours.' I scarcely dare to let myself accept the sweetness of her passionate endearments."[42]

At the same time, Maynard fretted over the nature of their relationship: "Is all this right? Is it taking the truly highest path? Surely it is all rather unusual?" Apparently, she attempted to caution Brooke: "I tell her, 'I will never let you give more than you ought,' but she [Brooke] sweeps this aside and says the marriage vows." At other times, Brooke would silence Maynard's doubts "with impatient" exhortations such as, "I am truly your wife!" Meanwhile, Maynard verged between assuring herself that their college rave was a phase, "I shall be happy to let her [Brooke] go to the right man," and then voicing guilt about her usurping of feelings that perhaps Brooke "should *only* give to a man."[43]

Although Maynard was troubled by the depth of her carnal intimacies with Brooke, she had no means of understanding her same-sex passion beyond that which she had already experienced. Her lover-husband-mother roles at Girton, and her "unhappy marriage" to Lumsden, as such, had been enacted in part within the context of patriarchal gender and sex norms; and in this instance, the "force" of passion passed through the "reverend" couple whose souls had touched. Maynard's use of the discourse of Evangelical social purity at this time was similarly interesting. She turned in particular to the ideas of social reformer, Josephine Butler:

> She [Butler] said, "The girl's passion for the man is the impulse toward maternity implanted by God, showing itself in the attraction of the other sex ... But she should appeal to the mind of a man since he leans to the physical side." *I* know how hard *this* is! I have felt it in every fibre of my being. I ask myself, "Why is the man's love fiercer than that of the woman?"[44]

Here, we might argue that Maynard "queered" the social purity scenario of the moral virtuous woman versus the physically excitable man. *She* had experienced the "fiercer love of a man" in her love for a woman. Meanwhile, Brooke's "intoxicating passion," Maynard claimed, was at odds with Brooke's feminine "incarnation of purity and sweetness when she l[ay] asleep [after passion] in [Maynard's] arms."[45]

Inevitably, Maynard's struggle to justify her desire through science and social norms steered her towards using her faith as a further means of self-understanding: "I long to give every inch of my heart and body to MGB, just I did with L [Lumsden]. But *this* love which, though as strong, is love without the keen edge of discord." The difference, Maynard surmised, was God's Blessing for her work at Westfield. She taught the Bible and had stood the worldly test. When "the question of dancing was raised," she nearly threw aside college rules or "external" restrictions: "I thought, 'Why not dancing? They would enjoy it!'" She added, "I was saved just in time by MGB, who said, 'It is better to make the line rigid.'" This was a sign, "I thought, 'God has offered MGB so I shall put away my last fear. While guarding the *external* restrictions, I shall set aside the *internal* restrictions and believe that what forces itself unasked upon me is meant to be.'"[46] In short, it was more important to guard against worldliness at Westfield than to debate God's (private) gift of love.

Maynard's idea of passion and desire as God's reward for "good" *public* deeds seemed to be emotionally freeing for her in the 1880s. In many ways, if she had replicated her first term, she quite possibly could have run a small Christian-based college with a loving female partner for the remainder of her working days. This inclination was evidenced in 1901 when she wished to found a Divinity college with Marion Wakefield at her side. Nonetheless, Westfield's particular erotic milieu under Maynard's hands seemed to incite sex- and power-based struggles. In 1883, for example, Maynard failed to recognize that Kate Tristram's increasing moodiness paralleled her relationship with Brooke. When Tristram admitted her desire for Maynard in April of 1884, she employed religion to explain to Maynard her aching heart: "No! Don't touch me! I do not feel like a Christian."[47] Was Tristram, one wonders, embracing Maynard's faith-based norms or subverting them?

The problems surrounding sexually-based jealousy and ambition were complicated by growing enrolment. Even so, Maynard faced for the only time in her thirty-one years as Mistress the nervous breakdowns of two students. In the first case, Emma Maunder's tirades and "wandering" up and down the hallway at night left Maynard fearful for everyone's safety. Maunder had only been at Westfield for ten days and her behaviour was disturbing. Indeed, to protect her students, Maynard "lay in Maunder's arms all night listening to her mutterings...about [their] *marriage* making [them] a part of each other forever." Maynard's classification of Maunder's "unhealthy affection" as desperate "madness" was markedly distinct from her effusing about Brooke's "wifely" love.[48]

Maynard's worry over Maunder did reflect Victorian ideas of women's "irrational" nature. In 1866, physician Jules Falret had classified "the 'deranged' woman as one who engaged in disruptive acts to possess her love." Meanwhile, as noted above, Maudsley was among those who cited higher learning as one cause of female hysteria. Here we see additional problems facing educational pioneers. If we take Maynard's green book at face value, Maunder was likely unstable even before entering Westfield. Yet Maynard worried that Maunder's emotional breakdown might fuel criticism of Westfield during these early years. After all, she was quick to distinguish her calm demeanour during her Girton Tripos with what Davies' and others called Lumsden's and Dove's hysterics. In 1877, she emphasized that her stress under Lumsden was diagnosed as physical fatigue. Later, in 1902, she assured the reader that Marion Wakefield was neurasthenic, not hysterical. In Maynard's view, women may struggle with new professional challenges, but this did not mean they "would go insane."[49]

The second and final Westfield student to leave due to stress related problems was Minna Colville. Talented and quite possibly an overachiever, Colville set herself impossibly strict time schedules for taking both The London Matriculation and Intermediate. Although Maynard's diaries are vague on the matter, Colville was also incensed by what she viewed as Maynard's inappropriate behaviour with students in the name of faith. In fact, Colville adopted Biblical language to accuse Maynard of being "a hypocrite and whited sepulchre; fair outwardly, but vile within." Maynard, in turn, retaliated by using her position of power to ridicule Colville in public before sending her home.[50] Time taught Maynard to modify her religious-based expectations, but her new-found power left her reluctant to curb her erotic-based favouritism. Her failures with a vulnerable Emma Maunder and a talented Minna Colville would always leave a sting.

Maynard's struggle with her role was further complicated by her own ambition and tendency to take on too much. Although overly busy with college matters, she continued to attend the S.A., C.W.E.U., and Girton meetings. Maynard found this pace impossible in future years, so it was not surprising that by May 1883 she spoke of "frequent headaches and insomnia" in both diary and green book. Brooke's "love" only exacerbated matters because Maynard "no longer consider[d] '[her] sweet child' [her] intellectual equal." Brooke now questioned

Maynard's behaviour as Mistress, particularly during the Colville affair. Maynard confessed to "feeling hurt" since Colville's words, she feared, did have a ring of truth: "Work is good," she wrote in her green book, "but it is not one's whole being, and love leaves a sad craving." In short, her relationship with Brooke had illuminated her need for "a strong masterful woman upon whom [she] could lean," or so Maynard wrote in her autobiography.[51]

Such a woman had already entered Maynard's life. In February 1882 she had received a "stiff, precise note" from a second-year Newnhamite named Anne W. Richardson (Nannie), which requested a meeting "with the author" of *Cultivation of the Intellect*. They had met the following June at Henry Sidgwick's venture Newnham, in Cambridge. Maynard was taken with the compelling dark-haired twenty-three-year-old who had been raised in an aristocratic Quaker home in Moyallon, Ireland, and Richardson was similarly drawn. She called on Maynard in London two weeks later to offer "fellow sympathy and support" for her college.[52]

Richardson was one of Westfield's first visitors in October 1882, stopping en route to Newnham with a gift of six small study lamps for each student's room: "That visit was the beginning of our lifelong friendship," Maynard wrote in her autobiography. "I realized that we were both aiming for the same work for God." Thus, while seeking emotional comfort from Brooke, she frequently wrote to Richardson for "strong masculine" academic advice. Here, at last, was someone who was not only a Christian, but also shared her class-based views and intellectual aspirations.[53]

When the Council agreed to hire another resident tutor, Maynard hoped to snag Richardson. However, Richardson, not yet qualified, was expected to oversee her father's linen mill after college (although she did become a lecturer at Westfield in 1887). Of note, here, was Richardson's guiding Maynard to the fateful hiring of genteel Christian, Frances Ralph Gray, who was expected to excel in her upcoming Classical Tripos at Newnham. After meeting Gray (Ralph), Maynard was clearly smitten with the beautiful, tall, blue-eyed brunette: "Her gentle face and low replies gave me a feeling of steady reliable force," she recorded in her green book, "and so, as young as she was, I felt my search had ended."[54] In fact, Maynard's professional and personal "searching(s)" were both ending and, at the same time, merely beginning.

Constance Maynard's mediation of ambition and passion proved an important process for her during the early 1880s. It involved a complex questioning of gender, sex, and class, and culminated in Maynard's synthesis of it into a singular professional- and faith-based aim. If she had known that this uneasy blend of values would create "years of desolation and emptiness," she might have heeded her misgivings when Richardson brought Gray to view Westfield in June 1883. She knew, even at this time, that they saw her Christian nurturing approach as somewhat lacking in public spirit and authoritativeness.[55] Nonetheless, Maynard's determination and ambition forged Westfield's success into the twentieth century.

Maynard's new-found position as Mistress of Westfield afforded her enormous control over young women. This circumstance was implied in the way that she conducted herself in the nightly Pie, and was evident in the ways she toyed with and controlled Margaret Brooke (and quite possibly Kate Tristram, Emma Maunder, and Minna Colville). While Maynard truly believed in her duty to convert her loves, her means of persuasion did, in some ways, mirror that of Campbell's in 1872 and 1880. Just as he had played on her sexual naivety, so she guilefully manipulated those to whom she was attracted and hoped to save. Just as she had adopted faith to avoid confronting Campbell's behaviour, so faith became a means to justify her own.[56] Even though her family would be of concern throughout her Westfield years, Maynard now knew that she could never go back. Tissy and Gazy might feel obligated to village work, nursing their father, or assisting Dora with her second pregnancy, but her "heart always seemed to fly back to the work [she had] left behind."[57] In sum, her priorities in love, duty, and faith were college-based rather than enacted in the domestic sphere. Her "family," regardless of how it was "publicly troubled" and emotionally wronged, serves as an analogy of the situation and of the power that some college women had living together.

Chapter Six

"Years of Gloom" 1883–1894

Maynard's autobiographical account of her "years of gloom" at Westfield began as a tale of woe, forewarning the sad chapter in her life that would follow:

> Throughout the writing of my autobiography I have never wanted to discuss Westfield. Why not? The story is an old one. The one I loved with undisguised passion failed me. The good friend who might have brought relief turned away, for my prolonged grief became to her wholly uninteresting.[1]

Although Maynard's professional role contributed significantly to her stress, the root of her grief stemmed from love: "Just as I dislike some people at first sight," she exclaimed in her green book, "I knew I loved Ralph [Frances Gray] from the moment I saw her." Indeed, the genteel Irish-born Gray offered Maynard the "total love [she] had always imagined." Gray was not only beautiful and devout, but had "gained distinctions in both English and Divinity at Newnham."[2] Thus, when her relationship with Gray unravelled, Maynard succumbed to extreme forms of suffering for human passion.

As we have seen, the diversity of Maynard's raves reveals the complexity and malleability of identity formation(s) that were forged in the new college milieu. Passionate friends, heterosexual lovers, wife-husband and mother-daughter role-playing were interchangeable, and yet, Maynard's "marriage" to Lumsden was not. Vicinus' observation, "One woman, one kind of love, did not automatically exclude other lovers or kinds of love," comes to mind here. Maynard's archives suggest that her same-sex experiences did not automatically change the meaning of female-female intimacy for Maynard.[3] Nor would her possibly sexual encounters with Gray alter Maynard's view of sex as heterosexual, even though her understanding of same-sex desire did slowly evolve.

To better understand the pious Maynard's conflict between "knowing" sex as heterosexual while exploring same-sex sexuality, we turn to the insights of queer theory. Frederick Roden is among those who propose that during the late 1880s Christianity intersected with new scholarly interests in Classicism to help shape what became the broader language of homosexuality in the fin de siècle. Intellectuals drew upon ideas from ancient times to re-examine their "bodily" same-sex desire.[4] This chapter explores Maynard's conceptualization of her desire for Gray through Hellenist discourse as a successful but lonely educational pioneer. Her failure with Gray led to Maynard's ill-conceived decision to adopt Stephanë Rosabianca (Effie); a child for whom Maynard could not take full responsibility. Maynard's power-based bonds with Gray and Effie coalesced with Maynard's faith and vision as Mistress of Westfield in complex ways.

A fluid approach to the erotic uncovers interesting aspects of Maynard's relationship with Gray. Feminist theorist Audre Lorde reminds us that women have been denied the "power of their erotic," because society often reduces it to the sexual, rather than "the doing" of say, faith. For example, while Victorians classified women as passionless, they acclaimed faith-based passion between women as normal to female development. When we consider Maynard's bond with Gray, Roland Barthes' view of eroticism(s) as an effective valence of obsessiveness, theatricality, and pleasure comes to mind. Intense erotic relationships, Barthes notes, involve such emotional extremes as domination and submission, restraint and eruption, or idolization and self-torture.[5] The erotic dynamics of restraint and eruption, and of idolization and self-torture, were bound to Maynard's religious-professional principles when she fell in love with Gray.

In order to contextualize Maynard's "gloom" with Gray, we must view the erotic dynamics between the two as problematized by Maynard's professional values. Still, Maynard's approach to running Westfield was a necessary strategy for a woman's college in late-Victorian England. Emily Davies and others supported their students initiation of such "male" college rules as "Sitting on High," the use of surnames, and formal dress for dinner. However, Davies discouraged Girtonians from "overt behaviour" and social evenings that male students could attend. Meanwhile, Newnham's Anne Jemima Clough was among those "maternal" leaders who advocated higher learning for women as she "fussed" over her students' health and letters home.[6] Maynard, for her part, established college rituals that reinforced Westfield's "genteel" feminine milieu:

> [T]he open fireplace in each student's room; the maid bringing the bowl of water every morning; breakfast and lunch served in hot dishes on the service table; formal dress for dinner; the ritual of marmalade making; the strawberry teas; the walking out with a companion til' 1905, when we could walk out alone![7]

It is not surprising that pioneering college women struggled to merge the emotional "feminine" with the "masculine corporate." Gray's criticism of one early student's work, for example, was viewed by the student as a betrayal of their female bond rather than sound academic advice. Such values endured. In 1894, Somerville's (Oxford) Agnes Maitland spoke of the merits of women's opportunity to embrace "life in a [male] corporate body." Even so, she assured society that "feminine unselfishness was a plant that flourishe[d] exceedingly well" in women's colleges. Maynard justified these values at Westfield, claiming they were "the best possible shelter for the new aspirations."[8] Nonetheless, it must be noted that the hesitant beginnings of these early educational pioneers laid the groundwork for major reforms for women socially, economically, and politically.

Moreover, when we examine in more detail the Westfield of the mid-1880s, it seems evident that Maynard hoped to distinguish Westfield from other women's colleges through her interconnection of religion and higher learning. Evangelicalism had particularly suffered under the twin foes of secularism and ritualism during the mid-1870s; but from this ebb a reinvigorated Evangelicalism emerged, inspired by new ideas about devotion and stressing "Holiness by faith" rather than struggle as the path to sanctification. By the 1880s, many Evangelicals found in this new spiritual language a means of coping with religious and cultural changes.

Maynard, too, was drawn to Holiness through the huge Mildmay conference held yearly for Christian workers. However, the fact that Mildmay invited clergymen to speak against the new teaching is telling. Maynard was among those who still maintained that the "true

6.1 This photograph of Westfield College group at Marsfield Gardens, 1889, reveals the ways in which college women merged the feminine with the masculine corporate. Constance Maynard is featured pouring tea while resident staff member Mabel Beloe and Anne Richardson are prominent in their B.A. gown and hat. As London graduates, Beloe and Richardson had the right to wear the "masculine" academic dress denied to Maynard and others who completed their studies at Cambridge. Courtesy of Queen Mary University of London Archives/Westfield College/WFD.

believer" was in continual conflict on earth: "Holiness st[ood] for life, only life – not for 'the faith,' only for faith":

> I held a deep religious devotion and an intense desire both for increased personal knowledge of God and for opportunity to succour others in their search for religious truth. I had eaten of the Tree of Knowledge of Good and Evil [at Girton], and recognized that though it may be a necessary step in our advance towards holiness, that step was "the Fall." The great task lay in teaching theological "Truth."[9]

In the words of former student and teacher Anne Richardson, Maynard was "convinced of the importance of mission, without which one's power of achievement would be lacking." The power of achievement, for Maynard, lay in her hope that women would spread God's word in an increasingly "masculinist" world motivated by secularism and capitalist ideals of wealth and "progress." Since the new spiritual language was anti-doctrinal as well as "materialist," Westfield students would evangelize the world with their scholarly knowledge and "theological 'Truth.'"[10]

Maynard was not the only late-Victorian intellectual woman to challenge "masculine" worldliness through "spiritual" woman. As Jacqueline deVries and Joy Dixon argue, the materialist patriarchal age concerned female reformers whether they were conservative Evangelicals or non-mainstream spiritualists. Indeed, some used "masculine" secularism to advocate for women-centred issues. This was evident, for example, in a debate on Bible interpretation in the feminist *Women's Penny Paper*: "It is time for women to restore…the integrity and Truth of the Bible. We want women to be…the expounders and teachers and preachers of the Bible." Maynard's goals for women found powerful form in the weekly Sunday evening "Function" meeting, which was a modification of the "personally-conducted Pie" of early Westfield days. After a Bible class, discussion turned to college matters such as course work or volunteer missionary work. In later years, Function became an important platform for promoting women's mission work, both at home and overseas.[11]

The annual "At Home," which had evolved from a small "Thursday At Home," was now a lavish affair. Indeed, much like the Girton Party, the At Home was known for its distinguished guests, fine food, and entertainment. The "Annual Banquets" for graduates were equally splendid, and Maynard wrote glowingly about these:

> This time was as pretty a sight as ever I saw, all dressed in white with yellow poppies. Two students shouted in unison, "we want Miss Piper" and all the rest of the names. It was simply compelling. The long avenue looked charming as one B.A. after another fled down the white lane in her blade gown.[12]

Maynard's reference to the "white lane" and "blade gown" seemed oddly analogous to her view of feminine independence. The graduate as a pure and virtuous woman – like a "bride of Christ" – was an emerging triumphant contestant in the public sphere. Yet the symbolic power of the "blade" gown also evoked the "male" combatant who, while victorious in battle, was nonetheless drawn towards the white light of Christ. In later years, Maynard asserted that God ultimately "brought" man and woman together in the "perfect man." As patriarchal as this seems, Maynard's views were progressive for the times. Since gender did not separate one believer from another, she argued, why then should higher education.[13]

In terms of Maynard's professional achievements, her diaries and Westfield Council Minutes portended Westfield's great potential. Of the original five pioneers, Alicia Bleby and Emily Thompson had already gained The London Matriculation. They would successfully pass the Intermediate or precursor to the B.A. The Intermediate – similarly to Girton's Intermediate – required students to write papers on Latin and Roman History, Greek, English Language, Literature and History, Mathematics, and a modern language. Westfield students (similarly to those at Girton) then selected three out of five subjects for the B.A.: Latin and Roman History; Greek and Grecian History; English and a modern language; Mathematics, either Pure or Mixed; or Mental and Moral Sciences. However, in contrast to the Girton Tripos, the Westfield student could actually gain the degree alongside men. In 1886, Westfield's three pioneers, Marie Pechinet, Emily Thompson, and Anne Richardson (who had transferred from Newnham in 1884) were among the first thirty-six women in England to sit alongside men for the B.A. examination.[14]

The fact that girls' secondary education had vastly improved since the 1870s helped dramatically. Westfield now "gave preference to those candidates who had passed The London Matriculation and who intended to read critically for a degree." This shift in girl's education sharply contrasted the "girls' accomplishments" that had been taught two decades earlier. Over half the students enrolled at Westfield aimed to take the B.A. or B.Sc. The latter, instituted at Westfield in 1885, indicated the development in science alongside Classics at girls' educational institutions in general. For the B.Sc. there were ten subjects, of which three had to be offered: Pure Maths; Mixed Maths; Experimental Physics; Chemistry; Botany; Physiology; Zoology; Animal Physiology; and Physical Geography and Geology. By the time that Maynard retired in 1913, she could proudly note that up to ten B.A.s and six B.Sc.s "were sent in" for "Capping Day," the graduation ceremony during each May and November.[15]

"A Great Deal about Love"

When Frances Gray began teaching Classics at Westfield in October 1883, her impact upon Westfield and its Mistress was twofold. Maynard's Council *Report* of 1887 clearly conveyed Gray's academic and economic contributions: "The cost per student head for the B.A. is £13 lower than it was in 1882. Increased enrolments and more resident lecturers will further reduce costs." The hire of Gray revealed that resident staff who taught at the Matriculation level could cut tuition costs drastically.[16]

Gray's new position at Westfield forewarned personal change for Maynard as well. From the outset, Gray gave her the emotional support that she so desperately needed. She followed Maynard's college "rules," and she buffered Maynard from her critical Council. On the other hand, Gray seemed "almost *too* noble" to the adoring Maynard: "I am content with the sight of her, for beauty itself can go no further!" Facing an "aloof Madonna" was a new experience for Maynard. Her love for Lumsden had been reciprocated, and Brooke eagerly demonstrated her passionate wifely role. Indeed, Maynard's "ardent encounters" with Brooke continued even though Brooke knew that Maynard was smitten with Gray.[17]

In her green book review of 1883, Maynard attempted to contextualize her mired and "deeply rooted hunger for human love."

> I have learned a great deal about "love" this year. M [Brooke] generously moves away from me. I have hurt Kate [Tristram], who says that she will not love again so easily. I have seen Alison [student] try to love K, and yet K is unable, like me with M, to like A better [than me]. Ralph is stirred by [my] passion, but she thinks that love degrades.[18]

Oblique as Maynard's account of love was, with its allusion to exploitive love triangles, we should not underestimate college raves. Vicinus has shown how college women supported each other through tremendous social opposition in their demands for independence. Maynard's records reveal that some raves were never broken. For example, early students Maria Parry and Katherine Porter supported each other's independence through forming a life-long partnership.[19]

Of course, college bonds were not always meek and tender. In Sharon Marcus' view, Victorian pornography, fashion culture, and doll stories exemplified the varying levels of dominance-submission that existed among mainstream women. But raves could be highly negative experiences for college women – as evident in Maynard's relationships with Tait and Lumsden – and tragedy best describes Maynard's bonds with Brooke, Gray, and Marion Wakefield. Meanwhile, Tristram's threat to leave Westfield due to unrequited love was yet another example of the damaging emotional swathe created by Maynard.[20]

However, any problems with raves seemed far from Maynard's mind in her review of 1884. Gray was "the one," and promised Maynard intellectual equality as well the erotic passion she had explored with Brooke:

> Her [Ralph's] perceptions are more helpful than anyone else's and she spends most evenings on my sofa. A warm point was when I asked her if she loved me. She said she wanted to be sure before saying the words but she could do so now. We stayed in a long, close embrace while she told me.[21]

Maynard's romanticization of "total love" with Gray had already proved idealistic. She had disliked "serving under" Dove and Lumsden at Cheltenham and St. Leonards, but she felt "even more subordinate to Gray. R is much cleverer than I am, *and* she's a true Christian!" It seems that Gray had already tired of Maynard's strict Christian asceticism and corresponding maternal-erotic view of Westfield as "a happy, confiding family." Maynard, in turn, resented her "weak tears' over the *least* provocation" with Gray over such college rules as dancing and novel reading. An incident concerning the January *Report* (1884) further exemplified Gray's power. Maynard had asked Gray to rewrite it after struggling with it for weeks and, while dismayed at Gray's (re) focus on "hard work over conversion," had sent it in to the Council "without comment."[22]

Gray's friend from Newnham, Anne Richardson, fuelled the fire as far as Maynard was concerned. Certainly, Richardson had proved a "bright spot" since her enrolment as a student in October 1884, and added sparkle to debates and games. Yet her "'latitudinarian' manner" meant that they often disagreed. This was evident in Richardson's instigation of Bible criticism at Westfield. Maynard knew that Bible criticism was fairly common practice in intellectual circles. She admitted, "Even *I* allow myself irritation over damages in the Bible." Nonetheless, she wished "to avoid creating unsettling doubts among students." Westfield's motto "The Sower" was, of course, a means by which she could "emphasize that 'seeds' [students] became 'hard' if occupied *only* with science." Unfortunately, neither Richardson nor Gray shared Maynard's views on the conflict between worldliness and Christianity.[23]

Maynard's struggle with leadership and power reduced Richardson and Gray to negotiating roles themselves. Richardson particularly disliked Maynard's "overbearing" behaviour with students. Her comment, "your power last year made you unsympathetic," suggested her disapproval of Maynard's former "personally-conducted Pie" (and possibly Maynard's harsh treatment of Minna Colville). Her final teasing comment, "you are *not* to continue like that," indicated that even as a student Richardson considered herself to be powerful. Gray's problems with Maynard were somewhat similar. She controlled Maynard through her sexual allure and "aloofness," but faltered over professional issues. When she accused Maynard of over-working her, or of underappreciating her, she felt compelled to profusely apologize: "Oh Mistress! Your *perfect* magnanimity after I spoke like that. Oh! It is *most* Christian. I love you, *truly*." Maynard, for her part, keenly felt her failings as leader-lover, and no guilt-ridden affectionate apology could appease her.[24]

In her autobiography, Maynard confessed that she always pined for the maternal atmosphere so emblematic of Westfield's first term. She then asserted, "But I knew this rule must be replaced by an equally valuable public spirit." Although she encouraged corporate spirit at Westfield, her dislike of "impersonal" leadership often led Maynard to revert back to her preferred role: one-on-one intimacy with a sweet student who could be converted to her faith.[25] The interpersonal conflicts of Maynard's own creation had already revealed this, and such problems continued:

> May [Maria Parry] came today to tell me that she was converted. She was so excited that I made her lie down, and I listened while her heart poured

> itself out to mine in passionate love. I'm not sure that I'm doing the right thing. Yet it is leading her closer to God, it really *is*, and surely this should be the test, *shouldn't* it?[26]

Not every student responded favourably to Maynard's subversive, coercive approach:

> Margaret and I discussed E [Evelyn Moore]. When I confessed to being repelled by E's coldness M said, *most* approvingly, "E hates demonstrative affection. She thinks the way we behave is disgusting even though we are Christians." I felt very upset. Are we fools in our demonstration of "Xianity"?[27]

In this instance, Brooke avenged Maynard's rejection of her through faith. Meanwhile, Moore's comments, similarly to Minna Colville's in 1882, challenged Maynard's perhaps inappropriate behaviour with students in the name of faith. As Maynard admitted, "I can lay my reason and ambition for Him alone. And my heart? It is soft, and responds to 'touches' with an intensity of pleasure that is almost pain."[28] Maynard did not wish to curb her behaviour because her spiritual-erotic longings were so great. In a sense, her social freedom as Mistress provided for Maynard a means to express the sorts of forbidden desires she had long craved.

Maynard's freedoms and conflicting unease in her role as Mistress created conflict with the Westfield Council; a relationship that gleans insight into one early educational pioneer's battle with blatant sexism. Maynard had sought to "keep well in with them" because of Lumsden's bad experience at St. Leonards. She thus assumed they would "give her a housekeeper" in late 1883, given her overwork in general. The Council not only denied her request, but complained about her household expenses: "I did not want to remind them that I worked for no salary at all," Maynard lamented. "I kept silent and my heart sighed." There is no evidence of this interaction beyond Maynard's autobiography. Since the Council Minutes do not mention Maynard's salary until later years, she had perhaps agreed to work without pay until "the scheme went."[29] Unfortunately, this situation left Maynard vulnerable to the Council's continued disrespect of her femaleness; an attitude that reflected Victorians' treatment of female professionals and women in general.

By late 1884, Maynard was convinced that the Council sought ways to disempower her. She was inflamed by the Council's decision to depose her as Honorary Secretary, although it was possibly meant to lighten her burden as Mistress. Her relations with Council members flared again when she verbally attacked Fanny Metcalfe's "lordly" reprimand about her poor book-keeping. Maynard felt "so uneasy about [her womanly] disgrace" that she apologized to the Council for her angry outburst. However, Dudin Brown's "fit of 'pique'" about the event forced Maynard to relinquish her seat on the Council. For Maynard, this was indeed a bitter pill to swallow. Bernard sat on Girton's Council as did Frances Dove on St. Leonards. So "now [she] was the sole exception."[30]

These were difficult years, for as Maynard noted, "I was repressed by my Council in so many ways." The Minutes and diary confirm that Mistress and Council wrangled over numerous issues throughout 1885 and 1886. Maynard understood "that science [instigation of the B.Sc.] was a top priority at Westfield, and yet [the Council] only passed the B.Sc. in June [1885] after much demurring." When she suggested the hire of Newnham graduate Josephine Willoughby to develop the B.Sc. and give Kate Tristram more time to pursue her B.A., the Council agreed on the condition that both become part-time lecturers without pay for the October Term.[31] Maynard had to fight to institute salaries for both women in the ensuing terms.

The ongoing tensions about the B.Sc., salaries, and suitable students, together with the Council's criticism about Maynard's "negligence" as Mistress, led the former to institute sub-committees for household management, college promotion, student admission, and faculty hiring. In this, the Council likely wanted to help. The records imply that Maynard was not simply overworked, but that she was a poor manager or was perhaps victim of her class and gender. She neglected to settle accounts (neither she nor her sisters had ever handled money); she avoided reprimanding domestics and students (she had never overseen domestics at Oakfield or students St. Leonards); and her bias towards enrolling daughters of friends and clergyman compounded her problems. Maynard interpreted the Council's actions as a sign of distrust in her. She also resented her growing loss of power and control.[32]

"The Tormented Lover"

Not surprisingly, Maynard's ongoing conflicts with the Council affected those closest to her. It seems that professional and sexual pressure at the workplace had proved too much for Gray. In 1885, she announced her intention to live with her family who had moved from Ireland to London. Reading between Gray's words, Maynard suspected that *she* was the cause of Gray's flight. A green book entry in December 1885 highlighted her torment:

> Go, Helen, Go! You fetter me and you joke me. In my folly I led you to my side and drank in your beauty. I did not know that your hands would keep me down from my work, and paralyse my will. Oh, My Ralf! Your long sweet kiss is on my lips still, your head on my knee in the firelight, your voice singing in my ears. Because I have loved you far too well, God has taken you from me.[33]

The above reveals once again how Maynard interlinked cultural materials to describe her same-sex feelings. She interwove familial husband-mother role-playing with Amy Mantle. She used the Scottish love ballad to explain her maidenly love for her mannish Lord Lumsden. With Brooke, she had adopted the discourses of social purity to explain her fierce, masculine passion for an atypically passionate girl. In this instance, she presented an oddly hybrid religious-Greek mythological language to convey Gray's rejection.

Maynard's interplay of Hellenism and Christianity to explain female-female passion in the mid-1880s was not entirely unusual. Queer theorists such as Frederick Roden and Yopie Prins posit that the establishment of Greek history and religion as an alternative transcendent value to Christian theology at universities gave some intellectuals opportunities to re-conceptualize their same-sex desire. For example, Prins' analysis of educational pioneer Jane Ellen Harrison led Prins to conclude that Harrison linked her research on ancient Greece with her Christian faith to ponder same-sex "fleshy love."[34] Of note is that Harrison was both a student and Tutor of Classics at Newnham. Perhaps Gray as an ex-Newnhamite in Classics shared with Maynard similar ideas about same-sex carnality.

The sexual undertones in Maynard's account of her love for Gray seemed implicit. She as "tormented male Greek lover" had fallen victim to Helen of Troy, and so must "relinquish *everything* to God" for salvation. Nonetheless, even as she condemned ancient Greece for its "sexual decadence," Maynard confessed, "I have some of it in me." After all, "thrills" and electric "sparks" between college women could evolve into dangerous forms of sexual feeling. Caught perhaps willingly in erotic dynamics of a self-tortured lover who idolized in vain, Maynard's green book became filled with grief over Gray, interspersed with smatterings about Brooke's "misery" over *their* love. When a dejected Brooke left Westfield in January 1886 without her degree, Maynard lamented, "*Nothing* makes any impression since *she* [Gray] has left!"[35]

When Gray accused Maynard of overworking her, Maynard fell completely apart. In a conversation to Richardson about Gray, Maynard tried to explain Gray's anger through the language of faith: "I said, 'I don't want to seem to excuse myself, but I really believe R's problem is due to her want of love for God.'" Richardson had different thoughts on the matter. In 1884, she advised Maynard to visualize her "love" for Gray as a form of Arnoldian-like professionalism: "Ralf has a nature formed by duty and a tendency to disregard the love of others… She needs a fearless hand over her Miss." This time, Richardson was far more direct: "I have seen with you [Maynard], Margaret and perhaps even myself, waywardness. Has there not been something wrong? Now again Ralph has come to feel that in *personal* absorption there is a danger and 'a something wrong' that she can scarcely express, but *feels* intensely."[36]

Did Maynard realize the sexual implications in Richardson's caution? That *this* propensity on Maynard's part was what troubled Gray? Quite possibly she did, given her pondering of inner desire(s), and what became her ongoing interconnection of Hellenism and Christianity. In 1928, for example, she remarked, "Faith would be easier if Christ had sat at decadent Athens, but I think we must always have some of the Greek." One wonders about green book entries in 1885 as well: "I know my desire for L [Lumsden] was deeper than that for Lewis," followed by another after Gray's departure from residence: "I could almost read their [the Council's] nasty thoughts, but I'm sure they are wrong."[37] Nonetheless, Maynard still sought to reconcile her "something wrong" within the language of her faith:

> We discussed what we would do. I advised R [Gray] to continue as she had done. R asked, "and you?" I replied, "I will *see*." She wanted me to explain, but I just said, "when anyone is called to the kind of work I do, it is very lonely, but one should only satisfy that loneliness through God's permission."

In the end, if "God gave" Maynard love she would accept it, no questions asked. She "clung" to R's parting words, "I don't think either of us will starve," to avoid further analysis of her feelings in her green book.[38]

However, when Gray remained distant throughout the fall of 1886, Maynard lost all hope. Her green book entries virtually ceased and her yearly review was brief: "The first six months of the year explain the last six, which I do not wish to discuss." After August all entries ceased until January 1901, when Maynard was "in throes of passion" for her new love Marion Wakefield. It's unknown whether Maynard tore out the interim pages of this record as she threatened to do in later life, or if someone else did.[39] We do know that Maynard bequeathed her memoirs to five close Westfield friends, a list which included Gray. Given that Gray had first access to the documents, she perhaps destroyed records that she found uncomfortable. Catherine Firth, the second to receive the records, claimed that entries between 1887 and 1901 were missing when she was given them.[40] In any event, gone are the multifaceted narratives that could have provided a rich account of Maynard's life experiences in the 1890s.

Maynard's self-portrayal in her autobiography over these years continued to be that of a tormented "queer" lover. This was a Christian, albeit bestial-like figure, who "battled whistling winds" for temptation of the flesh through self-flagellation: physical pain, enforced sleeplessness, fasting, and solitude. Raised to suppress "the will" and "blindly follow God," a distempered Maynard recalled Rachel Cook's fateful words at Girton, "You make your faith and believe it." She added, "Rachel was right! I did not *want* God. I wanted Ralf." In desperation, she went to Gray's flat to "pour out her soul. A forbearing but *not* loving [Gray] suggested [they] had better part"; that perhaps she herself should leave Westfield. For Maynard, Gray's attitudinal finality "was a staggering blow. I experienced a form of 'amputation.' I adorned a lace cap to symbolize 'death of youth.' For those who asked, I said, 'I love Ralph so much that I could die for her.'"[41]

The pain of love threatened to destroy Maynard's professional life. She considered leaving Westfield, and even came close to resigning, but there were reasons to remain. When reading her diary and Council Minutes over these years, one is struck by Maynard's remarkable investment in her students. For example, in 1890 she noted: "Professor Walker came in the afternoon to talk about Alicia Bleby. Then long talks with Sarah White and with Priscilla Wood about their possible prospects." Bleby became the principal of a girls' high school in Cape Town and remained there until her death in 1911. Maynard's "long talks" with the talented White and Wood also paid off. Wood was the first Westfield graduate to receive an M.A. in Classics in 1896, and White

6.2 Westfield College staff, 1888. Maynard, aged thirty-nine, is in the centre of the group wearing her symbolic lace cap. Anne Richardson is standing to the left, and Mabel Beloe is on the right. Frances Gray is seated in front and to the right, and Josephine Willoughby is to the left. Courtesy of Queen Mary University of London Archives/Westfield College/WFD.

was the first to achieve her B.Sc. degree. White then received an M.D. from London in 1896, after which she ran a private practice in Belfast.[42]

It is also noteworthy that another talented student, Mary Cornford, broke off her B.Sc. in 1888 in order to transfer to medicine at London. Several who followed her example later worked as medical missionaries, and perhaps owed to Westfield not only their grounding in the basic sciences but also their vocation. At the same time, the Westfield College Register implied that Cornford was among the increasing numbers of students who came from middle-class professional families. This was a stark contrast to the earlier predominance of daughters of clergymen or the gentility.[43]

In January 1888, two years after her "official" break-up with Gray, Maynard was formally invited back to Council meetings, which gave her new leverage. This change was particularly evident in her defence of high B.Sc. tuition (the Council threatened to close the program because of it), and in her demand for higher salaries and less teaching hours for her staff. Indeed, her "unconstitutional" instigation of a sixteen-hour teaching schedule, in face of the agreed upon eighteen, could almost be seen as an act of defiance. When the Council decided that "the College should not be dropped" Maynard felt the biggest battle had been won. By October 1888 Westfield had taken over two adjacent houses, and the Council planned to purchase a large estate as its future home. Maynard's strong ties to Old Students from the G.P.M. Ring would help to garner invaluable support for the "new" Westfield, both financial and promotional.[44]

Her successes at Westfield aside, Maynard was quick to remind the reader about her ongoing "silent torments." She had convinced the Council to hire the talented Anne Richardson as resident Classical lecturer after her graduation in May 1887. At times, Richardson was an emotional "oasis for [Maynard's] barren desert"; or as Barthes might explain, an "eruption" to Maynard's emotional restraint:

> I was in bed when I heard a knock on the door. Nannie came in and lay down beside me. To feel her close was as if all the frost melted into summer. I lay in the darkness fully content, my starving ended. It was with utter relief that I fell asleep, and the next day had a new strength with which to face life.[45]

These fleeting visits, which were perhaps both pleasurable and perfunctory for Richardson, left Maynard craving more. Richardson not only disappointed on that score, but even worse, had become close to Gray. A tormented Maynard likened her situation to Dante's Purgatorio: "It [Purgatorio] was my favourite with the unwillingness of victims to escape from their pain." Her diary of the time affirmed her penance: "I hate this bondage"; and again, "I slip the collar on *quite* willingly." Dante's medieval works, of course, indicated romantic heterosexual love and the unavailability of the beloved. Maynard's "queer" Purgatorio meanwhile exacerbated her same-sex frustrations. She felt "hurt and irritated at least a dozen times" a day and had "to restrain [her]self from tearing up all the papers that surrounded [her] on her desk" at night.[46]

"God's Gift(s) for an Aching Heart"

It is perhaps understandable that Maynard's "loss and emptiness" led her to adopt a child at the end of 1888 for what lasted a brief six years.

The idea of adoption had become popular in the 1860s, following the Church of England's impetus to aid unwed mothers. The Women's Social Services, as an offshoot of S.A. rescue work, was the most effective rescue organization in Britain. The W.S.S. provided prenatal care for fallen women; made substantive efforts to situate them after they gave birth; and sought adoptive Christian parents for their illegitimate children. However, fallen women understood that a biological parent could not legally sever her ties from a child.[47]

Maynard knew of the W.S.S. through ex-Girtonian Ellen Pash, who worked for the S.A. in Paris: "I had considered motherhood for a while," she wrote: "Father's death [from a heart attack in 1888] led to even more serious thoughts about it." Her sisters were against her "taking such a step" and she "promised not to." It was Pash, Maynard claimed, who offered her an illegitimate six-year-old named Stephanë Rosabianca (Effie) born to a young middle-class Italian named Rosabianca Fazulo. When she first saw Effie, Maynard felt conflicted. She was repulsed by Effie's "tan [skin colour], crossed black eyes and pale swollen lips, and yet was attracted to E's intelligence and independence." She decided: "Brains my daughter *must* have." I now see "it's an unusual face, yes, even handsome." [48]

Maynard hoped for a "trial period" as a mother, but Pash informed her that "another had offered a home for Effie." After much deliberation with family, Maynard signed the deed of adoption on 16 November – or at least became responsible for Effie. She characteristically "saw Effie as God's gift for [her] aching heart." Perhaps more importantly, Effie could "tolerate living with strangers."[49] Maynard expected Effie to fit in with *her* life as Mistress, not vice versa, and she would only see Effie during vacation periods.

Six note books tell the story of Effie, together with entries in Maynard's diary and autobiography. The diary initially effused over Effie and her development: "When E hugs me and rubs her soft cheek against mine, I feel satisfaction in my heart"; and again, "E is transformed through bathing and a new wardrobe. I bought her glasses to help her squint." They "read Scripture together and there were lessons, walks, music and playing." Effie was sent to St. Leonards and when home, was "'shown' at Westfield." Maynard fully believed that her love for Effie was very strong. Yet, sadly, one is reminded of Maynard's "school ornament" situation at St. Leonards under Lumsden, for Effie's story quickly becomes one of tragedy. Effie was to Maynard an interesting project; a showpiece to be admired, controlled, and discarded when no longer of interest.[50]

Maynard's interest in Effie did not seem to last more than eighteen months. Effie was expelled from St. Leonards after one term and subsequently from middle-class boarding schools in Eastbourne and Highgate for "bad behaviour" and lies. Effie apparently only "behaved well" when she wanted a material reward. A disenchanted Maynard began to foist Effie on family members until "they refused E" on grounds of "lies, vulgarity and rudeness." Dora claimed Effie "corrupted her innocent children with her dirty mind." It was later that Maynard discovered Effie had "run" at one of her earlier working-class lodgings. Effie's freedom to run messages had introduced her to the vices of prostitution and petty theft that Maynard so disapproved of and could not understand.[51]

It is important to note that Effie's attention-seeking was also considered immoral, vulgar, and rude by Maynard, her family, and her social circle. The child was made to feel inferior and unwanted. When Maynard felt obliged to see Effie – because family members refused – they were never alone. Effie often played third to a favourite student, who was described as "beautiful, gentle and calm [pious]," While Effie was characterized as an "ugly little gnome" who was "a disgrace." In response, Effie threw temper tantrums. As biographer Catherine Firth suggests, Maynard did not realize that she herself drew out the worst in Effie. Nor could she teach Effie her own life principle. Effie was "not to be humbled" by faith because she sought worldly "approbation."[52]

It seems clear that the clashes between Maynard and Effie stemmed from Effie's temperament and Maynard's biased perspectives. Maynard was staunchly nationalist and classist, despite her claim that "All were equal in His eyes." She could not conceptualize Effie as her daughter because Effie was "inferior" physiologically, socially, and spiritually. As she later admitted, "It was her [Effie's] certain coarseness and breed that I always shrank from." This was also inferred from Maynard's instruction for Effie to address her as Godmother, Auntie, or Miss Maynard. In fact, by late 1890, Maynard wished she could relinquish all responsibility to Effie. Maynard's attitude, however, seemed evident in her decision to place Effie in lower-middle-class lodgings and attend a working-class Board School.[53]

Maynard's disappointment with and disinterest in Effie did not happen in isolation. Although her autobiography was silent on the matter, her diary implied a far greater joy in her life; namely, her reconciliation with Gray. Their rekindled relationship likely resulted from the growing rift between Richardson and Gray. Richardson had gained notoriety across England as a female public speaker on temperance and Irish politics. She was often absent from Westfield, and when there, was apparently discontent: "I hope N leaves," Maynard wrote in her diary: "I want R to move back into residence." Richardson, however, chose to remain at Westfield for over twenty more years although she remained restless.[54]

Richardson notwithstanding, Gray moved back into residence in January 1890, one may surmise, to renew her relationship with Maynard. We know through the green book of 1885 that they kissed at length on the lips in the privacy of Maynard's room. However, we only have access to Maynard's later experiences with Gray through her diary and autobiography. The diary of 1890 and 1891, while scant in detail, implied Maynard's pleasure in their renewed intimacy. She spoke of "delightful" nights or "*good* nights with *R*," and of Gray's tender ministering when she felt unwell. She appeared to allow herself to fall back under Gray's spell.[55] Their erotic encounters over these years are mentioned in her autobiography in the form of a single transcription of a green book entry, written on 14 April 1891:

> R was not well, and I went to see that she was rightly attended to. As I left she said with gentle hesitation, "You never bite my fingers now, as you used to do." "Oh no, never," I replied lightly. "You never snarl and growl like a jaguar when you can't express yourself. I never heard anyone growl as well as you." "No," I said, "it's useless. I've been cured of that." The sweet voice went on, "You never rock me in your arms and call me your baby." "No," I said in the same even tone, "I've been cured of that" ... I will not go into the desolation I felt when alone again. I was like a pot-bound root all curled in on itself.[56]

It seems that much like her relationships with Mantle, Lumsden, and Brooke, Maynard's explorations of passion with Gray were expressed through various forms of erotic role-playing. Yet if we compare the above entry with those about Mantle, Lumsden, and Brooke, it is admittedly a little more sexually explicit. Was it a code for sex? Would other entries about Gray seem more "deviant"? Does this explain the missing green books? The answer remains unclear. Nonetheless, Maynard's recordings about her adolescent crushes and college bonds suggest her same-sex sexual awareness from the late 1860s on. Indeed, we might argue that her relationships with Mantle, Lumsden, and Brooke forged Maynard's identity as a woman who could excite women, and who held atypical social power over them. We can conclude that intimacy between college women permitted a range of pleasurable feelings which may, at times, have subverted ideas about female bonds, but were not viewed by college women as homosexual acts.[57] What also seems clear, and should not been downplayed, was Maynard's wish presumably in 1891, and certainly in 1927, that her green book entry regarding Gray be viewed as a part of her penance for worldliness over her "years of gloom." When turning to the context in which we find this quote, we could surmise that Maynard's rejection of Gray's overtures resulted from Maynard's anger over allowing her "weakness in love" to override her values. Gray's focus on ambition had left Maynard feeling vulnerable, hurt, and very bitter.

Westfield had recently moved to its permanent home, Kidderpore, a large former mansion with a newly-built wing located in a two-acre estate about a mile from the old college. This change occurred not a moment too soon, for the college was "over-filled" with an enrolment of thirty. However, Maynard was apparently not happy about this change, and feared that Kidderpore was a symbol for Westfield's move towards a larger, secularist body. This had been evident in January 1891, when the Council had sent some Westfield members to Kidderpore, with the full move to take place over Easter. The dishevelment had proved stressful, but a terse diary entry following the Council's decision, "and *that*, I suppose, will mean R's going [to Kidderpore]," indicated Maynard's deeper concern.[58] It seems that Gray seized this opportunity to further her career as a House Mistress. Although Maynard's diary is vague on the matter, her Ring letter of 1891 evoked her resentment:

> This term we are physically uncomfortable for the Council allowed us to be cut off. Nine students are with Miss Gray at Kidderpore and are unbearably proud of it. With their thick walls, double windows and wide fireplaces, they … look with scorn on us whose steps are slippery and whose fires smoke.[59]

Maynard's irritation was compounded by a hurt that ran deep. She sorely missed Gray's bodily presence, but Gray was absorbed by her new responsibility, and the lovesick Maynard felt deeply threatened by it. Kidderpore students were allowed to dance and hold parties, and Kidderpore's first play "was splendid," Maynard noted in her diary. Indeed, in this record, Maynard implied her acceptance of Westfield's move towards secularist thinking. In her autobiography, however, she chastised herself for being "so miserably blind." Her account was vague, but it seems that Gray was furious over Maynard's "interfering" with her administration of Kidderpore. She accused Maynard of deceit, and then asked the Council for an extended Easter vacation. As a result, Maynard not only navigated a disastrous move over to Kidderpore alone, but faced Fanny Metcalfe's brutal scorn: "You are a weak leader, and lack duty to your faith." Metcalfe's latter comment seemed a deliberate taunt since she had never approved of Maynard's "staunch evangelicalism."[60]

Maynard's humiliation over the move, over Metcalfe, and over Gray, seemed to exacerbate her sense that the new Westfield "was *not*, by the widest stretch, the family." Where was the "confiding college" she had devised to train genteel women to evangelize? The core of the issue, for Maynard, was about faith and power. Her vulnerability in her love for Gray, she believed, had weakened all of her values: "Whether in dancing, or the rouge on 'Juliet's' sweet face, I had conceded here and there till I seemed to have no voice in the matter at all. I had consulted the wishes of my Staff too much."[61] Gray, as would any individual close to another, likely sensed the root of Maynard's frustration and hoped to reconcile their differences. But an angry Maynard, vengeful over her diminishing power and faltering aims for Westfield, seemed to have retaliated by informing the piqued Gray that she was cured of their erotic plays.

Whether or not they resumed their relationship remains unclear. Maynard simply noted in her autobiography after this evocative entry: "I had failed 500 times, here I try again, but then followed much misery." The diary meanwhile suggested that Gray alternated between being teasingly close to Maynard and then to Richardson. For example, she was close to Richardson from 1888–9; Maynard from 1889–91; and she grew close to Richardson again in 1892. Although Maynard was perhaps tied to her own seduction-resistance ritual, she abhorred Gray's shifts between intimacy and distance: "I felt like a prisoner in an empty cell. I was shut out from the joy of domestic life around me."[62] Heartbreak had led to anger, once again, at God's silence.

Paralleling her heartache for Gray, and her anger in general, was Maynard's increased upset over Effie. One wonders again about the connection. Did Gray affect Maynard's attitude towards Effie? Was Effie herself still causing problems? Or had Maynard's *use* for Effie run its course? It remains unclear. A green book entry in 1903 suggested

6.3 Kidderpore, a white neo-Classical stucco mansion, became the "second" Westfield in 1891. Courtesy of Queen Mary University of London Archives/ Westfield College/WFD.

Maynard's exploitation of Effie: "It was a drastic measure to take her... but, perhaps it was my only safeguard against despair." The diary presented another perspective entirely. Effie's behaviour had worsened, as far as Maynard was concerned. Yet her punishment of Effie – rooted in classism and racism – bordered on cruelty. Over one Easter, Effie had worked as a servant "to learn humility for her rude behaviour" and "aggrandisement of self." Another attempt to place Effie in the care of domestics for similar reasons failed: "I could *not* humble her, yet I sometimes humiliated her, then she became very cross - Oh, it is hard to know what to do!" Maynard wished to teach Effie to seek "True Spiritual life," but failed to see that her treatment of Effie was not the way to achieve these goals.[63]

Maynard's disfavour of Effie left Maynard unable to analyse her conduct as a mother. Her behaviour did not go unnoticed. When W.S.S.

6.4 Westfield College, 1894, showing the group of forty-nine students now enrolled. Maynard, who particularly disliked "the new" Westfield's "secularist" Ionic columns, is seated in the middle of the first row wearing her white lace cap. Frances Gray is seated to the right and Josephine Willoughby is to the left. Richardson is standing behind Maynard and Gray in her B.A. gown and hat. Courtesy of Queen Mary University of London Archives/Westfield College/WFD.

Officer Ellen Pash accused her of lacking in "mother love," Maynard reacted by sending Effie back to a middle-class school. This move led to disaster when Effie, aged twelve, was expelled for "teaching girls filthy tricks" [masturbation]. The tyranny of this "sin" fuelled Maynard's disgust since Victorians believed that "stooping to this vice" stunted both physiological and spiritual progress. Maynard sought legal advice on the proviso to discontinue her custody of Effie. She sent Effie back to an S.A. orphanage in June 1894.[64]

Maynard continued to support Effie financially, but she rarely saw her again. Her "attempt to spend a day" with Effie twice between 1894 and 1896 failed. Nor did she intervene with the S.A.'s decision to send Effie to work as a domestic. This not only introduced Effie to prostitution and petty theft, but also led her to become a "fallen woman" at age thirteen. Society would not have viewed Effie's sexual activities as consensual, yet Maynard only recalled "feeling genuine contempt for so feeble a character." Her diary substantiated her claim: "E is defiled! Worse than murdered! Since the 'outcasts' are their [S.A.] prize, they will keep her." The S.A. served two purposes. It could take Effie off her hands and at the same time ease Maynard's conscience. At age fifteen a perhaps desperate, Effie hoped to become an S.A. Officer, but was not accepted because of her bad behaviour and her onset of consumption. As far as Maynard was concerned, "Effie was a disappointment to the end" of her life in 1915. Effie must surely have felt just as disappointed in her "God-mother."[65]

Effie's situation notwithstanding, nothing could have prepared Maynard for the "chief event" of 1894. Gray accepted an offer to become Mistress of a new junior school for girls (later known as St. Katherines) at St. Andrews in Scotland: "This all sounds simple enough," Maynard wrote in her autobiography. "I wrote a heartfelt testimonial and spoke brightly of all that could be done." It was anything but "simple." A diary entry in February, "Ralph's telegram arrived, appointed," apparently concealed the rage within Maynard. According to another account in her autobiography, she plunged headlong into depression again, which left her exhausted and at times suicidal.[66]

Biographer Catherine Firth proposed that if Maynard had been aware of the study of psychology – at "the stage which it had reached by the end of the nineteenth century" – she may have better understood her "suffering" and loneliness as an educational pioneer.[67] Certainly, there is no evidence in Maynard's diary to suggest her knowledge of late-nineteenth-century sexology. As historians now argue, few British knew of Havelock Ellis's *Psychology of Sex*, first published in 1897. Even a decade later, Ellis's classification of "normal" versus "perverse" sexual predilections were mostly met with ambivalence.[68] Maynard, it seems, could not have easily known of the new sexological discourses during her tenure at Westfield.

Turning to the time of her crisis in February 1894, it's evident that Maynard sought ways to achieve "psychological" strength through forms of ritualistic deification. She recognized that her penchant for Dante's "'Purgatorio' was a deliberate refusal to escape her pain." She also fully believed that "atoning for suffering helped" what she called her "mental salvation." Present-day psychologists theorize that physical "pain" can relieve emotional pain, and in both diary and autobiography, Maynard declared that "bicycling extremely hard led [her] to a brighter, happier space." On "good days," she could appreciate all the gains she had made as Mistress.[69]

Maynard also fought pain by seeking closure. In August 1894, she visited St. Andrews ostensibly to help Gray unpack, although nothing is written about the trip. Maynard's reference to Gray's "tense visit" to Westfield the following April likely inspired Maynard's "cycling tour" that ended at St. Andrews in July 1895. A brief diary notation, "Ralf seems perfectly happy with her new life," inferred that Gray's demeanour was not one of regret over her decision. But Maynard held onto deep regret. Even in 1927, she could "still hardly look that way." It would be "a long time, if ever, before [she] dared to sort [her] feelings over." Meanwhile, Frances Dove's poignant lament at St. Andrews, "I put all my eggs into one basket [Lumsden] and they broke," bespoke the longing and loneliness particular to many late-Victorian educational pioneers.[70] The visit to St. Andrews possibly facilitated Maynard's own process of emotional disengagement. Though perhaps Maynard's greatest love, Frances Gray, would be shelved alongside Campbell and Lumsden as a dusty, unresolved love of the past.

Chapter Seven

"Glorious New Spring" 1896–1913

"Is this enough?" murmurs the heart afraid, as bending left or right she leans her weight upon the sweetest of earths glories, *Love*![1]

Love's "force unmeasured" carried Maynard from the heights of bliss to the depths of sorrow as she struggled to reconcile passion, ambition, and faith with Campbell, Lumsden, Brooke, and Gray. Love was to soar again in 1897 to salve her desolate heart. Marion Wakefield "penetrated [her] winter" and inspired in Maynard "a dream whispered about for years;" the founding of a Divinity program at Westfield. These were among the happiest years of Maynard's life since her new love – at least initially – shared her aims and passionate nature. Yet the price proved high. This time, Maynard faced the "hollow pretences of human love and divine love" as a new century and era of thinking dawned.[2]

This chapter of Maynard's professional life was her last appeal for "the vital connection between faith, higher learning, and Blessed love." Her hopes lay in a beautiful young Westfield student half her age who promised her a "glorious new spring of hope and love." Maynard believed herself to be reborn as "the new Evangelical" who would combine higher learning with Biblicism to lead society towards Truth. As a "Divine female [she] would send out disciples [Westfield graduates] to convert the world" through the Doctrine of Atonement. God, in turn, would reward her with Marion Wakefield as her lifelong partner and successor of Westfield.[3]

It would be easy to dismiss Maynard's aims as outmoded, given her cultural context. In a turn-of-century age that combined incarnational thinking with human agency and scientific and technological development, Maynard's views seem self-serving and limited. Yet as historians like John Maynard, Jacqueline deVries, Callum Brown, and Jane Rendell note, the religious climate was as complex as the emergent secularism. Women who combined Victorian modes of piety with secularist thinking were, in fact, successful advocates for social change and for women's rights.[4] This chapter argues that Maynard's view of faith as a necessary component to higher education was progressive. Faith had also inspired her forging of women's capabilities as missionaries both at home and overseas.

Faith had a large impact on Maynard's relationship with Wakefield. In this instance, Maynard advocated extreme forms of physical penance for their carnal encounters. Their bond also raises interesting questions about what historians call mother-daughter love. Maynard had engaged in lover-husband as well as mother role-playing with Amy Mantle at Girton, and her self-reference as lover-husband-mother to Wakefield was as erotic: "The husband and wife are constant, and the child added to the mother's heart [is] intoxicating." Implied here was Maynard's sense of finding in Wakefield "complete love." It was a love that some feminists find troubling, given the history of sexual abuse against women and, in particular, an erotic configuration modelled on "incest." Yet Victorians themselves viewed incest as a vice. When Maynard gave Wakefield a ring she asked that Wakefield view their betrothal as "the married kind," rather than that of mother and daughter.[5] How then do we conceptualize their erotic partnership?

Vicinus and others posit that Victorians' view of mother-love as "the supreme bond" became both the strength and weakness of these sorts of intimate friendships. For example, a woman's "motherly responsibility" for her "daughter," who felt unworthy of such great love, created friction and oscillating shifts in power between close friends.[6] These forms of tension seemed apparent in Maynard's entries about Wakefield's indolence and low self-esteem, which left Maynard frustrated and disappointed over "her child's" failures. Yet Maynard's physical desire for Wakefield, the woman, meant that Maynard could never really view Wakefield as her daughter. Barthes' and others' view of pleasurable feelings as wide-ranging, suggests the complexity of erotic exchanges that can exist between two individuals, no matter what gender or age. In this instance, forms of domination and submission, coupled with desire and its resistance, shaped Maynard's bond with Wakefield.[7]

Queer theorists would likely consider Maynard's complex relationship with Wakefield as a form of shared femininity as well as an example of the ambiguity of the homo/hetero binary. Julian Carter proposes that queering mother-daughter love "makes room for the possibility that a familial paradigm and metaphor for same sex-love might coexist with the explicit knowledge of and gratification of sexual passion."[8] As this chapter argues, Maynard's adoption of religious-Greek mythological language not only implied her sexual control over Wakefield, but that of a woman who held atypical social power as an older educational leader. Meanwhile, Maynard's interweaving of floral imagery with religious language evinced her knowledgeable pleasure of and desire for the female body as a late-Victorian.

Even as we enter this final stage of Maynard's experiences as Mistress of Westfield (1896–1913), she tells us with confidence that "The sky was clear," referring to both her personal and professional life. She explained that the vacancies in Classics and science left by Frances Gray and Josephine Willoughby had been filled by well qualified second-generation university women. Among them were the talented Caroline Skeel (Classics) and the dedicated Lillian Whitby (Mathematics), who took on administrative duties during Richardson's leaves. The year 1896 was another "successful Capping year" with nine victories, including Westfield's first M.A., the talented Priscilla Wood.[9] It is little wonder that Maynard's Ring letter of 1896 evinced the new-found pride and confidence that she felt:

> Now we are at work again and college looks much the same, still the crowd round the letter table in the morning sit, still the lion roaring as we rise from the table, still the packing into the small lecture halls. Indeed, they still wear the same flannel blouses, only their faces are different.[10]

Less stress in the workplace had helped Maynard to recover from her "spells" of depression. In 1894, she had regarded cycling as her "mental salvation" for her grief over Gray. Writing in 1928, she firmly connected mental salvation to faith: "It's just like when one pours a bath. Sin is taken away by the defiled water." Her use of the bathing metaphor also attests to Maynard's association of cleanliness to sexual purity. By this time, of course, physicians were examining the causes of emotional states and unresolved longing. However, since Victorians had focused on the cure, the devout Maynard assured the reader that her "defiled" grief was washed away by faith, not science. She also emphasized that her mindset in 1896 was one of self-purpose. She was more relaxed around students who, in turn, felt more confident about consulting her on various college matters. This improved "Westfield's public spirit" by creating more congeniality, trust, and understanding.[11]

In terms of the larger public spirit, Maynard's diary reveals how Victorian educational pioneers supported each other through powerful organizations. Flourishing bodies, such as the Association of Headmistresses, drew hundreds of representatives from colleges, high schools, public schools, and board schools to its yearly conferences. Lively debates that centred on such issues as training and working conditions reflected the ongoing concerns of the era. Maynard found a "lecture on salaries most useful" because it gave her leverage to gain for her staff better pay and fewer teaching hours.[12]

The move to widen access to female education was, of course, common to educational pioneers. Maynard was a board member of the Church Schools Company that was founded in 1895 with a religious emphasis in mind. Her diary recounted how girls' high schools and women's colleges were flourishing in northern towns like Streatham, Wigan, Brighton, and Bournemouth. Maynard's choice of qualified and experienced Christian teachers for Westfield revealed the number of women who had by then attained degrees and taught for a number of years.[13]

Maynard also served on the committees of the Women's Grosvenor Institute and Penny Bank. She pronounced training for such working-class occupations as cooking as "good enough work." This elitist observation reflected her mocking of "shoppy" peers at Girton, and her ongoing disdain of her adopted daughter Effie. Her view of an ex-Girtonian's running of a Settlement Home was evidenced in her Ring letter of 1898: "It's not working because the lowest class have *no* tastes to which we can appeal to raise *them*!" Here Maynard distinguished between "respectable" workers and "unrespectable" paupers, although she viewed workers, in general, as "wretched people." Meanwhile, "the very impressive" Wycombe Abbey that opened under Frances Dove in 1896 offered upper-middle-class girls an educational focus similar to that for boys, just as St. Leonards had done.[14]

Sunday Function best demonstrated Maynard's religiously-based aims. As Catherine Firth recollected of this pivotal experience, "Every Sunday we assembled in the Mistress's room. The seniors sat in armchairs in a semi-circle facing her while the rest sat mostly on the floor of the dimly lit room." The setting and the aims evoked Maynard's

7.1 Constance Maynard, 1897, aged forty-eight, seated at her desk in the Mistress's room. Courtesy of Queen Mary University of London Archives/Westfield College/WFD.

lifelong goals: self-expression, evidence, and Truth. Meanwhile, the intimacy of the fire-lit room and "hooded candle at her side" symbolized the "strong bond of affection" that she sought in her public and private life.[15]

By the late 1890s, Function had evolved into an important arena for Maynard to broach missionary and allied topics. One is reminded of Maynard's self-revelation at Girton, "I fully believed that God had chosen me...to hold the most difficult post in the world." Similar to "the Church that [was] Girton," Function was a forum in which ideas about the future Student Christian Movement (S.C.M.) were spawned with the aim to evangelize the student world at large. Formally constituted in 1905, the S.C.M. represented the convergence of the Student Voluntary Missionary Union (S.V.M.U.), and the British Colleges Christian Union (B.C.C.U.). The B.C.C.U. had been established at Westfield in 1896, and regularly hosted the combined annual meeting of all London branches for female students. Meanwhile, the S.V.M.U. sent guest speakers to Westfield on a regular basis.[16]

The S.V.M.U. and B.C.C.U. echoed the goals of the Bible League that had been instituted in 1892; that is, the promotion of "the Reverent Study of the Holy Scriptures." These Christian-based organizations sought to resist the onset of Bible criticism that had challenged ideas about Infallibility and Sole Sufficiency as the Word of God. Indeed, the more liberal Evangelicals considered "Truth" as evolving through the inspirational experience of the people of God over time. The new approaches to Truth did, of course, reflect the Liberalist, scientific age with its capitalist thinking and emergent feminism. As a result, Holiness or the holiness movement had led many Evangelicals towards higher criticism as a means of coping with modernism. For Maynard, however, Function was a means of feminine independence, as well as a guard against broad "interpretative" analyses and possible "errors" in the Word of God. Certainly, she was drawn to such texts as *Lux Mundi* that "changed [society's] perceptions towards such areas of difficulties [as Infallibility]." Nonetheless, it was only through one's resistance to worldliness, she believed, that the "nature beyond us would abide in God" and transcend the flesh, world, and Satan that existed apart from God.[17]

"What a Glorious Thing Love Was"

If we turn from Maynard's diary, which spoke largely of her public life, what evidence do we have of her emotional-religious life at this time?

From whom did she seek day to day love and support? Since her green books are missing, we must consult her autobiography. According to this record, it was Anne Richardson, Maynard's long-term colleague and now senior lecturer at Westfield. In fact, her reliance upon Richardson left Maynard very frustrated. Of an incident in 1896, she wrote, "I was so happy when N persuaded me against emphasizing conversion over work in the testimony on Westfield's aims. Yet I felt quite at despair over succumbing to her." This conflict, according to Firth and Vicinus, was fuelled by Maynard's self-exaggerated grievances,[18] which was quite likely the case. Nonetheless, Maynard's relationship with Richardson at this time had some truly disturbing elements. Knowing full well Maynard's struggle with self-esteem, Richardson deliberately sought to undermine her:

> I had felt elated after hearing that Holloway lacked Westfield's cultivating spirit. When I told N she knocked me flat. She says "things are said about me behind my back of which I have not the least idea." My hands hung by my side at my sense of inefficiency. I left the room so I could release my tears.[19]

Maynard's recollection of her ensuing discussion with Richardson added more salt to the wound: "She said *now, suddenly,* she wanted to become a vigorous Protestant!" The pain, for Maynard, lay in Richardson's motivation as a Quaker. The Trust Deed had made the intention of founder Dudin Brown clear: "Westfield [and Mistress] must be linked with the most conspicuously Protestant side of the Church of England." Richardson remained a Quaker, which precluded her from the Mistress-ship, but Maynard felt bitter: "Why did N have this effect on me?" she asked the reader. "It was a strange and painful arrangement, was it not?"[20]

Reading between the lines, Richardson's avoidance of emotional entanglement with Maynard seems to have caused the latter the most hurt. While a lonely Maynard romanticized about Richardson, Richardson firmly distanced herself by way of new female friendships. But it was through Richardson that Maynard met someone who did respond to her passionate overtures. She metamorphosed "from feeling ugly, desolate, unloved, and unsuccessful, [into] a glorious new spring of hope and love."[21]

Maynard first met her new love Marion Wakefield in April 1897, when she planned an Easter retreat to Berka in Holland with some favourite students. When the leader of recreational and spiritual activities could not attend, Richardson proposed her young cousin, Marion for the position. She described Marion "as a pleasant, hearty, country girl, who was a dynamic spiritual influence in her local cottage meetings in Portadown in Ireland." Maynard could not write about Wakefield in her green book for a year, according to her autobiography: "When I did," she told the reader, "I poured out my heart in over twenty pages."[22] Maynard transcribed without comment only two incidents in her autobiography. The first entry, taken from the green book of 1898, suggested the intensity of Maynard's passion for Wakefield:

> Life made an appeal to me like a language of unanalysed happiness. I feared that I might love Marion, and yet what a glorious thing love was! The colours grew more brilliant as I thought of it. Meanwhile Christ stood beside me, offering me white, pure white. I must choose white, and I will, I dread love … M [Wakefield] had come to us so recklessly happy, and now there were tears on her cheeks. I had asked this child out for a holiday, and here I am tearing her soul to pieces. Am I a Minotaur that I must eat a maiden's heart?[23]

Maynard's intermingling of religious-Greek mythological language to describe her passion for Wakefield inferred a particularly aggressive form of same-sex desire. As we have seen, Maynard's transitions in sexual self-consciousness(s) and identit(ies) as a woman of power since the early 1870s were products of Evangelicalism in dynamic interaction with various secularist discourses. She not only challenged cultural norms as a female educational pioneer. Her role had perhaps afforded her too much control over students emotional lives, since no set rules of professional conduct yet existed in women's colleges. As noted in chapter 6, late-Victorian women were not ignorant of same-sex desire in classical texts. Christina Rossetti, Eliza Keary, and Jane Ellen Harrison were among those who applied classic and religious voices to challenge gender norms and proclaim their same-sex desire. However, Maynard's struggle to choose "pure white" over love, and the "tears" on "the child's … cheeks," implied her toying with the younger Wakefield's sexual naivety. Maynard's active rather than feminine-passive persona of the Minotaur conveyed her unbridled power. While Helen of Troy (Frances Gray) had rebuffed Maynard's male-like bestiality, the Minotaur overpowered this maiden (Wakefield). As a raging half man/half beast, he/she devoured her bodily and spiritual sustenance. Maynard had left Wakefield helpless, but quite possibly craving for more.[24]

According to Maynard's autobiography, she began her physical friendship with Wakefield in 1898 at age forty-eight. While Maynard felt uncomfortable about dallying with a twenty-three year old, she found Wakefield irresistible, possessed as she was with a "tall slender frame, creamy skin, cloudless blue eyes, splendid blonde hair, full red lips and white teeth." Wakefield, in turn, embraced her passionate love for Maynard. She had enrolled as a student and, according to Maynard, "was there to reach out to." Wakefield's overtures were endless: '"Oh! *Mistress*! my heart's choicest treasure, I *love* you, I *love* you!' What about me? I should hide my face in shame. I had fallen into worldly recklessness." Maynard's account of their trip to the Pyrenees further confessed to their erotic world: "Sometimes M bathed, a snow white Naiad in her native land, while I kept watch above ... Then we left for Porte de Venasque. Outside it was snowing and inside we had fire logs."[25]

Although Maynard's autobiography is vague on the matter, the Pyrenees trip fuelled Wakefield's passion. With a "heart on fire," she struggled under Maynard's high expectations: "She [M] worked too hard for Matriculation, and then she became sick. She stole in each night to seek shelter in my arms." Maynard not only referred to Wakefield's academic anxiety here: their physical encounters had become "far, *far* too much." According to Maynard, they must pray, practice celibacy, and fast for eternal salvation.

Whether Wakefield initially embraced resisting the flesh for God is unclear (even though she was eager to follow Maynard's faith for salvation). Maynard noted Florence Wakefield's sisterly concern, "You [Maynard] don't *know* how M suffers." She then exclaimed, "Yet M came to *me* again and *again* as her one comfort! Why?" The reader was to infer that Wakefield sought comfort, even pleasure, in enforced celibacy and fasting. In any event, Wakefield soon tired of Maynard's faith-erotic restrictions: "I hate suffering. I *play* at self-denial for *your* [Maynard] sake. I do not *want* to believe in the death of the self. It's *impossible*!'"[26]

Maynard recorded without comment the second entry from her green book to perhaps further disclose the nature of her relationship with Wakefield. This passage, written in June 1899, implied what Barthes might describe as intense acts around restraint and eruption:

> Oh! But love - L'amour tout simple - is a dreadful thing, a knife without a handle cuts the owner more than it does the opposed ... We say the Cloister is a mistake, but would millions make the same mistake century after century? I am supposed to take the steady side since it is *I* who has

lighted M's fire. Oh! Let us try for Passion pure in snowy bloom through all the years of blood![27]

Maynard's account of same-sex passion seemed sexually implicit in its interweaving of floral imagery, faith, and "virginal" and "violent passion." As Roden, Vanita, Vicinus, and others argue, some late-Victorian women used natural images that drew attention to their desire for the female body, such as lush gardens, tidal oceans, or rounded jewels. The word "bloom" could invoke female genitalia: "I felt I had coloured the white rose red," Maynard recalled. Her comparison of the rose's "worldly scent" with the honeysuckle's "out of world scent" was as telling, for the honeysuckle was Westfield's emblem. Meanwhile, Maynard's mention of the Cloister and "blood" of passion suggested her disavowal of same-sex desire in what Roden would term "a queer" heterosexual love of Christ. Ultimately, she was like "a moth to Wakefield's flame." In the end, Wakefield fled their heated passion and its troubling binary. She followed her family to Europe later that summer, claiming that she needed two months of rest from the pressures at Westfield.[28]

Had Maynard known that her separation from Wakefield in 1899 would span eighteen months, she probably would have been distraught: "I loved her strongly all the time!" she exclaimed in her autobiography. "In truth, I loved her for about 14 years."[29] The test of love had proved very costly in other ways. While her autobiography was silent on the matter, both diary and Council Minutes revealed the growing hostility between Maynard and Westfield Council throughout 1898 and 1899. This serves to remind us of the trials particular to early Victorian female educational pioneers and those, like Maynard, who were also devout.

The Trust Deed prescribed no fixed term for office, and so Council members like Fanny Metcalfe had remained. Familiarity, in Maynard's view, had "bred contempt from those who felt 'knowledgeable' of college matters." Although she perhaps had a point, the Council's grievances with her had some merit. Some Council members pressed for Westfield's recognition "as a School of the University by applying to become one of its bodies" (as Holloway and Bedford Colleges were in the process of doing). In a fairly recent postscript in *Cultivation of the Intellect*, Maynard had clearly reasserted Westfield's "intellectual aim"; but "this *new* objective," she feared, "w[ould] compromise Westfield's cultivating spirit." Nonetheless, when a number of students failed their

7.2 Constance Maynard, aged forty-nine, 1898, with Westfield College group. Maynard seated second row in centre with Richardson on the right. Courtesy of Queen Mary University of London Archives/Westfield College/WFD.

B.A. in October 1897, the Council insisted that Westfield become a School of the University. To begin this process, they instituted an education sub-committee which determined that the Council would select teachers, and that students would have more preparation in the Classics.[30]

Were Council members justified in their concerns? Had Maynard's distraction over Wakefield caused her professional neglect? Or were the academic problems a result of poor quality students and a rise in educational standards? According to the Minutes and to Maynard's records, it was a combination of all. In April 1898 Maynard had to account for more failure, this time in The London Matriculation and the Intermediate. She was to learn that the Council was not convinced by her explanation of "student illness," and ensuing grievances between Mistress and Council likely resulted from Maynard's acts of insubordination. She had not kept her account book updated; she had been absent during term-time without the Council's consent; and she had appointed two non-resident lecturers without consulting the education committee, which had been established for that purpose.[31]

Nonetheless, the hostility between Maynard and Council is worth closer investigation, and is perhaps best represented by the long battle over electric lighting. The Council only agreed to the expenditure in 1895 after a student was badly burned by a gas lamp, and then start-up problems were ignored. It took Maynard until 1897 to rescind "switching off the electric current" at 10:30 p.m.; until 1898 to install higher wattage bulbs in students' rooms (they had fallen back on candle light); and until 1899 to get electric lighting in her own rooms. In 1900 she "felt obliged to contribute £40 towards a second light bulb in every room because students *still* complained about the lack of light."[32] One has to wonder if the Council would have moved faster on these changes had she been the male Principal of a men's college.

Despite these differences between Council and Mistress, both agreed to take action in lieu of the high rate of examination failures in the late 1890s. Unfortunately, Maynard failed to inform her staff that they "would have outside expertise" on their marking for The London Matriculation – perhaps she had resigned herself to the Council's ongoing sexism. In any event, it caused outrage from Skeel and Whitby, who were more vociferous about women's rights than Maynard's generation of pioneers: "We have gained the certificate for 'Recognized Teacher' under the new statutes. This signifies our ability to teach at the degree level. We do not mind consulting with experts, but *examination* of our work is not consistent with the dignity of our position." Fortunately, the conflict was resolved for everyone's benefit. The Council apologized to the staff; students benefited from extra Matriculation coaching; and Maynard or another staff member in her absence was given "power of suggestion on all educational matters."[33]

The dignity of position notwithstanding, Westfield's conservative, genteel etiquette continued under Maynard until she retired in 1913. She was described as a kindly (Victorian) Mistress who liked "social customs" and connected "to students through games of 'Snatch' [Scrabble]." The maternal-like tone was reflected in "Westfield's garden with its hedges of rhododendrons and rose gardens," and in Westfield's annual At Home, complete with its "fine dainties," china, rented furniture, and orchestra. It was at the 1897 At Home, with 500 guests in attendance, that Maynard was interviewed by author Alice Zimmern, who published her powerful *Renaissance of Girls' Education* the following year.[34]

At times, Maynard's genteel conservatism and faith held her back from the scientific spirit of the age. This was evident in her ongoing reluctance towards Westfield's becoming a School of the University. Certainly, she feared Westfield's "disappearance" as yet another secular body of the University. As Westfield's "motto" (the Sower) proclaimed, "The good seed [faith] is wasted if hearts only 'patter' on the hard soil [science]." Anne Richardson strongly disagreed with Maynard. Without its status as a School of the University, Westfield remained inferior to Holloway or Bedford. Nonetheless, other female activists followed Maynard's views. For example, Evangelical Frances Power Cobbe believed that "hardness of character [science] had greatly damaged religious faith [and morality]." Oddly enough, Maynard did not share Richardson's support of suffrage, although many Christian reformers claimed that "it tapped those deep reservoirs of spiritual devotion."[35] Perhaps Maynard thought it wise not to rock the boat of higher education on the sea of public acceptance.

The topics included in the formal college Debate reflected Maynard's class-based imperialism; that is, her father's view of paupers and indigenous peoples as slothful and degenerate, and in need of governing: "Debate on independence of the colonies," she noted in 1902. "Imperial Federation won by a *great* majority, of *course*!" Student Irene Biss's recollection of an experience in 1907 suggested that Maynard's sociopolitical views were not always shared: "I spoke about a Bill allowing 5 shillings weekly to poor people out of work. I'm *glad* to say that the votes were in favour!" Biss was likely unaware of Maynard's delight over the "motion lost" on a Debate on socialism five years earlier. Apparently, Maynard's view of workers' social rights (or lack thereof) had not changed either.[36]

Her genteel conservatism aside, Maynard's commitment towards higher learning for women and for women's independence deserves great praise. Alongside degree success, which continued until Maynard's retirement, the Debate, as biased as it appears to have been, had underlying strategic aims: "The dignity of [Maynard's] argument," Firth recalled, "was intimidating to the bravest student as she rose to put forward her own." Firth recognized Maynard's intent to teach women to overcome their socially-induced timidity. This spirit was echoed in sports. By the early 1900s there were games clubs of all kinds, except football, and the yearly tennis tournaments were taken very seriously. Westfield was the first women's college at least in London to purchase a boat for a rowing team, which practised on the lake in Regent's Park in London after 1911.[37]

"The New Evangelical"

As mentioned, Maynard's vision for Function was highly ambitious as a way to promote her global evangelizing through the Bible. The Student Voluntary Missionary Union and the British Colleges Christian Union helped Maynard's cause through Biblical reverence (rather than criticism). However, neither the S.V.M.U. nor B.C.C.U. was particularly committed to early-Victorian Evangelicalism. This is not surprising. By the late 1890s the Atonement was, of all doctrines, the most vulnerable to the attacks made by higher criticism. In an age of Liberal thinking, many rebelled against a "barbaric" doctrine that ascribed earthly suffering under a tyrannical God. Doubt in the Atonement grew following the discovery of the practice of sacrificial offerings among "savages." The so-called "unique Christian message" about sacrifice on earth now seemed obsolete. Nonetheless, Maynard "held the [Atonement] doctrine to [her] heart." In fact, she felt driven to "spread the doctrine worldwide, for any center of Truth [was] surely there."[38]

Interestingly enough, Maynard's renewed conviction of Truth seemed evident through her green book, which resumed in full force on 1 January 1901. The opening lines began thus: "We have social reform, missionary conquests, universal education, and the discoveries of science and medicine." The reader is then told,

But the green book pages don't dwell on this topic...They follow an individual life "amid the vast web." I wait only on God, and to sit in the desert and starve if must be... I need only two external temporal gifts this year. One is Health, and the other is Marion. *May* I have them? Health is indispensable if I am to go on with the college. I really *want* Marion, but will this destroy any aspect of our [Maynard's and God's] relationship?[39]

As ever, the green book contrasted both diary and autobiography in its oblique, faith-based lament about love and aim. We are told that after Wakefield had fled Westfield, in 1899, she was diagnosed with depression and declared "unfit for a degree." Since Wakefield could not be Maynard's successor as Evangelical Mistress, "plans must change," Maynard wrote. "I want her [Wakefield] as my Secretary." Wakefield was not as sure. She had kept Maynard at bay for eighteen months, despite Maynard's "hunting her down" in Switzerland during her six-month Leave from Westfield in 1900.[40]

Maynard's autobiographical account situated her uncertainty about Wakefield and Westfield within the context of her revived faith: "It was *real* love, yet a block to the *nobler* things I desired." During her six month leave Maynard had met Evangelical minister Reverend Fawkes in Egypt. Their discussions about the "evils of worldliness" had rekindled Maynard's belief in the power of the Doctrine of Atonement: "The lesson choice," she believed, "was in [her] hands":

The Evangelical church is not dead. We have few clergy and there is timidity everywhere, but we have many good women who do parish work, rescue work, missions and the Y.M.C.A. In my youth I felt I would be called to be a prophet, to do some real teaching and leading of others by the power of God. I hear about the work in America and the prospect is inspiring and splendid.[41]

Fawkes had told Maynard about a new, all-male American Bible College. Maynard's role seemed clear. She as prophet was to be "the New Evangelical" who would combine modern learning with the Bible to convert "the sinful world." Just as in 1875, when she was inspired by Moody and Sankey; and in 1881, when the S.A. had "revived [her] Christianity," she felt "a [spiritual] longing."[42]

Maynard was drawn to the work in America because it proclaimed "the Infallibility" of the Bible. As historian David Bebbington points out, most English Evangelicals refuted inerrancy of the Bible as it included the axiom that history was error-free. Inaccuracy of detail in the Bible was unavoidable, many thought, in face of so many ages of development. In contrast, American Evangelicals were stern in their repudiation of error in a book given by God, and acclaimed literal interpretation of the Word of God: "The Bible *is* one single God," Maynard declared. "No one should tamper with it. It has served us for centuries."[43] For Maynard, the Truth of the Bible lay in the Atonement:

> I look in vain among [British] "experts" [on the Bible] for a single saint, a real soul of prayer and of that careful walking with regard to the world, that sense of aloofness that is to me so lovely, that type of soul which was produced again and again by the stern, literal, uncritical views of our [Evangelical] fathers.

She concluded, "I stand here in the face of all this resistance. I am wonderfully alone. I cannot find a single woman doing the work I do."[44]

We should not underestimate the complexities of Maynard's religious belief and commitment to religious duty, despite her adherence to a patriarchal God and "Evangelical fathers" who advocated earthly suffering for salvation. Nor should we dismiss her spiritual longings as conservative or non-feminist. Late nineteenth- and early-twentieth-century religion has been simultaneously blamed for perpetuating the discourse of domesticity, and accredited for women's entrance into the public sphere. However, as historians Jacqueline deVries and Jane Rendell remind us, the religious climate was as complex as the nuances in women's fight for social rights which, when combined, was a powerful platform for action.[45] Maynard's perception of faith as both liberating and oppressive was unique in shaping her self-understanding as an elite educational pioneer. Her commitment to higher education had already gained for women the university degree. Her woman-centred spiritualism, as ascetic as it seemed, had enriched her private life and had established women as teachers and preachers of the Bible worldwide.

Maynard's imagined role as a female prophet suggested another powerful form of self-envisioning. She was inspired by the rise in premillennialism in America; that is, the belief that Christ would return in person once the preaching of the gospel had established reign in all lands. She was a "Divine female," called upon by God to help convert and prepare the world. God, in turn, would reward her with love (Marion Wakefield). As she also admitted, "It is thoughts of the

7.3 Constance Maynard, aged sixty, 1909, wearing her black preaching dress with Bible in hand. Courtesy of Queen Mary University of London Archives/ Westfield College/WFD.

responses of a crowded, hearty Evangelical congregation that give me the thrill." One recalls Susan Warner's thoughts in *Wide, Wide World*: "those darkly, erotic male evangelicals who [could] charm congregations" to their will. Since Warner's fictional women "lusted to preach like them [male evangelicals]," perhaps Maynard too wished to emulate such power.[46]

In 1900, Maynard was determined to forge her scheme in a Divinity program at Westfield: "For this, God would give her M, surely?" It is notable that Maynard's longing for a Divinity program at Westfield was not shared by the Council. In a brief entry about "a stormy meeting" with the Council in May 1901, Maynard exclaimed, "Theology exists!" However, according to the Minutes of Council, Council members were more concerned by the "academic deficiencies" that prevented Westfield from becoming a School of the University: its "scanty little library"; a laboratory "equipped only for courses in Intermediate science"; and the problems arising from subjects not taught "by 'Recognized Teachers' under the new Statutes."[47] In fact, it seems that the Council's determination to upgrade Westfield versus Maynard's focus on a Divinity curriculum signified the beginnings of a serious divergence of interest between Council and Mistress.

Any thought of dissonance between herself and the Council was far from Maynard's mind in October 1901. She exclaimed, "I have Westfield, I have Divinity, and best of all, I have love!" After months of broken promises,

> Marion suddenly walked into Westfield on 12 October and, we went into my darkened room so that we could hold each other, and then she said, "I am to live with my mother and come here as your secretary." I am overjoyed. My little bed, which has seen extremes of agony, now sees hours of content. It's like going from midnight to a new dawn. Can anything be better?[48]

Maynard recalled this time in her autobiography, "I had health, love, the ever-expanding work and presage of success; it was *wonderful*!" Her "kindly staff" oversaw Westfield, leaving her to "arrange [her] life and not stumble along." She delivered seven Divinity classes each week that aimed to equip her students with the weapons to fight "the 'evil' that was secularism." Divinity, she explained, centred on the problem of worldliness and the attack on Christology. While Maynard warned her "delicate clergyman's daughters [about] the unfriendly relations of science [evolution theory] and religion," her staff thrust Westfield towards secularism. The gifted Eleanor McDougall and Marion Delf, hired in 1902 and 1905 respectively, forged both the Classics and Sciences at Westfield.[49]

"Even if I Die in the Account"

In her green book retrospective of 1901, Maynard exclaimed, "her name [Marion] is not written across the year as it was two years ago. This year, she was given not only to my heart but to my arms! Very few people know what love really is, but I do." Yet while enthusing about a "life filled with the best of earthly treasures," it was "not the perfect subjection to God" that she hoped for: "They say that bringing *every* thought to the obedience of Christ is an impossible aim. To all this my heart says, 'No! It is not - even if I die in the account!'" Here we see the echoes of Maynard's upbringing on Irving's homily: "Fallen creatures should repent by a sort of moral self-torture." Maynard knew that since the 1850s most Christians viewed "Christ as redeemer of humankind," but the true Christian should "Forsake *all* and follow God."[50]

Maynard's despair over the "inefficiency of [her] soul" seemed to follow her torment over her increasingly passionate encounters with Wakefield. According to an entry on 3 January 1902, Maynard convinced herself that she and Wakefield,

> needed spiritual more than physical health. I told her [Wakefield], "We must go back to the ultimate basis of our friendship. By this I mean that love is to be second, not first, to our search for the Saviour. We must pray for resistance and we must fast for spiritual guidance."[51]

One presumes "physical health" meant the well-being gained from their passionate encounters, although it remains unclear. In any event, human love had distracted Maynard and Wakefield from their religious objectives: self-denial was their only means to Divine love. While the entry suggests Maynard's hope for a shared form of Evangelical piety, Wakefield felt sufficient pressure about "living the Cloister" that by February 1902 she suffered another onset of acute anxiety. Maynard was clearly unsympathetic about her plight: "She [Wakefield] says she has lost her missionary spirit and is 'in fluctuation"'; and, "She [Wakefield] has evolved from being a light hearted secretary into a morose individual, who tends towards indolence in everything!"[52]

A desperate Wakefield adopted the discourse of science to escape from Maynard's faith-based prescriptions. She told Maynard that she had seen a physician, who "alarmed by [her] low pulse and low weight, had diagnosed [her] with neurasthenia." She was to undergo a "six-week Cure of bed-rest and overfeeding" that would cost Maynard a term's work (£83 and 8 shillings). Maynard disliked the idea of placing her "delicate 'Chela-bird' in a 'Cage,'" but save "M from harm she must." When Wakefield left for her Cage Maynard was told, "You cannot call on her, nor can she write to you, but letters to her are welcome."[53]

Was Maynard aware of the detrimental effect that she had on Wakefield? Did she feel guilt about the psychological pressure that she placed upon her? A queer approach to Maynard's various dialogue(s) about Wakefield in her records reveals the fluidity of one late-Victorian women's desires. In general, Maynard's records evince her relief upon learning that Wakefield's "neurasthenia was not complicated by hysteria." Neurasthenia was a "respectable" middle-class disease, and a catchall for fatigue, anxiety, or stress. Maynard's claim that "M's sickness resulted from her battle between faith and science" once again reflected Victorian thinking about the disease. In 1877, when her faith flailed due to Lumsden's agnosticism, she was advised not to physically over exert herself. In 1902, Wakefield's physician arranged Wakefield's "Cure" by improving her physical health through enforced weight gain.[54]

However, physicians no longer fully believed that neurasthenia resulted from a spiritual crisis or was entirely physiological. A closer look at Maynard's diary and green book reveals her deep discomfort over Wakefield. Maynard's diary describes her reaction to Wakefield's Cure following her demand to see the quarantined Wakefield:

> She *is* better! Exactly eight pounds heavier than when she came! It was all right as long as she was in bed, but now she must leave. Dinner is a pitiful sight with the consumption patients being forced to eat large portions of meat ... The atmosphere of "Cheer up! You're getting on famously!" is not for M at all.[55]

Horrified by the extremes of the treatment – as evidenced by her analogy to force-feeding through the bars of a prison cell – Maynard likely manoeuvred Wakefield's "being pronounced cured" and sent home. She then proceeded to voice both concern and vexation over

Wakefield's continued apathy and disturbing symptoms: "I am told that M is found blue with cold under her blankets!"[56]

Meanwhile, Maynard's green book hinted at her struggle to sanction her behaviour and same-sex desire. She explained that Wakefield suffered from "religious 'excitement,'" and then confessed to her own "excitement" with Gray, adding, "It wasn't only religious. I am capable of supreme excitement both in religion and love." Were these twilight moments for Maynard? Was she aware of Ellis' ideas about "the intimacy of spiritual and religious complexes"? While neither Church nor State had tolerated the "sin" of male sodomy for centuries, scientists were now rethinking female-female desire. Ellis' theories on the "Auto-Erotic Factor in Religion" suggested the possibility of sex between women. As Joy Dixon notes, Ellis' interconnection of faith and sex targeted women more than men due to historical links between femininity, religious mania, and hysteria. We return to Maynard's above assertion that Wakefield's faith-based "neurasthenia was not complicated by hysteria [female insanity]."[57]

Yet we are reminded that as Ellis's admittedly monumental *Psychology of Sex* circulated within British society in 1897 it was mostly met with scepticism. Nor was Ellis' characterization of "auto-eroticism" or association of masochism with the passive feminine widely known until the 1920s. Had he known Maynard, Ellis would have likely coined her behaviour with Amy Mantle, Margaret Brooke, Frances Gray, and Marion Wakefield as that of a "monstrous sadomasochist." A woman who engaged in sadomasochism was "a rare pathological female" who sought to control women through power and faith.[58] Maynard, however, did not view her behaviour as such. Nor did she mention the terms "sexology," "masochism," or "sadism" at this or any other time in her records. It was not until 1926 that she referred to the new language of psychoanalysis.

This is not to suggest that Maynard did not struggle with her sexual feelings. In 1901 she wrote, "I said [to Wakefield], 'I do not want anything from you. I do leave you free.' She closed her eyes tight, and then, suddenly clinging to me and kissing me, said, 'free for this?'" Maynard added, "I am quite desperate! I am no better myself in terms of perfect subjection to Him." Desire conceptualized as religious despair metamorphosed into blame: "It was not [her]self, but God, who had let [her] down in love." She asked, "Can *God* do no better?"[59] We can conclude that Maynard is an example of those cultural dissidents who found within her Christian faith a haven against what were the beginnings of changes in sex norms.

In her autobiographical account of 1902, written in 1929, Maynard tried to downplay her guilt perhaps because the value of psychotherapy was now being stressed for disorders like neurasthenia and anorexia nervosa. For example, she claimed that Wakefield's *physiological* "cure in the Cage had 'saved' M [from] a 'devil-like' curse."[60] Nonetheless, writing about her past same-sex relationships in her autobiography had become difficult for Maynard. While her green book of 1902 conveyed her hope with work, love, and faith, her autobiographical account voiced otherwise: "A young graduate had just questioned [her] about [her] past Westfield friendships," but she knew her "craving was ... *toward God*."[61] Her autobiography ended shortly after on an abrupt, disgruntled note about her trial of work, love, and faith. The reader is thus left to analyse Maynard's emotional-sexual experiences with Wakefield through her green book.

In "'One Life,'" Vicinus argues that Maynard's intimacy with Wakefield "seemed most satisfactory when it remained analogous to a mother and daughter,"[62] but the quote cited by that author from the green book in 1901 does not substantiate this claim:

> Marion was given to me, and I found all, yes, more than I had ever dreamed of, put into my hands ... The husband and wife are constant, and the child added to the mother's heart, with the almost intoxicating joy *it* brings, does not detract from God's share but allows the *content* to be full.[63]

I infer, rather, that Maynard adapted "maternal" love to justify earthly passion to God. As a good and nurturing mother she *should* be intoxicated with love. At the same time, neither diary nor autobiography indicated that she ever saw her love for Wakefield as entirely motherly. Wakefield apparently felt likewise, "Oh my love! I am all yours, every inch of me! I go on loving you every minute in a different way to what I do other people."[64] Maynard (and Wakefield) felt as comfortable with Maynard's lover-husband-mother role as Maynard had been with Mantle in 1874, and with Brooke and Gray throughout the 1880s.

In 1904, on their seventh anniversary of meeting, Maynard gave Wakefield an opal ring as a token of her commitment to their same-sex relationship:

> I told her that a love like ours was a wonderful thing; ... that never for a moment had a shade dimmed our love; and she said "no, never, never." I reminded her how often I had called her my daughter, as I had been very

> chary of the least allusion to married love, but that what we both felt really was of that kind; she nestled in even nearer. I said that I could never plan a future apart from her; that was impossible ... I put the ring on her finger and we prayed together.[65]

Deviant and as incestuous as this may seem in modern day, it would not have seemed so to Maynard and Wakefield. Respectable Victorian society rarely confounded intimacy between middle-class women with the polygamous or incestuous arrangements they attributed to "lesser races."[66] Maynard used Victorian ideals of marriage to justify her own mission: to secure a loving partner and hopefully a successor for Westfield and Divinity. She aimed to solidify her commitment by providing for Wakefield in her will. I would posit the perhaps radical idea that Maynard's fluid conception of Wakefield as daughter-wife interconnected with as well as subverted Victorian notions of marriage as a reproductive imperative, and as an organization for the transmission of property and profession to the next generation. Wakefield promised to return to Westfield as her secretary for the October Term of 1904. They would try for the third time.

However, the ring proved ill-fated. By mid-October Maynard complained about Wakefield's "careless" work. There were other changes too: "Without a word, M resolutely shuts her door at night," Maynard lamented. After symbolizing her unavailability to Maynard, Wakefield declared herself in love with a new student named Mary Armitage, who felt the same way, and that they were leaving Westfield.[67] A heartbroken Maynard once again analysed Wakefield's "expression of love" within the context of faith:

> I had expected this someday and I had encouraged it, telling her that she must have children and really love them ... I am not jealous of Mary, but upset that M has handed on everything I have given her to someone else ... Because I was over 50, and she was first experiencing love, to her it was only "the presage to a victorious region she was just entering." Can I expect otherwise? When she wanted to express love she knew no language but what I had taught her ... She did not know that it was a treasure that she would never find again.[68]

Maynard's inference to Wakefield's expressing *their* language of faith and love with Armitage was curious here. It suggested that Wakefield now had the position of power in a passionate same-sex relationship.

Although Maynard wrote about her anger, jealousy, and her breaking heart, she knew she had no future with Wakefield. By 1908, Maynard referred to her as "a failed daughter," which seemed to help Maynard through her process of loss. She chastised Wakefield for her "poor academic performance," and then sadly admitted, "You have no life with me my sweet love inspiring child." The fact that Wakefield enrolled in Bedford College and gained a B.A. in Philosophy spoke volumes, and she would later gain an M.A. in Psychology, and then pursue a Ph.D. in History at University College London. Maynard's anger seemed more of a projection of her own failure in faith, love, and duty as a mother. Yet she never ceased to view Wakefield as a lover she had lost: "*No-one* can look at her lips in their heavy fullness and not be almost frightened by their weight of feeling."[69]

"Empty Visions?"

Alongside her sad references to a "failed daughter" was Maynard's lament over the failure of Divinity. It had few students, it was bankrupt, and the Council had informed Maynard that it could continue only at her own expense. Although her green book was vague on the matter, the Council had dismissed her Divinity curriculum since January 1902: "Why do you [Maynard] focus on the speculative subject of evil? They [students] will not get teaching anywhere." When Maynard explained her intent to "reform the creed of the Evangelical Church" through the doctrine of Atonement they "were alarmed." They declared it "most dangerous," adding for emphasis, "We need 'proper' instruction of all theological doctrines presented in a 'direct' way." The Council clearly did not share her vision of Westfield graduates who would preach her Word to "crowded, hearty Evangelical congregations" world-wide. In fact, they likely viewed her "mannish" Evangelicalism rather odd, perhaps even perverse.[70] Moreover, her faith-based goals seemed outdated given the theological climate of higher criticism and broad theology. After all, Westfield was to become a more secular School of the University.

Nonetheless Maynard's Divinity program can be considered forward thinking for the early 1900s. Her insistence upon the authority of the Bible carried out by female prophets challenged women's place in a patriarchal society. Indeed, it revealed the potential for religious- and women-centred thinking as a platform for action and change. Thus, when the Council gained Westfield its status as a School in May 1902,

Maynard voiced irritation about "aligning Divinity's syllabus with that of the University of London." Divinity was now based upon "masculinized" High Church Anglicanism "that had echoes of Rome" similar to that of Ritualism and Holiness. It was a way of believing that, in Maynard's view, threatened to "destroy the soul."[71] She gradually lost interest in Divinity, or at least rarely mentioned it in any records.

In October 1908 Maynard suddenly declared, "I no longer distinguish between converts and unbelievers. I look on with complacency." She had not long since returned from giving a Divinity lecture at Newnham College, Cambridge, where she "was advised to give serious consideration before speaking about Scripture. Most said they would 'rather listen to new interpretations of the Testament.'" As far as Anne Richardson was concerned, Maynard's "grandiose scheme [atonement-based world-wide proselytizing] was 'empty visions'"; and Richardson's views were echoed by Westfield's Council. "I am to shrink back into helping Westfield," Maynard lamented, which appropriately described her diminishing influence on college life.[72] Her goal as the new Evangelical prophet was not to be fulfilled.

When we turn to the Westfield that Maynard was "to shrink back into helping," we find that the addition of a wing and library in 1905 had increased student enrolment from forty to being "overfilled" with sixty in residences. The new Westfield was bound by a "Scheme of Provision" for course work, admission procedures, and fees, all of which benefited Westfield's science program, degree success, salaries, and scholarships. History as an Honours subject was relatively new in London, thus it is remarkable that four out of the five first candidates were from Westfield, and that Catherine Firth placed in the First Class. Despite these successes, Maynard's lament over "the loss of Westfield's cultivating spirit" filled pages of both diaries until her retirement in 1913. She resented the middle-class "'high school' girls who won scholarships over the 'real gentle-women.'" She also mourned for the past golden days "when, in [her] stiff black dress [she] preach[ed] the gospel in [her] own way." Immersed in this spiritual milieu, one that possibly no longer existed outside of herself, Westfield had fled her domestic meadows for the more public pastures of professionalism.[73]

Maynard had planned to retire in 1917, at sixty-eight. However, she was made to feel that she *must* retire in 1913 since it was, for the most part, Richardson's wish. While Maynard had been deeply distracted by Wakefield and Divinity, Richardson had formed a close friendship with the talented Eleanor McDougall who, as mentioned above, had joined the faculty in 1902. Thus, when Maynard built a retirement cottage in 1911, Richardson seized upon this as opportunistic moment. She prodded Maynard to retire so that McDougall could become Mistress while she (Richardson) could rule behind the scenes, as she had always done. Maynard resented the old formulaic, ever at play, which "pressured" her to accede to others wishes: "11 years of R, and nearly 30 of A. They have been *good* for college ... But *how* the weaker nature suffers!"[74]

Matters came to a head in May 1912. Without warning, Richardson informed Maynard that McDougall was to be her successor, but would leave if Maynard did not immediately send in her resignation. Maynard "staggered under" the blow of "being kept in the dark," and then "being told by the Council that yes, [she] was no longer wanted." She judged that she had no other choice than to retire as Mistress. She handed in her resignation at a Council meeting in October of that year, effective May 1913. The experience epitomized her grievances: "Very little regarding my resignation, but *much* discussion about a successor ... To think that for 30 years I have worked *despite* my Council; their personal criticisms; their total lack of appreciation."[75]

Neither Maynard nor Richardson could have predicted the subsequent events. A Girton graduate named Agnes de Selincourt, who was highly regarded by some Council members for both her scholarship and missionary work, was voted the most qualified candidate.[76] McDougall immediately resigned and took a job in India, which led Richardson to have the first of a series of breakdowns that would end her career in 1925. Although Maynard judged Richardson's plight as a "retribution of sorts," her feelings of revenge only left her bitter. The circumstances of her retirement took a toll. An onset of neuralgia in the form of shingles that nearly blinded her in one eye denied her most of her final (Lent) Term at Westfield. She managed to attend her farewell party and receive her generous parting gift of £800 from the Council, which she ironically donated "as a special fund" for the "terrible city [lower middle-class] girls." She gave her last Function taking the subject delivered at her very first Westfield Bible class, the "Parable of the Sower."[77]

When Maynard retired she took with her the interconnection of faith and intellectual endeavour to which she had dedicated her thirty-one years as Mistress. Westfield produced more missionaries during the first thirty years of its existence than any other college of comparable size and standing. Of over 500 graduates, at least 50 served in countries like India, Japan, China, Africa, and Canada as missionaries and medical missionaries. Maynard was as equally supportive of the hundreds who entered the teaching profession and social work in Settlements and Children's Homes. By 1913, at least a dozen held the prestigious position of Headmistress, while many others taught in private schools and girls' high schools across the country and overseas. No matter what her graduating students' decision – whether missionary work, teaching, social work, or homemaker – Maynard wholeheartedly supported it.[78]

Soon gone from Westfield were the domestic intimacies that Maynard had maintained: the nightly cocoa parties; the marmalade making; and the strawberry teas in the garden. She was disappointed to discover that only months after her retirement "Scripture classes, which were [once] so cozy around [her] evening fire, [were] held in the morning hours in the ordinary lecture room under bright lights." Perhaps these changes were necessary for the evolution of Westfield and women's colleges at large. De Selincourt largely followed Maynard's main objectives, but her methods of obtaining them were different. She advertised Westfield both in the press and *The Record*; she introduced public lectures on such topics as "Liberal Education"; and at times, "professional" male theologians gave a Divinity lecture based upon a broad doctrine of theology and critical opinion. We can conclude that Maynard's excessive demands had their source from her upbringing. At the same time, her way of running Westfield revealed the strain under which she and her generation worked and, not least, her feminist orientated determination: "I never gave away *my* pulpit to clergymen," she remarked of her Westfield days.[79]

Maynard's emotional entanglements over her years as Mistress left her struggling with the idea of "something wrong," even though female bonds were not yet labelled deviant. As this study has shown, Maynard's self-search as a female educational pioneer was a complex, fluid process. Over a period of forty years, she had adapted various culturally-specific, historical, mythical, scientific, and faith-based discourses to express her aims as a pioneer and her desires as a woman. At the extreme, she found justification for love as God-given, but then punished herself and her loves for preferring human love over divine: "The room where [she] had suffered so much" was rid of its many painful memories by her symbolic "destruction of old letters," from adoring ex-staff member Kate Tristram, to "long passionate outpourings" from Amy Mantle, Louisa Lumsden, James Robertson, Margaret Brooke, and Marion Wakefield. The mistakes surrounding faith, aim, and love would not be forgotten, however: "All of A's, R's and the M's, and those with Effie," would haunt Maynard for the rest of her days.[80]

Conclusion

"Shadow of 'Outer Darkness' Close to Me"

After great pain, they say, the mere absence of it is positive joy,
and that you can feel enwrapped in bliss, –
well, it is something like that in the outer life and I'm content.
But within I still long with a great and sore longing.
I can never *quite* find that someone along the same lines.[1]

This study ends as it began with Maynard's lament about her struggle between faith and worldliness, a struggle that influenced her life in distinct ways. Although faith sanctioned her ambitions and passions, atonement-based duty predominated over her thoughts and feelings. Even so, in a strange and contradictory way, her faith afforded Maynard a means in which to combat the immense hurdles that faced her as an educational pioneer: from acceptance as a professional, to the loneliness such acceptance engendered. At the extreme, Maynard's shun of earthly love threatened her health and that of others. Her submission under Campbell, and to a certain extent, Lumsden, led her to adopt more dominant roles in her later relationships. One result of this transition was Maynard's manipulation of such young women as Girton student Amy Mantle, St. Leonards student Mary Tait, Westfield students Margaret Brooke and Marion Wakefield, and teacher Frances Gray. Whether contrived or not, Maynard's behaviour became an important aspect of her experiences as a Victorian woman.

What may we say about the older Maynard's experiences during her retirement years at her home The Sundial? She certainly embraced life. She was an avid writer. She was a keen reader. She travelled extensively. She attended conferences. She gave numerous lectures. As she

8.1 Constance Maynard, aged eighty-five, 1934. Courtesy of Queen Mary University of London Archives/Westfield College/WDF.

said of her approach to life in a lecture in 1920, "it's 'always interesting!' I deal with education, England and the world (the awakening of India and China)."[2] Her unceasing energy was evident in her purchase of "the latest tricycle" to cycle across England, and in her interest in the "great waves of thought" from the Zeitgeist to Christian Science.[3] Ambitious to the end, she sought to be recognized at the M.A. level. In an interview for the *Daily Mirror* her words rang loud and clear: "After the University preserved a silence...for some 53 years, suddenly, in 1928, we were informed that we might write the letters M.A. after our names, and wear the appropriate gown and hood."[4] Little wonder then that Maynard wished that the story of her life be known.

"I Have a Message to Give"

Maynard's "missive" to society in later life took form in publishing: "*This* [publishing] is THE REAL CENTRE of life," she exclaimed at seventy-six. "I *have* a message to give. I *am* a prophet."[5] Her message was most evident in her exhortation in the living of a Christian life. Short sermons, such as "The Perfect Law of Liberty" (1913), tied faith to morals like sincerity and courage. *The Prophet Daniel* (1914) advised Christians to focus on such principles of conduct as self-control. The fact that all her publications contained Biblical illustrations revealed the Biblicism that had marked Victorian Evangelicalism.[6] They also reflected Maynard's particular views on the Truth: "I cannot believe that the ethical struggle is the *real* value in God's eyes," she remarked in her green book in 1925. "It is *no* effort of Will." One recalls Maynard's reaction to Campbell's link of Will with agency and God. In 1873 she wrote, "Lewis has no religion at all, only a noble code of ethics!"[7] In 1925 she still claimed that "the Atonement remind[ed] us that we ha[d] something to do."

Nonetheless, Maynard's anxious plea reflected the times, for the unity of Evangelicalism had broken down. The movement had always been notable for its variety in doctrine, attitude, and social composition, but the schisms that began in the 1850s had deepened. The 1920s had seen a series of crises about "Infallibility of the Bible" created by higher criticism. Indeed, the more conservative Evangelicals believed that Biblicism was under serious threat both at home and overseas. Doctrinal debate centred on two "problem" areas; the Atonement and Christology. Liberal Evangelicals' contended that the omniscience of Christ must be given up; particularly the idea of Christ's worldly suffering as exemplary for one's own. Meanwhile, Maynard's and others' understanding of the Atonement as "handed down by Evangelical fathers" was refuted through claims that such terms as "substitution" and "vicarious punishment" were not in the Bible.[8] One can understand why Maynard's hope for Divinity failed amidst these religious challenges, despite her women-centred visions and aims to evangelize the world.

The parting of Evangelical ways was being hastened by the increased growth of High Church sympathies; ritualism; attention to Eucharist; and beauty in worship. Unsurprisingly, the revision of what became the "High Church" Prayer Book created controversy. After all, fifty years earlier in 1871, the Maynards' wished to "revise" the Prayer-Book precisely *because* emerging theological views "echoed those from Rome." Ritualistic worship must "be avoided" they believed, as it "destroy[ed] the soul."[9] A factor that played a more active part in encouraging division was debate on the relation of science and religion, particularly the re-remoulding of theology around the new scientific truth. Nonetheless, some strengths of conservative Evangelism remained, as evident in the large audiences who gathered to hear about Biblical Truth. Maynard always attended the annual Modern Churchman's Conference because eminent clergymen "spoke in defence of the gospels."[10]

In contrast to Maynard's seemingly outmoded message of faith, her publication of *We Women: A Golden Hope* in 1913 proclaimed her lifelong radical support of women's higher education, taking into account her views on gender, faith, and science:

> Man, as a race, has used us very badly, accounting us (taken collectively) as hopelessly inferior to himself ... The debt I owe to the pioneers cannot be paid except by heartfelt, lifelong gratitude ... We [women] have natural power of both reason and conscience. But beyond this again there is another source of knowledge that we call revelation, a guiding line given us from on High.[11]

Maynard's conclusion in *We Women* was noteworthy: "There is no longer 'man' and 'woman.'" God, she claimed, "brought the whole of human nature together in both Adam and Eve." Maynard's dismantling of gender and sex alluded to the Pauline Christ that recognized neither male nor female in religious belief. In Maynard's view, education should not separate gender either. The "seeds" of women's higher education "had been well scattered. It [wa]s up to the next generation to reap the harvest."[12]

Even so, one is reminded of the lines in Maynard's much-loved Parable of the Sower: "Most of the good seed scattered is wasted if hearts are already occupied. *Good* means not having these defects." For Maynard, the seeds of good change meant retaining certain feminine values. Her advice in *We Women*, "Remember, the mother is the true centre of the home, and sister of Jesus," evinced the Evangelical privileging of women's pious domesticity in order to deflect heathenness.[13] Maynard's views on social reform and suffrage were equally steeped in domestic and religious metaphor:

> By the vote we can suppress the evils of vice; by the vote we can secure good housing, sanitation, and national education, both general and technical; by the vote we can make idleness and cheating difficult, and honest labour attractive ... Do not neglect your vote, my sisters, but use it for these ends.[14]

The moral undertones in *We Women* reflected Maynard's sociopolitical elitism. She supported women's political engagement in nation-building, education, health, and "morality." She had unwavering praise for the women who dedicated their lives to the imperialist missionary enterprise. But feminist involvement in labour was another matter, because "the government doles we[re] the source of England's misery." While feminists and such groups as the Fabians fought for class rights, conservative Evangelicals were among those who believed in saving souls rather than creating programs for change. In Maynard's view, doles could not reform a class that was "slovenly, idle and immoral." The poor must "rise from their evil" and seek salvation in the Hereafter.[15]

In terms of Maynard's own spiritual journey, *The Life of Dora Greenwell* (1926) proved fascinating in its "queer like" reflection of her worldly test. Indeed, Maynard worked on this biographical study for over twenty years. Oddly enough, *Dora Greenwell* featured a drug-addicted Victorian theologian of that name who was on a life-long quest for Truth: "Her re-editing of ancient books, historical inaccuracies and scientific contradictions were, in the end, negligible," Maynard asserted. "She always wove her varied treasures into a crown for the head of the suffering Redeemer."[16] For Maynard, of course, the "varied treasures" for the suffering Redeemer included suffering oneself.

In a chapter entitled "Two Loves," Maynard cited "a very curious poem" by Greenwell. According to Maynard, this poem attested to

Greenwell's firm belief that one's "nature would finally be redeemed by Christ." As Maynard confessed of her own failings, "In a passionate nature there are instinctive elements that make it *impossible* to choose the Cloister." Christ, she hoped, would redeem her weaknesses before God. In light of cultural changes that stemmed from science, perhaps Greenwell's ideas proved a balm for Maynard, reaffirming her justification of passion and ambition without classification within the context of faith.[17]

When comparing Maynard's thoughts in *Dora Greenwell* with her diaries, one turns to the green book since it contained much of her current thoughts on life. Of note is Maynard's straddling between old and new ideals to analyse the "varied treasures" that she felt she had gained and lost as an educational pioneer. She was immensely proud of Westfield's steady growth and academic success throughout the 1920s. The enrolment was now at 100 and most students gained the degree. In 1924, for example, thirty-one candidates obtained the B.A. Honours, and four the B.Sc. Honours. It was at this time that Westfield Council dissolved its Education Committee and looked "more harmoniously towards its Principal Teachers" for academic advice. This seems ironic – even rather sad – given the Council's treatment of Maynard over the years. Maynard of course recognized that higher education had already gained for women more social equality and respect. She also appreciated the fact that third generation university-trained teachers were considered "qualified enough" to engage in academic research.[18]

Nonetheless, Maynard deeply resented Westfield's shift towards secularism. In her view, the scientific age had shunned talk of good and evil and had renounced all notions of morality. Sunday Function, now perhaps irreverently referred to as "Princ's Func," had long since been voluntary for students. They could engage instead in academic study or such pastimes as walking. Moreover, Westfield's current Principal Eleanor Lodge was keen that Westfield be considered an integral part of the University of London, and that students understand the importance of academic work: "Students have more power, and more choice in selecting subjects," Maynard lamented. "No one seems to care about their individual souls." No longer could she impress upon "*these* modern young women a sense of sin they ought to feel and did not." Westfield had clearly diverged from the "confiding [Christian] family" she had devised forty years earlier that aimed to train genteel women to spread (her) Truth.[19]

Green book entries about Anne Richardson provide more context for Maynard's professional hurts over Westfield. We learn that Agnes de Selincourt's untimely death in 1917 left Richardson once again "suffering" over love and leader; but that upon her recovery Richardson had "moved with the times" under Bertha Phillipots' (1919–21) and Eleanor Lodge's (1921–31) more secularist leadership of Westfield.[20] In Maynard's view, Richardson's attitude made her a "successful, but 'more callous' pioneer":

> I went to Westfield's first commemorative day in June [1922]. I found it strange that the history of the college, exactly 40 years, had no mention of me at all. There was ovation for Miss Phillipots and Miss Lodge. Yet I, who had 31 years, sat there unnoticed amongst the audience. It was Anne's doing. She goes on hurting me until I feel quite weary.[21]

As to whether this slight or oversight was Richardson's fault remains unclear, but it revealed her continued impact upon Maynard. Yet Richardson's formulaic for success was perhaps more fragile than Maynard's, since Richardson's "role" was to rule backstage for her adored one. When she could not get close to Lodge, she suffered another breakdown and was forced to retire in 1925. Maynard gained satisfaction from what she called Richardson's "hopeless mental incapacity." Richardson was remembered for her "strong presence at Westfield" and yet, similarly to Maynard and others, she struggled to negotiate "feminine" passion and ambition.[22]

Despite her irritations over the "worldly" Westfield, Maynard's own reticence about spreading her "message" at Girton, in 1926, revealed her own sense of failure and struggle with the changing times:

> When I stood on Girton's great platform in front of 300 unknown faces, it was the opportunity of a lifetime, but before so many agnostics? I spoke vividly about freedom and touched lightly on the difference of thought between home and college. Now I feel the stress of not speaking Christ's name more.[23]

It happened again at Westfield in 1934:

> The beginning was okay. I told them how Character was more important than Ability or Attainment, valuable as these were, and I gave them the main ingredients. The next necessity was Religion, to speak of how the outer shell was of no account ... Yet I could not deal with what true Religion really *was*. It was as if hands were laid over my mouth. I forgot everything.[24]

Silenced by the changing religious climate, and by her own self-doubt, Maynard felt keenly her loss of power. Her Girton Prayer Meeting had dwindled as had her beloved Ring letter. Even the burgeoning Student Christian Movement (converged S.V.M.U. and B.C.C.U.) accepted the new approach to the Bible. Speakers linked higher criticism with a broad doctrine of theology. However, the failed promise of Divinity left for Maynard the biggest sting.[25]

As narrow-minded and possibly self-serving as Maynard might have been, it is important to remember the gains she made for women. She can be considered a highly successful woman by any standard, leaving permanent models in research and higher education.[26] The founding and ensuing success of Westfield was due to Maynard's intellectual ability, her leadership skills, and her tenacity. These qualities were apparent in her unwillingness to compromise, and in her determination to first provide English women with the opportunity to take the B.A. and B.Sc. degrees at University College London. Her commitment to this goal stood her in good stead against the sexist disregard of women's education at large in society, and even latent in the Council that oversaw Westfield. While brought to desperation at times, she gained voice through perseverance and strength rather than retaliation. Her achievements afforded her success as Mistress of Westfield and dignity as an individual, despite the gender disparities of her culture.

"My Inner Turmoil of Feelings"

Besides its value in tracing Maynard's later professional life, the green book remains a striking account of Maynard's varied emotional "treasures." Treasures, she believed, that were "given and then taken by God." Certainly, we learn of the passing of loved ones like Gazy, and about the loneliness and trials of old age, such as bad teeth, gout, painful rheumatism, and a weak heart: "The time which suggests armchairs, Shetland shawls and avoidance of all conflicts of life." But an entry in April 1920 that suddenly exclaims, "I have fallen in love," is somewhat shocking. This time, the seventy-one-year-old Maynard referred to local nineteen-year-old Jim Gillett, whom she was tutoring as a favour to his middle-class parents. It was a "spiritual connection" which, for Maynard, was important. Few from her local village Bookham responded to her attempts at conversion and, as noted above, she hesitated to mention faith in academic circles. Faith was also attached to the emotional: "When his [Gillett's] lips in their pure youthfulness seek mine, - a flame not allowed often, - my whole being thrills.

I am a little ashamed to write such things. Yet may not the heart be kept young, quite unutterably young?"[27]

Similarly to her "little quiet outlet" (Mary Tait) at St. Leonards, Maynard wrote that she "naturally ke[pt] this *love* safe as a little hidden joy sent [her] from Heaven."[28] What is equally noteworthy was Maynard's continued view of this form of "*love*" as heterosexual or "sexual feeling": "I preserve that slight barrier to exist between man and woman, but he knows how to love, as some girl will one day know." Maynard's interest in Gillett impelled her to try to mould him into the Wakefield who had failed: "In him I see the future hands of myself. Chastity has built around him a 'crystal barrier' that allows thinking, and 'yet those lips' indicate 'his power of love.'" This seems a curious observation on Maynard's part. Did she think Gillett capable of "coaxing" adoring students towards the spiritual flame, just as she had done?[29] Faith justified Maynard's own passionate feelings for Gillett, of course, as it had with Campbell, Lumsden, Brooke, Gray, and Wakefield. Through the queer space of faith, desire was no longer entirely about gender or sex, or even about age: "God kn[ew] the inner most fibres of [her] being," the electric sparks, and "He c[ould] *do anything*." God could give her love and religious power.[30]

Maynard happily agreed to pay for Gillett's education at Oxford in 1923, but she soon grew resentful of his focus on academia and interest in peers over herself. In fact, Gillett's lack of faith forced Maynard to reconsider God's gift within the context of culture: "I have always longed for a son, but as my love grows, his slackens off." Maynard struggled with her desire for Gillett. After all, she had never simply viewed her love for him as that of a kindly mother (or grandmother). When she "found the courage" to speak to Gillett he told her, "'I have never felt love as much as you have.'" A disappointed yet worldly-wise Maynard added, "Somehow, I felt content with that." She likely knew she had overly romanticized Gillett, who in turn had possibly tolerated her evangelizing to get his expenses paid.[31]

The green book seems to evince a more guarded tone about heterosexual love after the Gillett episode. This was perhaps due to Maynard's admission a decade earlier about her discomfort over Fanny Campbell's "sudden discovery" of a copy of the sonnet Lewis Campbell had sent Maynard in 1872. She guessed that Fanny knew "the full meaning of Lewis' sonnet," and the individual that it was written for. Maynard admitted that she and Campbell had transgressed social mores, but was as quick to justify their behaviour: "We gave each other something the other could not otherwise have had." Until the end of her life, Maynard fully believed that Campbell was a key figure in her life. He had brought her pain and regret, but also opened her up to the world of ambition and love.[32]

Maynard's mulling over Campbell and Gillett paled in comparison to recordings about her past same-sex longings. Indeed, her frankness about fleshy love lends great historical value to both green book and autobiography, and their variations evoke deep reflection on those feelings. Her autobiography, in particular, discloses one late-Victorian woman's struggle to reconcile romantic friendship with twentieth-century ideas of sexuality. She still adopted cryptic religious metaphor to exonerate her past behaviour: her "upbringing caused [her] repression"; Lumsden was a "faithless tyrant who bound [her] to an unhappy marriage"; Brooke "took the blame [for passion] that was [Brooke's]"; Gray rejected her "love due to [Gray's] want of Divine love"; and she "saved M [Wakefield] from a real mental breakdown."[33] In 1919, however, her language metamorphosed into painful confessions about her "inner turmoil of feelings." She explained, "I felt *discomfort* over Amy [Mantle at Girton]. I told her, 'I can not respond to the private side that seems to give you satisfaction'"; and about St. Leonards student Mary Tait: "My heart was lonely and hungry beyond words." Maynard did not elaborate on either of these past relationships, but she implied that both had sexual elements.[34]

When Maynard re-examined her past same-sex longings in 1919, post-war Britain struggled to re-establish traditional norms in the face of new ideas about gender and sex. While many still declared Ellis' monumental *Psychology of Sex* obscene, his endorsement of self-expression and caution against inner sex "immorality" and "deviance" remained prominent in media and popular assumptions. In terms of growing awareness to female homosexuality, we can turn to Maud Allen's widely reported trial in London in 1918; or Marie Stopes best seller *Married Love* (1918), which acclaimed women's heterosexual passion – as opposed to submission – but warned women against "wrong" homosexual acts like genital contact.[35] Meanwhile, D.H. Lawrence's *The Rainbow* (1915) featured a chapter entitled "Shame" about college raves which, as noted, had not troubled biographer George Layard in 1901. The changing attitudes towards female bonds, in general, were illustrated by an attempt to make homosexual acts between women illegal in 1921.[36]

By the mid-1920s, English society was more knowledgeable of "deviance" and its application to women's sexual behaviour as well as men's.

Thus it is perhaps not surprising that Maynard admitted to her awareness of psychoanalytical terms in 1926. As noted in the Introduction, she suddenly voiced displeasure at the thought that "psychoanalysts" may now call her past same-sex feelings a "thwarted sex instinct."[37] In another autobiographical passage she confessed that,

> The early years (up to 1886) seemed okay. Then came "wrong excitements within." Why did I not speak out or consult someone? When I examine my feelings under the present light of psychology I suppose I had love within me which I could not give away. Someone has called this loneliness "sex feeling," but all I wanted was one life to stand beside me.[38]

A year later, she asked the reader, "If my craving *did* stem from 'repressed sex feelings,' why didn't my thoughts ever stray to a man?" Here, Maynard linked psychoanalytical thought with Victorian ideals of heteronormativity and domestic piety in an attempt to understand her struggle. She concluded, "No, my craving was not the instinct toward marriage, *surely not*, it was the *instinct toward God*, which can be satisfied with nothing less."[39]

Maynard's knowledge of psychoanalytical language may have been quite unusual. After all, her studies in the "Mental and Moral Sciences" at Girton was, as she claimed, "the beginnings of psychology." Nevertheless, scholars still debate the impact of psychoanalysis over sexology to the elucidation of sexual matters. Porter, Hall, and others propose that the few English Freudians who in the 1920s did adopt such terms as "repression" or "sublimation" did not necessarily provide any deeper rethinking of sexual categories. In contrast, such scholars as Susan Kingley Kent claim that many individuals gainfully employed Freud to postulate that "submission" to dominant norms could "repress one's primitive [same-sex sexual] instincts."[40]

Of note is that Maynard not only turned to psychoanalytical language for self-understanding in 1927. Equally provocative was her brief recollection of her same-sex feelings for Frances Gray after an S.A. meeting in 1892: "His [General Booth's] strange words, 'such a tender man, half a woman!' - seemed to explain my loneliness."[41] Maynard did not attribute her thoughts to Edward Carpenter's *The Intermediate Sex* (1908) that had greatly contributed to English sexological discourses on gender inversion. Yet her musing echoed his idea of the individual who bore the physical characteristics of one sex, and the emotional characteristics of the other. As Joy Dixon also notes, both Carpenter and Ellis identified a "positive organic relationship between spiritual development and the homosexual temperament." Carpenter claimed that the "blending of the masculine and female temperaments" could produce an invert "of intuitive mind." Indeed, his analogy of intuitive inverts "as diviners and prophets" can be compared to Maynard's sense of feeling "wonderfully alone" in her foundation of Divinity in 1901.[42]

Clearly, Maynard's dismantling of gender throughout the late 1800s and early 1900s interwove with her concept of same-sex desire as emotional-religious feeling, rather than "sex feeling." In a sense, Maynard was not alone in her creative carving of a same-sex sexual self-consciousness. A few modern women linked sexology with faith to validate same-sex love and claim women's social independence. Lesley Hall notes that credit be given to those brave women who battled a still profoundly patriarchal and sex-negative culture.[43] Nonetheless, as a late-Victorian, Maynard struggled with modern ideas about sex. She ended her musings on "tender man, half a woman" much like her appraisal of psychoanalytical thought: "I thought, 'I give up R [Frances Gray]! I want God only. How can I fear?'" Her past record "was mournful" she claimed, because she had chosen human love instead.[44] Maynard's entries are haunting portrayals of one older generation woman's struggle to navigate an era of change in sexual norms and friendship mores.

In contrast to the poignant dialogue in her autobiography, Maynard's green book beseeches forgiveness for her own and others' "inner turmoil of feelings." Entries following Louisa Lumsden's visits to The Sundial were particularly fraught with anger: "The mistakes she [Lumsden] made at St. Leonards! ... I told her that she 'had never been anything but a tyrant!' The sad part was that she didn't seem to realize this injustice." They also quarrelled about faith: "She [Lumsden] said, 'What does sentiment have to do with faith?' I did not admit *my* doubt. I said, 'I *still* believe in voluntary self-denial.'" Whether faith was a metaphor for their emotional past remains unclear. They rarely met again. But an entry shortly before Maynard's death waxed condescending: "Louisa may well have loved me, yet she remains the most *pathetic* figure in my life because there is no hope for her religiously." Still, Maynard could not help but "wonder at her *willingness* to remain with L" at St. Leonards. Her final comment on the matter, "It was 'partly love' and 'partly torment,'" suggests that Maynard recognized her pleasure in suffering under Lumsden.[45]

Anger, longing, and regret intermingled in entries about Frances Gray. We learn that in 1901, Gray took over until retirement St. Paul's

LOUISA INNES LUMSDEN, D.B.E., LL.D.

8.2 Dame Louisa Lumsden, date unknown. Courtesy of St. Leonards School Archives, St. Andrews.

girls' school in London. The school was "a *grand* venture with its marble floors, lofty rooms and solid oak door," and it soon '"turned to gold' in Ralf's capable hands." Although St. Paul's was a point of envy for Maynard – rather like Gray's reign at Kidderpore – Gray remained "nothing short of beautiful." After "a sad stay" with "the aloof" Gray in 1923 Maynard revisited their past: "It was the old story of Troy. I endured the worst, yet was content if Helen was within its walls." We recall Maynard's adaptation of the religious-Greek language in 1885 to describe her feelings for Gray. Her concluding comment, "Some of it I suppose was actual sin," is equally noteworthy. By this time, the Church linked religious and secular language to recognize homosexuality as both a sin and a medical condition. In 1934, Maynard declared herself "All over, *quite* done!" with Gray, but an entry in 1935 suggested otherwise: "R doesn't want my verses!" The verses Maynard referred to were love poems written for Gray throughout the 1880s and 1890s.[46] Until the end, it seems, Gray was quick to reject Maynard's overtures of love.

When comparing all of Maynard's relationships, entries about Marion Wakefield and Effie evoke the most guilt and pain. As noted in chapter 6, Maynard's disgust with Effie's behaviour had culminated in her "returning" Effie to the S.A. in 1894. Maynard's attitude, while coloured by her snobbery and faith, was fuelled when Effie's work as a domestic led her to become a "fallen woman" that same year at age thirteen. Maynard rarely saw Effie again, and the situation did not change when Effie was pronounced terminally ill with tuberculosis in 1914. Maynard, true to form, seemed caught between feeling revulsion and pity for Effie's "prolonged physical suffering." She did pay for Effie's medical care, however, and was perhaps justifiably enraged to learn that "two kind ladies [we]re also paying due to Effie's lies about being destitute." This was yet "another example of Effie's ongoing deceit." A green book entry written upon Effie's death was telling: "Forgive me darling. I gave you much, but I withheld what you wanted, undying love, and I do not wonder that you sought it elsewhere."[47] A sad end, it seems, to a sad relationship.

Green book entries about Marion Wakefield are a similarly disquieting read, but they were perhaps Maynard's most candid (and possibly liberating) observations of her sexual past. She recorded a particularly stormy encounter between them in 1923: "She [Wakefield] said, 'You did not see the harm you were doing me. When you thought that you were opening my mind, you were actually repressing me.'" Maynard sadly added, "I know the usual feelings *were* missed out of her life and

8.3 The original Westfield staff, 1905. From left to right; Frances Gray, Anne Richardson (seated), Constance Maynard, Kate Tristram, and Josephine Willoughby (later Adams Clark). In Maynard's opinion, Gray looked "imperial," Richardson looked "amused," Tristram looked "modest," and Willoughby looked "motherly." Courtesy of Queen Mary University of London Archives/ Westfield College/WFD/25/2.

given to me."[48] Their mutual desire, she seemed to admit, had diverted Wakefield from heterosexual passion. Wakefield had by this time gained an M.A. in the new field of Psychology at Bedford College, and was a Ph.D. candidate at University College London. She told Maynard about her newly-found interest in Nietzsche: "The charms of freedom are endless!" At the core of Nietzsche's rejection of repression was faith: "Dead are all Gods: Now we want...*our* ultimate Will." Wakefield, it seems, sought to deny Maynard her religion, and even more importantly, the faith-based "purity" of their passion.[49]

Did Wakefield share her thoughts on psychoanalysis at length with Maynard? Did Maynard take up the studies herself in the mid-1920s? It remains unclear. A green book entry in 1917 was perhaps telling: "She [Wakefield] says someday she'll tell me what her new work means, despite the fact that it will hurt me."[50] Two years later, Maynard voiced "discomfort" over her past experiences with Amy Mantle at Girton and Mary Tait at St. Leonards. By the early 1920s, she confessed to "wrong excitements" both for and with college women. In 1928, and after, she couched same-sex "recklessness" more directly in psychoanalytical terms: "I suppose when the natural channel is blocked, there must be some outlet"; and, "I realize that I did not really know what craving for human love meant."[51] Nonetheless, she remained ambivalent towards the new discourses on sex: "I analyse love, abstractly, but I will *not* discuss my feelings further."[52] In 1926 she wrote with assurance that her struggles were faith-based, and faith would remain a fluid means to conceive and justify past same-sex sexuality: "My only wrong was choosing human love over divine love."[53]

In 1934, at age eighty-four, Maynard's dialogue regarding same-sex longings did modify, if only slightly. She still expressed pain and guilt over her sins and "wrongs." After all, she had exploited college women on both professional and personal levels. Yet she had found through science some new forms of self-reconciliation. Her brief mention of Radclyffe Hall's *The Well of Loneliness* as "sad" is noteworthy here. Since its publication in 1928, Hall's novel advocated homosexual tolerance and established such "lesbian" stereotypes as the mannish invert.[54] For her part, Maynard hoped to be as "candid" with Wakefield about *their* past:

> For only a moment the door opened between us, for the sight was too painful. I dared not speak of my reckless satisfaction, or on the yet more solemn subject. I said, "I missed my vocation, I really was *too* lonely. Oh, M forgive!" She threw herself upon me, saying, "how *can* you say that? Look at the good!"[55]

Later in private Maynard confessed: "Yet, if Marion was still the same I would *still* love her; the skin, the tall frame, the splendid thick hair, the full lips and the white teeth-, all landmarks of what is lost."[56] While she might apologize to Wakefield for her transgressions in oblique psychoanalytical-religious terms, Maynard did not appear to regret their emotional past either.

In 1935, shortly before her death on March 26th, Maynard turned green book upon autobiography as her (last recorded) means of self-revelation. On 30 January she wrote:

> I have read over my autobiography written during 1915–1918. It all seems so new to me, as if it is about the life of someone else. My concentrated

> love of L and the utterly sleepless nights she gave me at Cheltenham, I look on the whole scene with a sort of compassion ... I was in the full tide of youth.[57]

She continued her thoughts on 8 February:

> ... as I go on it gets worse and worse – I ruined it by "falling in love" – Margaret Brooke, perhaps Nannie, Ralph Gray, and then, after a period of sore desolation came Marion Wakefield. It was wrong, yes, all wrong! Oh! If only I could have given that love, that preoccupation of the heart, to Christ alone! I had entered the Cloister voluntarily, and I perpetually transgressed its first rule. Yet God himself has written, "it is not good a man should be alone." So I do not understand why this actual starving for love should lead to sin. As I pursue the track, I see loss, waste and confusion around me.[58]

Certainly, Maynard had genuflected about her desire for college women from the 1870s onwards. This was evident in her conflict over carnal intimacies that she believed had surpassed her spiritual ideal. Yet far from hiding "behind a façade of self-effacing Christianity," she recognized her power as a woman and prophet-educational pioneer. She not only courted women, but also had a brief encounter with the married Campbell in 1881. When Richardson cautioned her against the "wrong" in her Westfield relationships, Maynard took pause. But despite her misgivings, Maynard claimed that her needs "were impossible to give up."[59] She pursued young college women until she retired in 1913. Towards the end of her life – as the above quotes suggest – Maynard struggled with her emotional history. Yet one might detect Maynard's frustration over opportunities lost. Did she think Victorians' incomprehension of female-female "sex feeling" a loss, and a waste, of sorts?

As argued throughout this study, Maynard's studies at Girton in the 1870s opened her up to ideas about the self and society. She explained this in her autobiography: "I still believe that besides the Intellect and Feeling, there is in me a 'mere unanalysable point.' It is a thread slight indeed, and yet just of sufficient strength to urge the Will on over the dark empty spaces that intervene."[60] This fascinating comment revealed Maynard's visualization of the self as both cultural navigator and powerful agent, despite her faith-based beliefs about submission of Will. Indeed, her thoughts almost reflect present-day queer theories on fragmented, unstable identifications.

Significantly, as a late-Victorian female educational pioneer, Maynard's complex views on the self lend more insight into her concept of desire "as God's will." Certainly, the new theories on sex did not resonate easily with her past experience of loving women (or Gillett). Yet perhaps her notion of the "mere unanalysable points" of the will left Maynard rightly ambivalent towards the essentialist-based ideas on desire that both classified and generalized "worldly" sex feeling. Of course, contemporary scholars still adopt psychoanalytical theories in their research, despite its sexist and arguably homophobic history, and so it must still offer insight into both past and present experiences.[61] Maynard's struggle at the bridge of this change should not be underestimated.

While influenced and yet troubled by the new scientific language in the mid-1920s and after, Maynard could not fully embrace the modern sexual terms. Would she have offered Gray her love poems shortly before her death in 1935 if she believed them "lesbian" orientated? It is doubtful in light of her cultural upbringing, unless the entry symbolized *Gray's* inability to be "candid" about their past. Maynard's archives only provide us with provisional answers.[62] What does seem clear, however, is that Maynard's understanding of her sexuality was markedly different from that of the following generation of women. She had no means of understanding her lifestyle choice as a cover for her desire, as it became for twentieth-century lesbian women. Moreover, her faith-based binary permitted her to behave in special ways with both men and women, despite her guilt and confusion.

In her autobiography, Maynard admitted that her upbringing had created "abnormal" forms of asceticism within her. Did she view what sexologists may term her "perverse feminine impulses" as outcome(s) of her staunch evangelicalism? Was she aware that Freud's "guilt paradigm" theorized one could "suffer" to experience sexual delight?[63] Did she associate aspects of her submissive-dominant (husband-wife-mother) role-playing at college with scientific definitions of sadomasochism? Her late records suggest that on some levels, she did. However, Maynard was neither fully able nor willing to re-conceptualize her beliefs within scientific discourse. In fact, her perhaps overly imagined or even privately relished concept of suffering and redemption was integral to her Christian sense of self. As Maynard warned us, the danger lay in allowing the behaviour to get out of control: "I could spend hours of resentment and tears recalling 'pain's most cruel sawing.' I felt it to the extreme and let it ruin my life for years."[64]

I suspect that Maynard yearned for a world that was ceasing to exist, one in which neither labels nor stigma surrounded women's passionate relationships. For Maynard, love was about emotional communication and the specialness of the other, and carried with it the hope of life-long devotion. It was a woman-centred, moral-religious-emotional conjunction, and she wished to give us a glimpse of that world. After all, as she asserted in her green book, "What I share with others must be shared and not hidden here."[65] The pages of that record do reveal the intensity of her relationships, as this study has shown.

To some scholars, who place value on the historically-constructed ideal of openly sexual categories, Maynard's retreat into faith to explain desire may seem non-progressive. Yet historians and queer theorists alike advise a fluid approach to past experience.[66] Maynard's self-identity emanated from multiple unstable norms around class, race, gender, and sex; identities that she interconnected with other discourses over a lifetime of experiences. In particular, however, Maynard chose to negotiate her(self) within the language of her ascetic faith. If we are serious about the scholarly enterprise of recognizing women's historical agency, we should be attentive to behaviours "outside" narratives that prescribe female ambition, sexual preference, or supposed sadomasochistic-like tendencies.

For complex reasons, then, historians must be careful not to utilize a modern identity to categorize an historical one, or even worse, obscure past sexual practices through blanket explanations and exclusions. Certainly, conceptualizing personal records as "real" life and "truth" is similarly reifying. We might debate the futility of interpreting past language in order to respond to it through our own. Yet however exaggerated or contradictory the green book, diary, and autobiography of Constance Louisa Maynard are, they present a remarkably in-depth account of her life experiences as an educational pioneer. The reader gleans fascinating aspects of one woman's struggles in another period. Maynard's dilemmas even offer us self-reflection and the chance to know ourselves better. In this researcher's view, the autobiographical-diary, "I," – however fugitive, partial, and unreliable – can be viewed as the privileged textual double of a real person, as well as a self-evident textual construct.[67]

We leave Maynard understanding that she was not only a remarkable woman for her times, but a woman who held enormous power. We can perhaps relate to her longing for love with an equal partner with whom she could share her passion, her intellect, and her faith. Unfortunately for Maynard, love not only suffered through her partly contradictory ideals, but materialized with one inequality or another in values, emotions, and intellect.[68] A single case study does not reveal the differing ways in which Victorian women reconciled passion and ambition within the context of faith. However, Maynard's life-story certainly raises new issues about power, faith, and ambition, and new questions about Victorian sexuality.

Notes

Introduction

1 Constance Louisa Maynard, Unpublished Autobiography, Part 7, chapter 48, "My Life Work, 1885," 1, written in 1928, Special Collections, Courtesy of Queen Mary University of London Archives/Constance Maynard/PP7/6, (hereafter cited as *A*, plus part, date, page numbers and years written). Maynard included her thoughts on love written in 1885 in her autobiographical account of 1885 to explain her conflict between earthly love and divine love as Mistress of Westfield.

2 Constance Louisa Maynard, copy of Last Will and Testament, Special Collections, Courtesy of Queen Mary University of London Archives/Constance Maynard/PP7. Copies of Maynard's unpublished personal documents, including her green book, daily diary, and autobiography, were available to me on microfilm from the University of Toronto. In May, 2012, Maynard's green book and autobiography were digitized at Queen Mary, University of London Archives. For access, visit, http://www.library.qmul.ac.uk/archives/digital/constance_maynard.

3 Catherine B. Firth, *Constance Louisa Maynard: Mistress of Westfield College* (London: George Allen and Unwin, 1949). Firth was the youngest of Maynard's five friends. No other biography exists on the life of Constance Maynard.

4 *A*, I, 1, "1849–60," 1, written in 1915. The autobiography evinces two main themes: how her childhood shaped her emotional-intellectual life, and how her upbringing inspired her commitment to female educational reform. She divided her autobiography into Parts (I–VII), with consecutively-numbered chapters from start to finish. Her dating system and page numbering is confusing, however. A number of Parts also begin at page 1 again.

5 The middle class that emerged during eighteenth-century technological and industrial development comprised of the lower-middle, middle, and upper-middle class. Hereafter cited as middle class unless specifically referring to individuals or particular groups.

6 For Maynard's hindsight views on class, gender, and sexuality see *A*, I, 1, "Childhood 1849–1860," 1–12, written in January 1915. For more on the limitations of prescribed middle-class femininity see Deborah Gorham's classic, *The Victorian Girl and the Feminine Ideal* (Bloomington: Indian University Press, 1983); and for masculinity see John Tosh, *A Man's Place: Masculinity and the Middle-Class Home in Victorian England* (New Haven: Yale University Press, 1999). For discussion on the rise of the middle classes see Leonore Davidoff and Catherine Hall's groundbreaking *Family Fortunes: Men and Women of the English Middle Class 1780–1850* (Chicago: University of Chicago Press, 1991).

7 See *A*, I, 1, "Childhood 1849–60," 32, written in January 1915. For Victorian's first-hand accounts of masculinity, femininity, and sexuality see, for example, Frederick Saunders, *About Women, Love and Marriage* (London: Hodder, 1868), 162.

8 For good discussions on the difference between early- and mid-Victorian Evangelicalism see Boyd Hilton, *The Age of Atonement: The Influence of Evangelicalism on Social and Economic Thought, 1785–1865* (Oxford: Clarendon Press, 1988); and David Bebbington, *Evangelicalism in Modern Britain: A History from the 1730s to the 1980s* (Grand Rapids: Baker Books, 1988).

9 See *A*, I, II, "Childhood 1849–60," 3–28, written in January 1915. Maynard explained that most social equals were deemed worldly and "frivolous minded." In contrast, her green book of the time laments over her inability to gain the Holy Spirit in order to vanquish the devil. For example, see Constance Louisa Maynard, Green Book, 16 April 1868, 192, Special Collections, Courtesy of Queen Mary University of London Archives/ Constance Maynard/PP7/2, (hereafter cited as *GB* plus date and page numbers).

10 Firth, *Constance Louisa Maynard*, 81–6. For Girton, see Rita McWilliams-Tullberg, *Women at Cambridge: A Men's University of a Mixed Type* (London: Victor Gollancz, 1975), 5.

11 See *A*, III, 23, "My Years at Girton 1874," 280, written in July 1915. The new field of "Mental and Moral Sciences" that foregrounded what became "psychology" in the early 1900s did counter Maynard's atypical upbringing. However, the assumption that Victorians were less religious due to science is false (see, for example, Lance Butler, *Victorian Doubt: Literary and Cultural Discourses* [London: Harvester 1990], 60–90, who drew this

conclusion based upon the 1851 census). In *Religion and Political Culture in Britain and Ireland* (Cambridge: Cambridge University Press, 1996), David Hempton challenges Butler and others by pointing out that newspapers and church records implied increases in church attendance until 1901. This time frame correlates with Maynard's optimism about her ability to evangelize both her society and the world in 1901.

12 See, for example, Dinah Mulock Craik, *A Woman's Thoughts about Women* (London: Hurst and Blackett, 1858); and George Somes Layard's later biography, *Mrs Lynn Linton: Her Life, Letters, and Opinions* (London: Methuen, 1901), 42.

13 For examples of Maynard's sense of religious-professional leadership and her negotiations with her parents see, for example, *GB*, 25 July 1876, 82; and 9 August 1876, 95. For Maynard's hindsight observations see *A*, V, 35, "St. Leonards School 1880," 462, written in May 1924.

14 Although post-modernist approaches to women's history challenge separate spheres as an analytical framework, historians do not dismiss its prevalence in Victorian society (see Amanda Vickery, "Golden Age to Separate Spheres? A Review of the Categories and Chronologies of English Women's History," *Historical Journal* 36 (1993), 383–414). For examples of works that detail how women challenged domesticity see, for example, Susan Kingsley Kent, *Gender and Power in Britain, 1660–1990* (New York: Routledge, 1999); and James Hammerton, *Cruelty and Companionship: Conflict in Nineteenth-Century Married Life* (London: Routledge, 1992).

15 *A*, III, 11, "Waiting 1872," 338, written in May 1915.

16 See Davidoff and Hall, *Family Fortunes*, 175–80. It is also worth noting that the *Englishwoman's Review* from 1873 to 1899 carried notices regarding various non-domestic-related female occupations (Penny Kanner, *Women in English Social History 1800–1914: A Guide to Research, Vol. II* [London: Garland Publishing, 1988], 110–11). Nonetheless, in *Independent Women: Work and Community for Single Women 1850–1920* (London: Virago Press, 1985), 121–211, Martha Vicinus convincingly argues for the significance of women's demands for higher education. The establishment of women's colleges attached to universities not only altered society's views on women's professional capabilities, but paved the way towards suffrage, which was a key political reform for women.

17 See Firth, *Constance Louisa Maynard*, 43; and Maynard's comment in Maynard, *The Cultivation of the Intellect* (London: Westfield College, 1888, first edn. in 1881), 21, "Any cultivation carried out apart from religion is dangerous …"

18 Firth, *Constance Louisa Maynard*, 5. In her Epilogue, 337, Firth stated that had Maynard lived her youth with the knowledge of psychology, "her

suffering would have been decreased." I wonder if the language of psychology would have repressed Maynard's same-sex desires.

19 Martha Vicinus, "'One Life to Stand Beside Me': Emotional Conflicts in First-Generation College Women in England," *Feminist Studies* 8, 3 (1982), 603–27. See also her *Independent Women*, 9, 186–96; and "Distance and Desire: English Boarding-School Friendships," *Signs* 9 (1984), 600–22. For move on college raves, which were also referred to as "gonages" or "pashes" see, for example, Sara Burstall, *English High Schools for Girls* (London: Longmans, 1907); and Burstall, *Retrospect and Prospect: Sixty Years of Women's Education* (London: Longmans, Green, 1933).

20 Vicinus, "One Life," 608.

21 Martha Vicinus, *Intimate Friends: Women Who Loved Women, 1778–1928,* (Chicago: University of Chicago Press, 2004).

22 *GB*, 4 November 1883, 138.

23 See Maynard, "Life of Stephanë: 1888–1915," vols. I–VI, Special Collections, Courtesy of Queen Mary University of London Archives/ Constance Maynard/PP7/5, for an in-depth account of Maynard's thoughts on Effie (hereafter cited as *Stephanë* plus part and page numbers).

24 For sexology and its impact upon Britain see, for example, Lucy Bland and Laura Doan, eds., *Sexology in Culture: Labeling Bodies and Desires* (Chicago: University of Chicago Press, 1998). Deborah Cohler's *Citizen, Invert, Queer: Lesbianism and War in Early Twentieth-Century Britain* (Minneapolis: University of Minnesota Press, 2010) challenges the idea of sexology as solely responsible for changing views on sex. She examines how discourses of imperialist nationalism also shaped representations of lesbianism. For Freud's theories on psychosexual development see *Three Essays on the Theory of Sexuality*, trans. James Strachey (New York: Basic Books, 1962).

25 For more on Maynard's beliefs in a dichotomy between the earthly and spiritual see, for example, *GB*, 23 July 1871, 208; and 20 June 1873, 85. For more on early- and mid-Victorian Evangelicalism see Hilton, *Age of Atonement*; and Bebbington, *Evangelicalism in Modern Britain*.

26 See *A*, 1, 1, "Childhood 1849–60," 12–14, written in January 1915; and *A*, II, 4, "Adolescence 1865–66," 65, 69, written in January 1915. Maynard's reference to "Pilgrims and Strangers" meant shun of society and the world. For Edward Irving's theology see James Fleming, *The Life and Writings of the Rev. Edward Irving* (London: Marshall, 1823), 1–12.

27 *GB*, 16 April 1868, 192; and 1 May 1868, 24. Maynard's fears seemed to echo Irving's decree that only "the power of the Holy Spirit operating within oneself independently of 'good works'... could vanquish the devil" (Fleming, *Irving*, 13).

28 See *GB*, 24 January 1935, 55; 5 November 1876, 113; and 31 December 1876, 127.

29 Quote from Maynard taken from Firth, *Constance Louisa Maynard*, 1.

30 Carroll Smith-Rosenberg's groundbreaking "The Female World of Love and Ritual: Relations between Women in Nineteenth Century America," *Signs* 1, 1 (1975), 1–29, argues that Victorians permitted a wide latitude of sexual feelings between women that, in Smith-Rosenberg's view, is lost to us today. Lillian Faderman's *Surpassing the Love of Men: Romantic Friendship and Love between Women from Renaissance to the Present* (New York: William Morrow, 1981); and Adrienne Rich's, "Compulsory Heterosexuality and Lesbian Existence," *The Signs Reader: Women, Gender and Scholarship*, eds. Elizabeth Abel and Emily K. Abel (Chicago: University of Chicago Press, 1983), 139–68, offer counter arguments to Smith-Rosenberg's depiction of a serene and sensual female world.

31 See Lisa Moore, "'Something More Tender Still Than Friendship:' Romantic Friendship in Early-Nineteenth-Century England," *Feminist Studies* 18, 3 (1992), 499–521; and Terry Castle, *The Apparitional Lesbian: Female Homosexuality and Modern Culture*, (New York: Columbia University Press, 1993). Ruth Mazo Karras' "Prostitution and the Question of Sexual Identity in Medieval Europe," *Journal of Women's History* 11 (1999), 145, is among those works that challenge Foucault's act/experience split in *The History of Sexuality, Vol. 1* (New York: Pantheon Books, 1978), 43. Meanwhile, Judith Butler's queering of drag as a "dramatization of the signifying gestures through which gender itself was established" led her to powerfully argue that both sex and gender were social "performances" (*Gender Trouble* [New York: Routledge, 1990], vii).

32 Vicinus adopts the term "lesbian" to highlight Victorian female-female eroticism, and so criticizes Rupp's "vague" use of "same-sex sexuality" in Rupp, "Toward a Global History of Same-Sex Sexuality," *Journal of the History of Sexuality* 10, 2 (2001), 287–302 (see Vicinus, *Intimate Friends*, xxii). One could argue that Vicinus' ahistorical use of "lesbian" fixes past sexual expression and restricts it rather than opens it up as a category.

33 As Julian Carter asserts in "On Mother-Love: History, Queer Theory, and Nonlesbian Identity," *Journal of the History of Sexuality* 14, 1/2 (2005), 107–138, our problem with mother-daughter eroticism is presentist in that "in our own time, overt sexuality between mothers and daughters is virtually unimaginable" (131). See Anna Clark, "Twilight Moments," *Journal of the History of Sexuality* 14, 1/2 (2005), 141, 156, for her interesting adoption of the "twilight metaphor." See Sharon Marcus' *Between Women: Friendship, Desire, and Marriage in Victorian England* (Princeton: Princeton University Press, 2007), 56, particularly chapters 3 and 4, which reveals the ways in

which mainstream femininity was openly homoerotic and aggressive. In a somewhat different vein, such scholars of the emotions as Paul Griffiths point out that while cultural factors shape such emotions as desire and guilt, these very emotions can also become nuanced "irruptive patterns of motivation" (Griffiths, *What Emotions Really Are* [Chicago: University of Chicago Press, 1997], 15.)

34 See John Maynard, *Victorian Discourses on Sexuality and Religion* (Cambridge: Cambridge University Press, 1993), 36; and Michael Mason, *The Making of Victorian Sexual Attitudes* (New York: Oxford University Press, 1994), for more on Victorians' interconnection of sexual ethics and moral conditions. For a groundbreaking study on the topic see Steven Marcus, *The Other Victorians: A Study of Sex and Pornography in Mid-Nineteenth-Century England* (New York: Basic Books, 1966).

35 See Frederick S. Roden, *Same-Sex Desire in Victorian Religious Culture* (Basingstoke: Palgrave MacMillan, 2002), 3; David Hilliard, "Unenglish and Unmanly: Anglo-Catholicism and Homosexuality," *Victorian Studies* 25 (1982), 181; and Patrick R. O'Malley, "Epistemology of the Cloister: Victorian England's Queer Catholicism," *GLQ: A Journal of Lesbian and Gay Studies* 15, 4 (2009), 537. See also Eve Kosofsky Sedgwick's seminal *Epistemology of the Closet* (Berkeley and Los Angeles: University of California Press, 1990), which challenged Foucault's reductionist analysis of Victorian sexuality within the discourses of the Augustinian confessional in *History of Sexuality*, 63, 120.

36 For a good discussion of English women's roles in religion, see for example, Julie Melnyk, ed., *Women's Theology in Nineteenth-Century Britain: Transfiguring the Faith of Their Fathers* (New York: Garland, 1998).

37 See Callum Brown, *The Death of Christian Britain* (London: Routledge, 2001); Sue Morgan and Jacqueline deVries eds., *Women, Gender and Religious Cultures in Britain, 1800–1940* (New York; Routledge, 2010); Vicinus, *Intimate Friends*; Joy Dixon, *Divine Feminism: Theosophy and Feminism in England* (Baltimore: John Hopkins University Press, 2001); Lesley Hall, *Outspoken Women: An Anthology of Women's Writing on Sex, 1870–1969* (London: Routledge, 2005); and Sandra Peacock, *The Theological and Ethical Writings of Frances Power Cobbe, 1822–1904* (New York: Edwin Mellen Press, 2002).

38 Morgan makes good points regarding Maynard's understanding of her same-sex desire through faith in "The Word Made Flesh," *Women, Gender and Religious Cultures*, ed. Morgan and deVries, 175–6. However, her adoption of Vicinus' "definition of *lesbianism* as an 'emotional, erotically charged relationship between two women'" to discuss Maynard's

same-sex relationships is not, in my view, particularly useful for a queer approach (175, italics mine).

39 Roden, *Same-Sex Desire*, 43–81; and Ruth Vanita, *Sappho and the Virgin Mary: Same-Sex Love and the English Literary Imagination* (New York: Columbia University Press, 1996). See Yopie Prins, "Greek Maenads, Victorian Spinsters," in *Victorian Sexual Dissidence*, ed. Richard Dellamora, (Chicago: The University of Chicago Press, 1999), 43–81, for more on the ways that Victorian educational reformers (in this case Jane Ellen Harrison) adopted faith with other discourses to understand their same-sex desires.

40 Susan Warner's and Mathilde Blind's work has been acclaimed as typical of the domestic-pietistic strain in Victorian women's poetry writing. However, this interpretation has been challenged by such scholars as Jana L. Argersinger, "Family Embraces: The Unholy Kiss and Authorial Relations in *The Wide, Wide World*," *American Literature* 74, 2 (2002), 251–285; and James Diedrick, "'My Love is a Force that will Force you to Care': Subversive Sexuality in Mathilde Blind's Dramatic Monologues," *Victorian Poetry* 40, 4 (2002), 359–86. For Richard Dellamora's recent analyses of Radclyffe Hall's writing see *Radclyffe Hall: A Life in the Writing*, (Pennsylvania: University of Pennsylvania Press, 2011).

41 In *Disturbing Practices: History, Sexuality, and Women's Experiences of Modern War* (Chicago: University of Chicago Press, 2013), Laura Doan imagines a queer critical history that does not '"look for' evidence of queerness-as-being in texts, but deploy[s] queerness-as-method to 'look through' the archives to see what is unknown at the present moment … rather than provide answers about sexual identities we already know" (90). For example, Maynard's "marriage" to Lumsden, in relation to Marcus' and others views on the term "female marriage" shall be discussed in chapter 4.

42 See Roden, *Same-Sex Desire*; and Dellmora, *Radclyffe Hall*.

43 *GB*, 27 March 1872, 123.

44 See *GB*, 15 December 1879, 157; and *A*, V, 32, "St. Leonards School 1878," 155, written in March 1918. See also Vicinus, "One Life," 613.

45 *GB*, 17 December 1883, 69.

46 For examples of Maynard's justification of her earthly passions within the context of her faith see, for example, *GB*, 6 November 1882, 49; 12 June 1884, 134; 21 March 1886, 109; and 8 June 1901, 62.

47 See, for example, *GB*, 31 December 1901, 98, and compare with *A*, VII, 55, "Westfield 1897," 138, written in June 1927.

48 See, for example, *A*, VII, 44, "Westfield 1883," 3, written in May 1925; and *A*, VII, 53, "Westfield 1891," 286, written in May 1925.

49 Havelock Ellis, *Studies in the Psychology of Sex Volume,* vol. 2, *Sexual Inversion,* 3rd ed. (Philadelphia: F.A. Davies, 1915), 157–9. Here Ellis wrote about the case of Florrie, who "craved" punishment and made sure that she "got it." For more on Ellis' analysis of the relation between pain, sexuality, and gender see Ivan Crozier, "Philosophy in the English Boudoir: Havelock Ellis, Love and Pain, and Sexological Discourse in Algophobia," *Journal of the History of Sexuality* 13, 3 (2004), 275–305; and Alison Moore, "Rethinking Gendered Perversion and Degeneration in Visions of Sadism and Masochism, 1886–1930," *Journal of the History of Sexuality* 18, 1 (2009), 139–63. Meanwhile, in "The 'Singular Propensity' of Sensibility's Extremities: Female Same-Sex Desire and the Eroticization of Pain in Late-Eighteenth-Century British Culture," *GLQ: A Journal of Lesbian and Gay Studies* 9, 4 (2003), 47–98, Katherine Binhammer proposes that a queer approach to *pain,* rather than gender or sex, may well disclose a "diversity of textual representations of female same-sex desire" over time (490).

50 There are a number of historically-based works on this. See, for example, A. Butler's classic, *Butler's Lives of the Saints,* new rev. ed. Herbert Thurston and Donald Attwater, 4 vols. (reprinted New York: R.J. Kennedy and Sons, 1962); Foucault, *History of Sexuality*; Maynard, *Victorian Discourses on Sexuality and Religion,* 10–12, 25–30; Caroline Bynum Walker's, *Fragmentation and Redemption: Essays on Gender and the Human Body in Medieval Religion*; (Berkley: University of California Press, 1991; and Vern Bullough, Dwight Dixon, and Joan Dixon, "Sadism, Masochism and History, or when is Behaviour Sado-Masochistic?" in *Sexual Knowledge, Sexual Science,* ed. Roy Porter and Mikulas Teich (Cambridge: Cambridge University Press, 1994), 49. Most of these authors argue that Christology theology has led many to inculcate a variety of gender neutral sado-masochistic-like behaviours long before sexologists classified them.

51 See *GB,* 22 May 1905, 92. For more on Maynard's discussion of her behaviour see, for example, GB, 3 May 1883, 71; 23 April 1886, 133; 31 December 1901, 98; and *A,* VII, 56, "Westfield 1888," 232, written in September 1927. For discussion on religious despair see John Stachniewski, *The Prosecutory Imagination: English Puritanism and the Literature of Religious Despair* (Oxford: Oxford University Press, 1991), 50–61, which proposes that "the burden of religious despair" can be so extreme that it leads some individuals to commit suicide. See also Hilton, *Age of Atonement*; and Allan Berger, "Choosing to Suffer: Reflections on an Enigma," *Journal of Religion and Health* 42, 3 (2003), 251–5.

52 See Moore, "Rethinking Gendered Perversion," 139, for classification of the "female sadist" implied by the masochist scenario, which was a

pathology that has been less commonly observed by present day scholars. See also Crozier, "Havelock Ellis," 293.

53 *A*, VII, 44, "Westfield 1882," 3, written in August 1926.

54 See *A*, VII, 52, "Westfield 1886," 172–4, written in June 1927. Roy Porter and Lesley Hall are among those historians who argue that Freud was not regularly discussed in Britain beyond a few academic circles in comparison to Havelock Ellis (see *The Facts of Life: The Creation of Sexual Knowledge in Victorian Britain, 1650–1950* [New Haven: Yale University Press, 1995], 189). In contrast, Ellen Willis and Susan Kingsley Kent posit that by the early 1920s many individuals were adopting Freud's ideas to explain their conflicts over same-sex desires (see Willis, *No More Nice Girls* [Hanover: Wesleyan Press, 1992], 12–14; and Kingsley Kent, *Making Peace: The Reconstruction of Gender in Interwar Britain* [Princeton: Princeton University Press, 1993], 102–3). I propose that Maynard was likely among the few aware of the new psychoanalytical theories in the mid-1920s. Her green book suggests that her knowledge of psychoanalysis stemmed from conversations with Marion Wakefield, her former love, who had enrolled at Bedford College to study the brand new field of psychology at the University of London.

55 See *GB*, 24 May 1935, 55, which was written three days before Maynard's death. As mentioned, Maynard's behaviour shall not be classified in this study, but the present-day sensitive issue of harassment is worth mention, if only once. I turn the reader in particular to Jane Gallop's *Feminist Accused of Sexual Harassment* (Durham: Public Planet Books, 1997). Gallop's perhaps queer view of her intimacy with female students as part of a "wide range of sexual opportunities" (50) seems controversial by today's standards. Nonetheless, her attempt to reconcile academic commitment and sexual charge is not unlike that which Maynard describes in her green book. Clearly, both women's experience suggests the complexity surrounding the professor and student relationship.

56 Although some may argue that this study is not a biography, bringing an obscure woman to wider attention is one goal of feminist biography, and of women's history in general. For more on life writing see, for example, Susan Ware, "Writing Women's Lives: One Historians' Perspective," *Journal of Interdisciplinary History*, 40, 3 (2012), 416; Bella Brodzki and Celeste Schenck, *Life/Lines: Theorizing Women's Autobiography* (Oxford: Oxford University Press, 1988); and Susan Groag Bell and Marilyn Yalom, eds., *Revealing Lives: Autobiography, Biography and Gender* (Albany: New York Press, 1990). For more recent work on Maynard's life, see Pauline Phipps, "An Atonement for Ambition and Passion: The Experiences

of British Victorian Educational Pioneer, Constance Louisa Maynard 1849–1935," Ph.D. Diss., Carleton University, Ottawa, 2004; Phipps "Faith, Desire, and Sexual Identity: Constance Maynard's Atonement for Passion," *Journal of the History of Sexuality* 18, 2 (2009), 265–86; and Phipps, "Constance Maynard's Languages of Love," *Women's History Review,* forthcoming, Summer 2015. In *Evangelicalism and the Making of Same-Sex Desire: The Life and Writings of Constance Maynard (1849–1935),* Ph.D. Diss., The University of British Columbia, Vancouver, 2011, Naomi Lloyd develops some of the theological-secularist-sexual themes addressed in my Ph.D., but does not connect them to Maynard's powerful experiences as an educational pioneer.

57 Firth, *Constance Louisa Maynard,* 5.

58 She noted this at least twice (see *GB,* 3 June 1886, 312; and 17 November 1892, 317).

Chapter 1

1 Maynard transcribed her sonnet from her *GB,* 8 August 1905, 50, in her *A,* VII, 49, "Westfield 1885," 345, written in June 1925, to explain her conflict between earthly love and divine love.

2 *GB,* 7 January 1866, 18. See also Constance Louisa Maynard, "From Early Victorian Schoolroom to University: Some Personal Experiences," *Nineteenth Century* 76 (1914), 1060; and Firth, *Constance Louisa Maynard,* 43.

3 See *A,* I, 1, "Childhood 1849–60," 2, written in May 1915. As Maynard remarked here, "I would keep it [green book] strictly private."

4 Certainly, Maynard's autobiography suffers under her selection of diary entries and prioritization of life events, but it proffers more insight into her experience. An example can be found in her account of Wakefield's struggle with neurasthenia in *GB,* 17 April 1902, 114, and her later observations about Wakefield's "mental" condition in *A,* VII, 65, "Westfield 1902," 488, written June 1925.

5 Compare *D,* 19 February 1886, 98, with *GB,* 20 December 1885, 94. The woman Maynard was referring to here was Westfield College teacher, Frances (Ralf) Gray.

6 As noted in the Introduction, Vicinus' *Intimate Friends;* Morgan's and deVries' ed., *Women, Gender and Religious Cultures in Britain;* Joy Dixon's, *Divine Feminism;* and Roden's, *Same-Sex Desire,* are among the few recent studies that discuss women's faith and same-sex eroticism together.

7 See *A,* I, 1, "Childhood 1849–60," 4–10, written in January 1915. See also

Firth, *Constance Louisa Maynard*, 50–9; and Mary King, "Reminiscences of the Henry Maynard family, 1837–1875," 1–22, in Maynard, *A*, I, 1 (hereafter cited as King, *Reminiscences*, plus page numbers). The so-called middle classes forged the wool industry in the 1500s, and continued to rise each century thereafter. The particular configuration of the Victorian middle classes was shaped by technological and industrial innovations during the 1700s. Henry Maynard's earliest known ancestor was his grandfather, Thomas, who made money as a malt distiller and was buried in Edmonton in 1757. Henry continued to develop the family business overseas, which became a part of empire building (see Davidoff and Hall, *Family Fortunes*, for more on Victorian entrepreneurs and empire).

8 Louisa Hillyard was considered genteel through title rather than landed wealth. Her ancestors had fled the large family estates in Civray in 1865 and settled in England as Protestant refugees. The estates were inherited by other family members, who continuing Catholic, remained there until the mid-1700s (*A*, I, 1, "Childhood 1849–60," 7, written in January 1915; and Firth, *Constance Louisa Maynard*, 9, 21–38).

9 *A*, I, 1, "Childhood 1849–60," 9–11, written in January 1915. See also Firth, *Constance Louisa Maynard*, 15–21. The Maynards' move from a more modest three-storey terrace in London reflected the economic growth of the time. The middle class tended to believe that such entrepreneurs as Henry forged Britain's reputation as "banker and workshop" of the world. For more on attitudes of day see, for example, T.W. Heyck, *Transformation of Intellectual Life in Victorian England* (Chicago: Lyceum Books, 1982).

10 *A*, I, 1, "Childhood 1849–60," 5–6, written in January 1915. For genteel girls' upbringing see Gorham, *Victorian Girl*, 155.

11 *A*, I, 3, "Childhood 1849–60," 36, written in January 1915; and King, *Reminiscences*, 30–1.

12 *A*, I, 3, "Childhood 1849–60," 38, written in January 1915; and King, *Reminiscences*, 32.

13 See *A*, I, 3, "Childhood 1849–60," 40, written in January 1915; and Maynard, "Victorian Schoolroom," 1068–1070. Popular advice books, such as Hannah More's *Coelebs in Search of Wife* (1808), advocated women's subservience to men and her place in the home (Gorham, *Victorian Girl*, 3–43).

14 *A*, 1, 3, "Adolescence 1863–64," 41, written in February 1915. Belstead, located in Sussex, was favoured by Louisa Maynard because of "its genteel domesticity" run by founder Mrs Umphelby, fondly nicknamed "Mamie." For more on girls' private boarding schools see Joyce Senders Pederson's,

"Schoolmistresses and Headmistresses: Elites and Education in Nineteenth-Century England," *Journal of British Studies* 15 (1975), 137–43.

15 *A*, II, 8, "Young Womanhood 1871," 196, written in April 1915. Maynard compared her situation with that of Harry who, as eldest son, would inherit the family business and yet was reluctant to do so. Unfortunately, Harry's poor business skills later bankrupted the family.

16 *GB*, 1 January 1866, 1–2. Louisa Maynard gave each child a "new year motto" which, based upon atonement theological principles, they were expected to follow.

17 There is no evidence in any of Maynard's records to suggest that her father ever challenged her mother's religious views. Mary King concurs in *Reminiscences*, 5–6.

18 As mentioned earlier, Victorians' interest in science does not suggest their irreligiousness. The Maynards were among those who consulted Hugh Miller's Christian geology that "traced three divisions - 1st vegetative life; 2nd creeping things; and 3rd mammals, including man ... Such 'days' encompassed thousands of years." The Maynards had found some form of correlation to this belief in "Smyrna, Rev. 2.8" (*GB*, 5 July 1871, 197).

19 Cited in Hilton, *Age of Atonement*, 286, emphasis mine. Maurice was an Anglican theologian who taught at King's College, London, and then Cambridge. Known as the protagonist of Christian Socialism, Maurice argued that the Incarnation doctrine determined the divine redeemer who, according to God's plan, united humanity with God.

20 See *D*, 13 March 1871, 23; and 20 July 1871, 44. For more on how Evangelicalism shaped and was shaped by mid-Victorian culture see Bebbington, *Evangelicalism in Modern Britain*, 2–11, 75–105; and Hilton, *Age of Atonement*, 289–305.

21 *GB*, 15 December 1905, 73.

22 See *A*, I, 1, "Childhood 1849–60," 36, written in January 1915; and also Firth, *Constance Louisa Maynard*, 29.

23 *A*, I, 1, "Childhood 1849–60," 36, written in January 1915. See King, *Reminiscences*, 6, for more on Louisa's piety. Compare Constance's experiences with that of Frances Power Cobbe in Peacock, *Writing of Frances Power Cobbe*, 28–9. See also Brown's account of the ways that women's religiosity was privileged in the mid-1800s (*Death of Christian Britain*, 59). For early-Victorian Evangelicalism and the idea of suffering see Stachniecoski, *Prosecutory Imagination*, 54–60.

24 *GB*, 3 December 1869, 7. For more on societal response to Paley and Irving, see Hilton, *Age of Atonement*, 104–5, 170–7. Paley's *Evidences*, which focused on historical evidences for Christianity, was highly acclaimed and

a required reading for Cambridge undergraduates into the 1900s. In contrast, Irving's "On the Humanity of Christ" remained condemned for its reference to Christ's "human" failings.

25 Cited from Maurice's *Theological Essays*, 1853, in Hilton, *Age of Atonement*, 286. Maurice firmly believed in the Church of England as a national church, where all members of society should unite as one.

26 In her *A*, I, 3, "Childhood 1849–60," 36, written in January 1915, Maynard noted, "Mother dissuaded all expression of faith when we read from our Bible." A faith that elicited sentiment prevented one from seeking divine grace.

27 King, *Reminiscences*, 32.

28 *GB*, 16 April 1866, 192.

29 Maynard's beliefs on the divine body echoed Irving's decree in "Humanity of Christ," 433, "that, only martyrdom, leading to…'final perseverance,' could suffice to vanquish the devil." For more on Maynard's idea of the divine state, see *GB*, 1 May 1866, 24; and 30 November 1866, 21.

30 Compare Maynard's argument in *A*, I, 3, "Adolescence 1865–66," 41, written in January 1915, with her comment in *A*, II, 5, "Adolescence 1867–68," 97, written in February 1915.

31 See *GB*, 22 February 1867, 192; 20 November 1866, 45; 2 February 1867, 45; and 22 February 1867, 192.

32 See *GB*, 1 April 1867, 98; 2 May 1867, 112; and 12 June 1867, 120. Paley believed that man's superior nature brought humans closer to God (Bebbington, *Evangelicalism in Modern Britain*, 22–40).

33 See, for example, Roden, *Same-Sex Desire*; Hilliard, "Unenglish and Unmanly"; O'Malley, "Epistemology of the Cloister"; and Sedgwick, *Epistemology of the Closet*.

34 *A*, I, 2, "Adolescence 1865–66," 28, 60–2, written in February 1915; and III, 11, "My first term at Hitchin 1872," 374, written in December 1915. For more on the Victorians' imagined role of prophet, see Maynard, *Victorian Discourses on Sexuality and Religion*, 201–2; and Richard Swindburne, *The Existence of God* (Oxford: Clarendon Press, 1979). For Victorian women's erotic sense of self as a "Divine female," see Argensinger, "Unholy Kiss," 254–9; and Brown's idea of discursive Christianity in *Death of Christian Britain*, 58, which reveals how women reworked religious ideas to forge their own experiences.

35 Constance Louisa Maynard, Diary, 2 February 1871, 12, Special Collections, Courtesy of Queen Mary University of London Archives/ Constance Maynard/PP7/2, (hereafter cited as *D* plus date and page numbers).

36 *D*, March 1871, 23. For Maynard's "Cycling Tours," see, for example, 13 July 1887, 78. For her fight over installing light bulbs at Westfield, see *Minutes of Council*, 7 June 1898, 285, Special Collections, Courtesy of Queen Mary University of London Archives/Westfield/WFD, (hereafter cited as *Minutes*, plus date and page numbers).

37 See *A*, II, 8, "Young Womanhood 1871," 200, written in April 1915; II, 9, "Adolescence 1871," 236–42, written in 1917; and *D*, 28 October 1871, 183. Jebb chaperoned Constance and Gazy in London when they took drawing lessons between 1869 and 1871.

38 See Firth, *Constance Louisa Maynard*, 39. For exponents of Victorian middle-class masculinity see Tosh, *Man's Place*, 189.

39 The middle-class work ethic advocated that "national progress [was] the sum of uprightness, as national decay [pauperism] was of individual idleness, selfishness and vice." Of course, atonement thinking individuals considered soul saving more important than eliminating pauperism (David Newsome, The *Victorian World Picture: Perceptions and Introspection in an Age of Change* (New Brunswick: Rutgers University Press, 1997), 131–2.

40 *D*, 3 July 1871, 23. Constance saw far less of her father when she went to Girton. Henry thus turned to Gazy for companionship, particularly after his wife died.

41 For more on the Evangelical literature of the time see Brown, *Death of Christian Britain*, 22–5; and Hilton, *Age of Atonement*, 299–301.

42 *D*, 6 September 1872, 22. Father and daughter had visited Edward Irving's tomb in Glasgow cathedral, which was close to the Glasgow slums. For more on the miners, see *D*, 3 July 1871, 23. Henry's views on gender, class, and race was shaped by his faith and the Malthusian and Darwinist theories of the time (see Heyck, *Intellectual Life*, 121–33, for more on Victorian reaction to these theories).

43 See *D*, 28 January 1872, 20; and June 1872, 33. According to Constance, Harry was distressed after visiting a consumptive hospital. He chose to distance himself from his parents' faith to follow an Evangelicalism that was "celebratory of all life," and focussed on self-improvement.

44 For more on revivals see George A. Rawlyk and Mark A. Noll, eds., *Amazing Grace: Evangelicalism in Australia, Britain, Canada, and the United States*, (Montreal: McGill-Queens University Press, 1994), 179–82.

45 For Boxall, see *D*, 15 March 1871, 52. For Maynard's comments on the destitute prostitutes, see *D*, 6 January 1881, 78; and 12 February 1881, 85. For her views on her "common" fellow Girtonians see, for example,

GB, 14 May 1884, 247. For Effie, see *A* VII, 50, "1888," 167, written in May 1915.

46 *D*, 28 May 1898, 96. The Settlement House, named Southwark, was renovated and rented out to the poor as a means of improving their lives. Maynard's biased predictions did prove correct. Southwark fell into bankruptcy because the workers failed to pay their rent.

47 For more on Evangelicals interest in higher education see Bebbington, *Evangelicalism in Modern Britain*, 134.

48 The Bill is mentioned at least three times a week in the diary. See, for example, *D*, 4 March 1871, 6; 6 March 1871, 8; and 10 March 1871, 10. See also Maynard, "Victorian Schoolroom," 1060–73, for more discussion on her self-studies.

49 After educational reform for middle-class boys began in the 1830s, educational pioneers became keen to begin a similar movement for middle-class girls. Alice Zimmern's, *The Renaissance of Girls' Education in England: A Record of Fifty Years' Progress* (London: A. D. Innes, 1898,) is a good first-hand account of the development of girls' education.

50 *A*, III, 11, "My Girton Years 1872," 344, written in October 1915. See also Senders Pederson, "Schoolmistresses and Headmistresses," 148. St. Leonards was followed by Roedean School (1885) and Wycombe Abbey (1896).

51 Emily Davies, "Women in the Universities," in *Thoughts on Some Questions Relating to Women, 1860–1908* (Cambridge: Bowes and Bowes, 1910). In this paper Davies recounted the struggle that ventures like Bedford faced from powerful individuals, like journalist W.R. Greg who advocated that "women know their place" (Greg, *Literary and Social Judgments* [London: Trubner, 1868], 56).

52 See Maynard, "Early Victorian Schoolroom," 1065–9; and J.G. Fitch, "Women and the Universities," *Contemporary Review* 58 (1890), 333–54. The situation was similar at Oxford, with the first women's residences, Lady Margaret and Somerville Halls, not being built until 1879, and degrees not being granted until 1921.

53 In her *A*, I, 3, "Adolescence 1863–64," 47, written in February 1915, Maynard explained that she could not see Fanny for ten years because her mother disapproved of the romantic language in their letters to each other.

54 See Craik, *Thoughts about Women*; and Layard, *Mrs Lynn Linton*, 25–6, 42. William Rounsville Alger's, *The Friendships of Women*, 10th ed. (Boston: Roberts Brothers, 1882), is another account of the mores of Victorian female friendship.

55 Firth, *Constance Louisa Maynard*, 52, 82; and Vicinus, *Independent Women*, 35–6.
56 Green book quote taken from Firth, *Constance Louisa Maynard*, 70.
57 See, *GB*, 12 June 1873, 66.
58 See *GB*, 10 June 1866, 32; and 21 May 1868, 69. As to why Maynard did not see Dalrymple after Belstead remains unclear.
59 *GB*, 26 March 1869, 89.
60 *GB*, 12 October 1880, 55.
61 See *A*, VII, 44, "Westfield 1881," 302, written in May 1926. Kate Flint's use of the twilight metaphor to queer women's encounters with each other "on the fin de siècle street" helped in my analysis of Maynard's descriptions of her chance encounters with Dalrymple (Flint, "The 'hour of pink twilight': Lesbian Poetics and Queer Encounters on the Fin-de-siècle Street," *Victorian Studies* 51, 4 [2009], 690).
62 See *GB*, 26 March 1868, 60; and *A*, II, 7, "Adolescence 1869–70," 160, written in 1917. Apparently, Louisa's thought that George's wish to read the Bible to his sick villager friend Willy Bishop was "unworthy" was both class and faith-based.
63 For Maynard's feelings toward Hetty Lawrence and others see, for example, *GB*, 28 November 1869, 53; and 21 March 1870, 138.
64 *GB*, 4 November 1869, 275.
65 Quote taken from Firth, *Constance Louisa Maynard*, 27. In *Age of Atonement*, 286, Hilton explains that Irving viewed evil as an independent force that had even tempted Christ. The Maynards adopted this view, which could explain Constance's fear and torment as a young girl.
66 See Brown, *Death of Christian Britain*, 59–61; Davidoff and Hall, *Family Fortunes*; and Gorham, *Victorian Girl*.
67 *GB*, 26 March 1869; 98; and 4 July, 1869, 43.
68 *A*, I, 3, "Adolescence 1863–64," 59, written in February 1915.
69 *A*, II, 4, 8, "Young Womanhood 1871," 206–213, written in April 1915. See also Firth, *Constance Louisa Maynard*, 67–8.
70 In *Epistemology of the Closet*, 140, Kosofsky Sedgwick theorizes that Catholicism gave countless proto-gay individuals "the shock of men in dresses, of passionate theatre, [and] of introspective investment." See also Hilliard, "Unenglish and Unmanly." For changes in Evangelicalism, see Bebbington, *Evangelicalism in Modern Britain*, 14–17, and 148–9.
71 *GB*, 24 June 1868, 145.
72 *GB*, 27 August 1869, 102. As Irving cautioned, "Christ's 'sinful substance' was perfectly holy no doubt, but ... not inherently so. If it were not so,

the doctrine of Atonement would have been void and meaningless" (Bebbington, *Evangelicalism in Modern Britain*, 93.)

73 Stachniecoski, *Prosecutory Imagination*, 64.

74 See *A*, II, 4, "Adolescence 1865–66," 59, written in April 1925. See Bland and Doan eds., *Sexology in Culture*, 188–9, 192–3; and Moore, "Rethinking Gendered Perversion," 138, for more on turn of the century sexologists' debate on female masochism. For Freud's definition of female masochism, see Sigmund Freud, "The Economic Problem of Masochism" (1924), in *The Standard Edition of the Complete Psychological Works of Sigmund Freud*, ed. and trans. James Strachey, 24 vols (London: Hogarth, 1953–74), 19, 159–70. Early twentieth century psychoanalytic writers, such as Helene Deutsch, elaborated on Freud's assumption about the naturalness of female masochism (Helene Deutsch, "Feminine' Masochism and Its Relation to Frigidity," *International Journal of Psycho-Analysis* 11 [1930], 48–61).

75 In Dixon's, Morgan's, and deVries' view, scholars' tendency to conflate both women and the spiritual with the private is partly the legacy of the early-Victorian Evangelical doctrine of separate spheres, which obscures the ways in which women of faith transgressed cultural boundaries (Dixon, *Divine Feminism*, 7; Morgan, "The Word Made Flesh"; and Jacqueline deVries, "Feminism, History and Religious Cultures," in *Women, Gender and Religious Cultures*, ed. Morgan and deVries, 158–210).

76 For green book entries on Maynard's mission to teach college girls to love God see, for example, 17 October 1882, 192; 26 September 1899, 156; and 8 May 1905, 200.

77 Maynard struggled to describe her physical interactions with young Westfield student Marion Wakefield (*A*, VII, 59, "May Term 1897," 411, written in April 1928). For more on Maynard's struggle see, for example, *A*, VII, 49, "Westfield 1886," 133–9, written in May 1926. As Clark suggests, we might conceptualize a past individual's struggle with fleeting sense(s) of "wrong" same-sex sexual feelings as "barely visible" perhaps only half understood "twilight moments" (see "Twilight Moments," 141).

78 Present day scholars tend to classify sadomasochism as behaviour(s) that encompass various dominant-submissive role-playing, from playful finger biting to more painful forms of sexual dominance-submission (see, for example, Wurmster's, *The Mask of Shame*, 45–6; and Melvin Lansky and Andrew Morrison, eds., *The Widening Scope of Shame* [Hillsdale: The Analytic Press], 1997). A queer approach to Maynard's language(s) of love allows us a more fluid space to imagine her particular behaviours and/or self-identities as a pious, rather repressed lonely educational reformer.

79 *A*, VII, 62, "Long Vacation 1899," 448, written in June 1926. For more on Maynard's ongoing struggle, see Phipps, Ph.D. Diss., 300–48, 410–70; and "Faith, Desire, and Sexual Identity," 265–86.

Chapter 2

1 *A*, II, 9, "Year of Crisis, Restraint and Liberty 1872," 36–7, written in January 1915. Maynard transcribed Tennyson's poem. "Oh love! Oh fire! Once he drew/In one long kiss my whole soul through/My lips, as sunlight drinketh dew."
2 *A*, I, 2, "Adolescence 1861–62," 40, written in January 1915. For an interesting comparison of Maynard's experiences with that of other Victorian girls see, for example, Susan Warner, *The Wide, Wide World* (1850; reprint New York: Feminist Press, 1987), 32–6. For norms on femininity and sexuality see Gorham, *Victorian Girl*, 54–5, 91–6, 160. For prescribed emotional behaviour see Karen Lystra, *Searching the Heart* (Oxford: Oxford University Press, 1989); and Peter Stearns' "Girls, Boys, and Emotions: Redefinitions and Historical Change," *Journal of American History* 22 (1993), 43–5.
3 *A*, II, 4, "Adolescence 1865–66," 56, written in January 1915. In *City of Dreadful Delight*, 93, Walkowitz notes that such movements as "social purity" challenged the double standard of sexual morality by targeting the promiscuity of bachelors. For more on masculinity and accompanying norms, see Tosh, *A Man's Place*.
4 *GB*, 19 February, 1869, 107.
5 Compare *GB*, 7 July 1868, 159; 21 February 1869, 109; and 12 March 1869, 134, with *A*, II, 6, "Adolescence 1868," 130, written in February 1915. For more on the idea of religious despair see, for example, Stachniewski, *Prosecutory Imagination*, 50–61, which proposes that early-Victorian Evangelicalism was Puritan-like in its decree that the Christian could never "suffer enough" for human carnality. Maynard's cousin, Mary King, claimed that Louisa Maynard's Huguenot-based faith did reflect Puritan ideals (King, *Reminiscences*, 5).
6 See *A*, II, 6, "Waiting 1869," 139, written in February 1915; and Firth, *Constance Louisa Maynard*, 63. According to Maynard, neither doctor was attractive or approachable.
7 *GB*, 17 August 1869, 91–103. In this lengthy entry describing her conflicting feelings about Collison, Maynard explained that her father had just "put aside £20,000 for each daughter."
8 Compare *GB*, 13 April 1869, 170; and 15 July 1870, 219, with *A*, II, 9, "Year of Crisis, Restraint and Liberty 1872," 195, written in April 1915.

Maynard's challenging of ideas about female desire can be loosely compared with works by such female Victorian writers as Christina Rossetti and Mathilde Blind (see Roden, *Same-Sex Desire,* 38–40; and Diedrick, "My Love is a Force," 361–2).

9 *A*, II, 9, "Year of Crisis, Restraint and Liberty 1872," 238–40, written in April 1915.

10 *GB*, 9 January 1872, 40.

11 See, for example, *GB*, 28 February 1872, 55; 6 April 1872, 63; and 3 March 1872, 67.

12 In her *GB*, 6 March 1872, 121, Maynard noted her delight when Fanny insisted on buying her a more fashionable dress of "thin book-muslin with narrow strips of embroidery and a white waist band." The dress was apparently worn "at every festivity after that."

13 *GB*, 14 April 1872, 133.

14 *A*, II, 9, "Year of Crisis, Restraint and Liberty 1872," 259, written in May 1915.

15 *GB*, 12 March 1872, 109.

16 See GB, 21 April 1872, 121; and A, II, 9, "Year of Crisis, Restraint and Liberty 1872," 258, written in May 1915.

17 See *GB*, 18 February 1872, 123; and 27 March 1872, 124. We could compare Campbell's views on "greatness" and belief with the poetry of Arthur Hugh Clough, for example, which questioned religious dogma and the belief system that it set in place (see Maynard, *Victorian Discourses on Sexuality and Religion*, 39–84).

18 See *GB*, 27 March 1872, 124; and 18 February 1872, 122. It seems that Campbell adopted the more worldly mid-century incarnational-based beliefs to challenge Maynard's atonement theology (see Hempton, *Religion and Political Culture* for more on faith, secularism, and masculinity).

19 See *GB*, 9 March 1872, 121. Advice literature of the time described how a woman fell in love with a man's "moral wisdom." The man, in turn, was drawn to a woman's "loving submissive nature" (Stearns, "Girls, Boys, and Emotions," 33). For Maynard's hindsight observations see *GB*, 9 March 1914, 236. She told the reader that Fanny was "faithful" as was Lewis, since he resisted having affairs. She then criticized Fanny's disinterest in Lewis' intellectual needs, which was not entirely true since Fanny did support higher learning for women.

20 *GB*, 27 March 1872, 123. Campbell told Maynard that he been "very much in love with" a male student named Herbert. There is no other information about Herbert in her green book or diary.

21 See *GB*, 29 March 1872, 128; and 28 April 1872, 136. In her *A*, II, 9, "Year of Crisis, Restraint and Liberty 1872," 275–81, written in April 1915, Maynard

described another moment when they were alone on the beach. Campbell had asked her "to go to sleep while he watched." She had complied, but was unprepared for his look of "deep lingering attention" when she opened them again.

22 See Saunders, *Women, Love and Marriage*, 162. See also Lystra, *Searching the Heart*, 60; and Tosh, *A Man's Place*, 70–7.

23 *GB*, 6 April 1872, 136.

24 See *GB*, 6 April 1872, 136; and *A*, II, 9, "Year of Crisis, Restraint and Liberty 1872," 286, written in May 1915.

25 See *GB*, 28 March 1872, 126; and 29 March 1872, 128. See also *A*, II, 9, "Year of Crisis, Restraint and Liberty 1872," 275, written in April 1915. For more on the ways that religion reinforced Victorian masculine power and hetero-and same-sex desire see Maynard, *Victorian Discourses on Sexuality and Religion*, 80–100; Roden, *Same-Sex Desire*, 12–30; and Donald Hall, *Muscular Christianity: Embodying the Victorian Age* (Cambridge: Cambridge University Press), 1994.

26 *GB*, 28 April 1872, 133.

27 *GB*, 28 April 1872, 132. In fact, in both green and diary Maynard fretted over her sinful emotions. For example, in her *D*, 5 May 1872, 134, she exclaimed, "Oh! Wash my feet from the sin of this day and keep me Thine."

28 See *GB*, 17 May 1872, 159. For more on the religious eroticism of Victorian male poetry and sonnets see, for example Hall, *Muscular Christianity*, 40–60; and Argensinger, "Family Embraces," 251, 255–8.

29 See *GB*, 18 August 1872, 195; and *A*, 1, 2, "Adolescence 1861–62," 35, written in January 1915.

30 Firth, *Constance Louisa Maynard*, 102–3. As noted in chapter 1, pioneering college women could not "take the degree" in England at this time even though they sat the same final examination that male undergraduates took to attain the degree.

31 Compare Constance Maynard, "My College Days," *The Girton Review* (1926), 7–12 with *GB*, 2 June 1872, 161. For her hindsight observations see *A*, I, 3, "Childhood 1849–60," 36, written in January 1915.

32 See *GB*, 10 May 1872, 136. Henry Maudsley's, "Sex in Mind and Education," *Fortnightly Review* 21 (1874), 466–83, was among those that warned society of the dangers of cerebral activity for women's health.

33 Maynard's entries about the examinations reflected her gendered education. She thoroughly "enjoyed Scripture, History, English and Drawing, but only just survived the dreaded geography and arithmetic." Euclid, she noted, "would have been perfect if only [she] had not had to begin again!"

(see *D*, 22 June 1872, 112–16; and *GB*, 10 June 1872, 165–6, for comments on the pressure that she felt as a Victorian woman).

34 Compare *D*, 26 June 1872, 111, with *A*, II, 10, "Year of Crisis, Restraint and Liberty, 1872," 300–10, written in July 1915. See also Lynne Walker's, "Vistas of Pleasure: Women Consumers of Urban Space in the West End of London 1860–1900," in *Women in the Victorian Art World*, ed., Clarissa Campbell Orr (Manchester: Manchester University Press, 1996), 70–85, for a good discussion on Victorian women's traversing of new public spaces.

35 *D*, 29 June 1872, 116. Her score of 78% in Scripture, 73% in History, 65% in Drawing, 65% in Composition, 57% in Geometry, 50% in Arithmetic, 46% in Greek, 46% in Geography, and 28% in Grammar, placed her in fifth place among the ten candidates.

36 It seems that Gazy also fell for Lewis' ploys and the secular atmosphere at The Scores. In her *GB*, 16 February 1873, 210, Constance perhaps jealously remarked, "Gazy is *still* reacting to her visit to St. Andrews. She *says* that she misses Lewis and all else! *I* cannot help her with this, only God can."

37 *GB*, 2 July 1872, 181.

38 *GB*, 4 July 1872, 183.

39 *GB*, 12 August 1872, 195.

40 *GB*, 14 August 1872, 198.

41 *GB*, 7 July 1872, 186.

42 *A*, II, 9, "Year of Crisis, Restraint and Liberty 1872," 181, written in March 1915.

43 Compare *A*, II, 10, "Year of Crisis, Restraint and Liberty 1872," 286, written in June 1915, with *GB*, 9 July 1872, 287.

44 *GB*, 30 October 1908, 23. For a similar comment, see 9 March 1914, 217.

Chapter 3

1 *A*, II, 10, "Hitchin 1872," 295–300, written in October 1915. Maynard recalled that Hitchin (formally Benslow House) looked like a "country home more than a college." Inside was tiny and dreary. The library was also the lecture room and the common room. The dining room, with its "barred windows and dank walls," served "repellent food." The dead pig that she took to college was a sewn up sacking containing such items for her rooms as cushions and curtains.

2 Vicinus, "One Life," 603–27. See also her *Independent Women*, 9, 186–96; and "Distance and Desire" 600–22. For move on raves see, for example, Burstall, *High Schools for Girls*; and *Retrospect and Prospect*.

3 See Carter, "Mother-Love"; Marcus, *Between Women*; and Flint, "'Hour of Pink Twilight.'" For more on the fluidity and malleability of identity formation, see Butler's groundbreaking *Gender Trouble*; and Rupp, "Global History of Same-Sex Sexuality."

4 See Nancy Partner's "No Sex, No Gender," *Speculum* (1993), 436–42; and Diana Fuss' *Identification Papers* (New York: Routledge, 1995), which explore the idea that identification cannot be securely distinguished from innate desire. For more on ideas about irruptive patterns of emotive states see, for example, Griffiths, *What Emotions Really Are*, 15.

5 The reformation of middle-class boys' public schools flourished after the introduction of examinations in the 1850s. Meanwhile, the nondenominational University College London offered a curriculum far broader than that of Oxbridge, and thus opened up new career opportunities to men from the middle classes (Heyck, *Transformation of Intellectual Life*, 62, 75).

6 Although Bedford struggled, it was the first women's college to be admitted as a School of the University of London in 1900. Notting Hill, London, was one example of the new type of girls' high schools founded by the Girls' Public Day School Company to establish "forward thinking girls' schools" across England (Senders Pederson, "Schoolmistresses and Headmistresses," 148).

7 See Davies, "Proposed College" in *Thoughts*, 102–5. As Vicinus notes in *Independent Women*, 121–211, over 240,000 women had entered such professions as medicine by the end of the century.

8 Davies wished Hitchin to stand distinct from Newnham in its claim as an attachment to the university, but she faced criticism. While *The Times* asked society "to give [Hitchin]...some serious consideration," the *Athenaeum* noted parents' "horror" over the idea of examinations for their daughters ("Instruction Relating to Girls," in *Thoughts*, 60–3). As McWilliams-Tullberg notes, even though Hitchin lay outside Cambridge, the Cambridge community was more suspicious of Hitchin than Newnham since it had a reputation as a women's rights foundation (*Women at Cambridge*, 68).

9 The other three pioneering students were Emily Townsend, Isabel Gibson, and Anna Lloyd. In "A Girtonian of the 1870s," *Girton Review*, May 1925, 3, Emily Townsend, nee Gibson, recalled their efforts to rebel: "We refused to all face Miss Davies [to eat] as we could not have good conversation in a row." Playing charades meanwhile gave them opportunities "to poke fun" at gender hierarchy. Some dressed as men were berated by "savage looking women," or were "besieged to sign the paper on Women's Rights" (see *D*, 26 October 1872, 53; 11 November 1872, 6; and 20 June 1873, 85–7).

10 Louisa Lumsden, *Yellow Leaves: Memories of a Long Life* (Edinburgh: William Blackwood, 1933), 1–15, 21–7. The pioneers felt disadvantaged by their poor education in the Classics, in comparison to male students, and because lectures were hurried due to Professors' commitments at Cambridge. Pioneer Anna Lloyd wrote that she, alongside pioneers Townsend and Gibson, left before their Tripos due to fatigue and anxiety. Girton's first Mistresses, Mrs Manning (1869–70) and Miss Austin (1870–71), faced similar difficulties (*A Memoir: With Extracts from her Letters*, [London: Cayme Press, 1928], 68–72). For more about Hitchin/Girton see Barbara Stephen, *Girton College 1869–1932* (Cambridge: Cambridge University Press, 1933).

11 Compare *D*, 28 October 1872, 56–9, with *A*, III, 11, "My Years at Girton 1872," 346, written in October 1915. However, Maynard's diary depicted her grim relegation to the "iron room," a shed-like unheated building located on the grounds. Hitchin only accommodated five students, and five were already living in nearby rented cottages.

12 See *GB*, 20 October 1872, 255, and 23 December 1872, 260.

13 *D*, 18 January 1873, 78. Sarah Woodhead was "the first out," with her Mathematical Tripos in 1873, followed later that year by Cook and Lumsden. As Maynard exclaimed in her *A*, III, 11, "My Years at Girton 1872," 392, written in November 1915, "These were special times when a new form of collective conscious left us shouting to be heard!"

14 Compare, for example, *GB*, 16 March 1874, 46; 5 February 1875, 88; and 6 June 1875, 150, with *D*, 23 October 1874, 99; and 17 May 1875, 593.

15 Bebbington, *Evangelicalism in Modern Britain*, 134–40; and Doreen M. Rosman, *Evangelicals and Culture* (London: Croon Helm, 1984). One only needs to glance through Maynard's *A*, I, chapters 1, 2 and 3, 2–97, to find references to faith and discussion on theology.

16 *A*, III, 11, "My Years at Girton 1872," 355, written in October 1915.

17 See *GB*, 22 February 1867, 192; and 27 October 1872, 240. In her *A*, III, 11, "My Years at Girton 1872," 360, written in October 1915, Maynard wrote, "I was disarmed time and again" by secularist arguments. Although Maynard could not relinquish atonement thinking, she was not alone in such belief. For example, Peacock posits that while Frances Power Cobbe often denounced her Evangelical upbringing on the Atonement as "the product of primitive thinking," she never strayed far from it (*Writings of Frances Power Cobbe, 1822–1904*, 80, 268).

18 See *D*, 7 December 1873, 180; *GB*, 22 June 1874, 60; Maynard, *Between College Terms* (London: James Nisbet, 1910), 31; and McWilliams-Tulberg, *Women At Cambridge*, 132–42.

19 As noted in chapter 2, Maynard challenged Lewis Campbell's assertion that the will gave one access to knowledge, since she believed only God could do this. Campbell's notion of spirit-faith-intellect reflected the concepts taught at universities and colleges, as Maynard herself was discovering (see Newsome, *Victorian World Picture*; and Hempton, *Religion and Political Culture*).

20 See *D*, 13 October 1874, 67; 20 May 1875, 78; and 20 February 1874, 54. Mill's influence seemed clear in Maynard's goals for Divinity: to incorporate critical thinking in Biblical teaching. Kant's unknowable God, in turn, confirmed her belief that only God gave one understanding. For more on Mill, Kant, and Coleridge, see Heyck, *Transformation of Intellectual Life*, 190–5.

21 See *GB*, 15 May 1873, 74; 25 May 1873, 424; and *A*, III, 12, "My Years at Girton 1873," 386, 423, written in December 1915, for more on their discussions about religion. Lumsden apparently told Maynard that she had been brought up on Scottish Calvinism and had eventually rebelled against it.

22 See, for example, *GB*, 27 May 1873, 425; 7 June 1873, 81; and 12 June 1873, 90. For more on their rave, see Vicinus', "'One Life,'" 603–27; *Independent Women*, 9, 186–96; and for the term Madonna, see *Intimate Friends*, 86.

23 See *D*, 4 June 1871, 84. For Maynard's discussion on evolution with the Cambridge minister see *GB*, 20 June 1873, 85; and 10 October 1873, 145.

24 See *A*, III, 12, "My Years at Girton 1873," 447, written in January 1916. Maynard's diary meanwhile symbolized her new worldly interests: "I wear my hair in the 'modern' style, like L does" (*D*, 18 June 1873, 88; and 21 July, 96). There is no mention of Louisa Maynard's disapproval of Constance's engagement in fashion, but Constance did note her discomfort over Gazy's comment, "I *might* have had all this [Girton] too, you know" (27 June 1873, 69).

25 *A*, III, 19, "My Years at Girton 1874," 748–9, 751, written in March 1916. See also Firth, *Constance Louisa Maynard*, 118.

26 See *GB*, 17 October 1873, 50; and McWilliams-Tulberg, *Women At Cambridge*, 94–7.

27 For more on Maynard's and Lumsden's husband-wife role-playing see *A*, III, 12, "My Years at Girton 1873," 428, written in January 1916; and Vicinus's *Independent Women*, 291, and "One Life," 610–15.

28 See *D*, 30 December 1873, 56; 16 March 1873, 75; 7 June 1873, 81; and *A*, III, "5, Easter Vacation 1873," 545–52, written in January 1916. Bentham believed that the moral worth of action was solely determined by its contribution to overall utility and happiness. As Newsome asks in

Victorian World, 62, "Could *any* Christian view the menacing influence of Utilitarianism with equanimity?" (emphasis mine).

29 See *D*, 12 December 1873, 71; and 7 June 1874, 28.

30 See Laura Mayhall, "Did the Victorians Accept Female Marriage?" *Victorian Studies* 50, 1 (2007), 79. Perhaps Marcus' analysis on the affinity between mainstream female-female longing, submission, and control seems farfetched, yet it sheds insight into the more atypical intimacy and power relations that existed between such college women as Maynard and Lumsden (Marcus, *Between Women*, 150, 152–9). Theodora Jankowski's approach to female power in *Pure Resistance: Queer Virginity in Early Modern English Drama* (Philadelphia: University of Pennsylvania Press, 2000) is also worthy of note. Jankowski proposes that during periods when gender binaries are extreme, "power positions occupied by members of the traditional female gender…must be regarded as queer" (34).

31 See *A*, II, 4, 8, "Young Womanhood 1871," 206–13, written in April 1915; *GB*, 14 December 1873, 180; and 7 June 1874, 81. For more on Victorian Evangelical parents' faith-based need to break their children's will, see Bebbington, *Evangelicalism in Modern Britain*, 14–17 148–9; and Stachniecoski, *Prosecutory Imagination*, 64. Meanwhile, in *Between Women*, 160, Marcus relates Victorian tales about dolls to Evangelical notions of suffering and redemption that were enforced by adult authority figures like parents.

32 See *A*, III, 19, 16 "My Girton Years 1874," 773, written in April 1916; *GB*, 8 February 1874, 205–7; and 15 November 1874, 159.

33 Dove was hired to teach mathematics and physiology half days (*GB*, 9 November 1874, 150; 27 November 1874, 164). Maynard noted that Davies sent her "to Belstead each summer" to promote Girton (*A*, III, 15, 16 "My Girton Years 1874," 542, written in February 1916).

34 *D*, 2 November 1873, 161. She never ceased to think that the agnostic Lumsden viewed her as intellectually inferior to Borchhardt. This caused a deep rift between them.

35 See *GB*, 5 November 1874, 265; and 2 March 1875, 278. The original Bible study group consisted of Elizabeth Welsh, Elizabeth Baker, and Mary Kingsland. When her study group began, Maynard noted, "I would give *anything* to be waiting for L, and actually it *must* be so before I leave" (23 October 1873, 37). Lumsden, however, never attended the meetings.

36 See *A*, III, 16, "My Girton Years 1874," 577–8, written in February 1916. Kingsland apparently read Maynard this excerpt from her green book. For more on the religious climate of the time see, for example, Bebbington, *Evangelicalism in Modern Britain*, 143–7.

37 See *GB*, 7 March 1874, 90, for Maynard's thoughts about Mantle and Paley's views on pleasure. Maynard had gleaned this insight from her mechanics class – the idea that "perpetual motion indicated fleeting, 'unknowable' knowledge" (*D*, 28 May 1874, 78).

38 See *GB*, 26 April 1874, 200; and 10 May 1874, 245.

39 See *GB*, 28 May 1884, 260; and 13 June 1884, 288. Maynard did not elaborate, but Mantle, it seems, spoke openly about sex, which would counter Maynard's and other women's upbringing. We gather through Maynard how the model for mother-daughter intimacy (and indeed female-female intimacy itself) could evolve through raves, and can compare this to Carter's "On Mother-Love," or Lillian Wald's, "Smashing: Women's Relationships Before the Fall," *Chrysalis* 8 (1979), 17–27. For erotic impulses see Partner, "No Sex, No Gender, 436–42; and Fuss, *Identification Papers*.

40 *GB*, 14 May 1884, 247.

41 *GB*, 25 October 1874, 762. In her *A*, III, 12, 16 "My Girton Years 1873," 438, written in January 1916, Maynard explained that Lumsden was furious because the committee had not told her, and had also kept her waiting over an hour. In *Yellow Leaves*, Lumsden downplayed her behaviour: "I confess that the two years of my tutorship were not happy ... The Girton committee treated me as if I was a mere stranger" (57); and regarding the rescheduled ceremony, "I was too deeply hurt to take any notice of the second invitation" (59).

42 See, for example, *D*, 29 November 1874, 90. Here Maynard wrote, "There was a flu outbreak and L was up most nights for a week." In her *GB*, 20 November 1874, 66, she noted that Mary Kingsland "felt miserable having to write 'Perfect rubbish!' for Euclid, which came from the mouth of her pupil [Elizabeth Burgess]." See also McWilliams-Tullberg, *Women At Cambridge*, 65–7, for more on the trials of early educational pioneers.

43 Quote from Lumsden taken from M.C. Bradbrook, *That Infidel Place*, (London: Chatto and Windus, 1969), 31. Compare Maynard's *GB*, 25 March 1875, 47, with *A*, III, 20, "My Girton Years 1875," 478, written in February 1916. Davies offered Lumsden's post to promising Girton student Elizabeth Welsh, who declined out of courtesy to Lumsden. Lumsden was so incensed by Davies' lack of decorum that she felt forced to officially resign.

44 In her *GB*, 25 March 1875, 47, 57, Maynard exclaimed, "We [Maynard, Moody, and Sankey] both have the same aim, and we both have tools from the same Bible." In "Family Embraces," 255–6, Argensinger proposes that this Evangelical masculine prototype was a proponent of the revivalist movement. For more on women's view of religious agency see, for

example, Warner, *Wide, Wide World*, 352; Susan Warner, quoted in Anna Warner, *Susan Warner*, 275 (letter of 18 April 1848) and 499; and Douglas, *Feminization of American Culture*, 18.

45 Bernard, appointed as Mistress in 1874, was condemned for her passive feminism (Vicinus, *Independent Women*, 134–5). For Maynard's organizing of sports, see *GB*, 25 October 1875, 85; and *D*, 6 June 1873, 46. Rain and mud often prevented outside games, but when they could play on the new lawn, male undergraduates pestered them. In 1874, they erected an old black barn until it collapsed in 1875 (Kathleen McCrone, *Playing the Game: Sport and the Physical Emancipation of English Women, 1870–1914* [Lexington: University Press of Kentucky, 1988], 25–34).

46 For more on free-thought see, for example, Laura Schwartz, "The Bible and the Cause: Freethinking Feminists vs. Christianity, England 1870–1900," *Women: A Cultural Review*, 3 (2010), 266–71. For more on Muller, see Dixon, *Divine Feminism*, 173–5. For entries about Maynard's egotistic behaviour, see *GB*, 31 March 1875, 140.

47 Compare *GB*, 31 May 1875, 160, with *A*, III, 20, "My Girton Years 1875," 610, written in June 1916. In her *A*, Maynard asserted that the free-thought would try and turn her little flock from religion through Bible criticism.

48 *GB*, 6 June 1875, 176. For more on the general decline in preaching on hell, see Bebbington, *Evangelicalism in Modern Britain*, 144–7. Perhaps Maynard's discomfort over the free-thought was based upon her sense of their ability to challenge faith. According to Schwartz in "The Bible and the Cause," freethinking feminist's helped to shape modern definitions of secularism.

49 Compare *GB*, 14 June 1875, 182, with *A*, III, 20, "My Girton Years 1875," 615–17, written in April 1916. In her *A*, she criticized her little flock for making "mistakes" that had created "superciliousness" amongst the free-thought towards "the weakest" flock members. Her *GB* meanwhile noted her jealous, grudging admiration of Borchhardt.

50 In the spring of 1874, and 1875, Sidgwick not only asked her to rewrite her essays on Kant and then Locke because of the "inaccuracies" in her arguments, but had declared her analysis on Cicero "unintelligent" (see *D*, 4 April 1874, 69; and 18 May 1875, 70).

51 See *A*, III, 25, "My Last Term, 1875," 758–60, written in July 1916. The Tripos began on 29 November. Maynard placed slightly above Mary Kennedy, the first from Newnham to sit the Tripos. Maynard's concerns about hysteria had some validity. As Joan Brumberg notes in *Fasting Girls: The Emergence of Anorexia Nervosa as a Modern Disease* (Cambridge: Harvard University Press, 1988), 76, physicians were beginning to propose that hysteria "created senseless delusion in women" that overused their brain.

52 In *Constance Louisa Maynard*, 122, Firth argued that Maynard's upbringing on seeking and accepting Truth led her to "learn knowledge without analysis." Firth was perhaps swayed by Maynard's hindsight deprecation of her talents (see *A*, III, 19, "My Girton Years 1875," 769, written in July 1916). Yet in 1875, Maynard recognized Girton's limitations as a pioneering college (see, for example, *GB*, 12 December 1875, 99). See also Williams-Tullberg, *Women At Cambridge*, 72, on the difficulties that early-educational pioneers faced.

53 See *GB*, 8 November 1874, 78; 12 May 1875, 151; and *A*, III, 15, "My Girton Years 1874," 501, written in March 1916.

54 *GB*, 24 October 1875, 138.

55 *GB*, 19 September 1875, 98. See in particular Irving's "On the Humanity of Christ," 421, which assures the Christian that Christ's Crucifixion proves the vital importance of "the doctrines of atonement, regeneration and redemption" for personal salvation.

56 See GB, 22 September 1875, 100. Maynard justified her treatment of Mantle through class and faith: "I feel the difference in our position too strongly, to admit any close tie; even spiritually I have treated her with an indulgence." For Maynard's change of heart, see 17 October 1875, 128; and 29 December 1875, 198.

57 Compare *A*, III, 25, "My Last Term, 1875," 763, written in July 1919, with *A*, III, VII, 52, "Westfield 1886," 172–3, written in July 1926.

58 *GB*, 6 January 1876, 99.

Chapter 4

1 *A*, IV, 27, "At Home and At Cheltenham 1876," 2, written in September 1916. Maynard began this part (IV) of her autobiography at page one again.

2 Ibid., 2.

3 *A*, IV, 27, "At Home and At Cheltenham 1876," 3, written in September 1916.

4 Rachel Cook continued her work as a reviewer for the *Manchester Guardian* after she married, as did Sarah Woodhead, who taught Mathematics at various Yorkshire colleges. Cook joined such ex-Girtonians as Henrietta Muller, Malvena Borchhardt, and Emily Gibson in the fight for suffrage. Gibson published a number of travel books and was noted for her insights into Fabianism and Fascism (*Girton Register*, 2–10). Meanwhile, Mary Kingsland's dedication to working women's bodily rights in factories was likely driven by her entrapment to a

physically abusive husband (*A*, IV, 33, "Cheltenham 1876," 230, 270–81, written in October 1916).

5 See *GB*, 14 May 1876, 37. Although gold had recently been found on the land, the firm had lost thousands over a six-month period due to Harry's poor business dealings. In the end, the family lost Oakfield.

6 For Cheltenham, see *GB*, 3 July 1874, 29. For Manchester High School, see 17 July 1874, 49.

7 *GB*, 18 April 1876, 14. As cited in chapter 3, note 43, Davies offered Welsh the post before Lumsden had officially resigned. Bernard informed Maynard that Welsh was "open minded" and thus more suitable. Welsh accepted Bernard's offer, and eventually became Mistress at Girton.

8 *GB*, 20 July 1876, 66. Constance convinced her father that George needed hydropath therapy for his knee – wrapping the joint in hot and cold sheets – but the treatment did not work.

9 *GB*, 25 July 1876, 69–75. Maynard "clung to L's assertion, 'You must see that I'm *not* irreligious or materialist in thinking.'" Although she felt guilty over not supporting Lumsden at Girton, she seemed impressed that the family mansion, Glenbogie, was situated by a town called Lumsden. Snobbery, it seems, also drove Maynard's interest in joining Lumsden at Cheltenham.

10 See *GB*, 25 July 1876, 82; and 9 August 1876, 95. In her *D*, 9 October 1876, 89, Maynard explained and likely told her parents that "L hope[d] to teach advanced work with just enough payment to keep her."

11 *A*, IV, 30, "Cheltenham 1876," 140, written in December 1916. See Firth's brief comment about Lumsden's power over Maynard, followed by, "are not these things written ... in the Green-books and the Diaries?" This seems a tantalizing request that we form our own conclusions. Firth failed to analyze Maynard's life at Cheltenham or St. Leonards, focussing instead on Maynard's courtship with Robertson (Firth, *Constance Louisa Maynard*, 155, 135–67).

12 *GB*, 12 October 1876, 117.

13 See Marcus, *Between Women*, 225–226, and also 201, 261–2, 196–203; and Laura Mayhall's challenge of Marcus in "Did the Victorians Accept Female Marriage?" 79, 75–80. Mayhall may be correct in her assessment of Marcus' overstating the normativity of female marriage, but we should not dismiss Marcus' observations either. See, for example, Claudia Nelson's recent review of Marcus' *Between Women*, which applauds Marcus' effective use of life stories to argue that "female marriage [gained] a considerable degree of sanction both for its similarities to...heterosexual marriage and for its greater flexibility and parity" ("Between Women:

Friendship, Desire, and Marriage in Victorian England," *Journal of the History of Sexuality*, 20, 2, [2011], 413).

14 Based upon my analysis of Maynard's records, I would posit that both family and friends viewed her marriage to Lumsden as socially respectable (see, for example, *GB*, 19 November 1876, 127; and 25 November 1876, 132). In *Intimate Friends*, 9, Vicinus notes poet Elizabeth Barrett Browning mentioned the term "female marriage" to a friend who replied, "Oh, it is by no means uncommon." We should not assume that Victorians understood female marriage as normative, but we can conclude that ideas about female-female intimacy were as complex as those who experienced it.

15 See *GB*, 24 December 1876, 126–7; and 19 October 1876, 119.

16 *A*, IV, 30, "Cheltenham 1876," 222, written in February 1918. For more on the science versus religion debate, see Hempton, *Religion and Political*, 66; and Gerald Parsons, *Religion in Victorian England* (Manchester: Manchester University Press, 1997), 87–90.

17 *GB*, 5 November 1876, 113; and 31 December 1876, 127.

18 See *GB*, 29 October 1876, 113; and 10 December 1876, 120–7. In her *D*, 12 November 1876, 99, Maynard wrote, Beale "says my Latin class is loud and useless."

19 *A*, IV, 30, "Cheltenham 1876," 162–4, written in January 1918.

20 Compare *D*, 19 November 1876, 78, with *GB*, 20 November 1876, 119; and *A*, IV, 30, "Cheltenham 1876," 165–8, written in March 1918.

21 See *GB*, 31 December 1876, 128. Apparently, Fanny Campbell told Maynard that she must be part of the St. Leonards package. However, Campbell likely supported Lumsden's wish that Maynard teach "the simple gospel's" – published religious texts for young adults – rather than atonement theology from the Bible.

22 See Lumsden, *Yellow Leaves*, 61. For more on the general decline in preaching on hell and eternal punishment see Bebbington, *Evangelicalism in Modern Britain*, 145.

23 *St. Leonards School Gazette*, 2, 3, (1927), 27, Special Collections, courtesy of St. Leonards Archives, St. Andrews, Scotland (hereafter cited as *SLS Gazette* plus volume, year, and page numbers). Thomas Arnold's initiation of Rugby in the 1930s with the above-mentioned goals had reformed middle-class boy's education (Newsome, *Victorian World*, 69; and Heyck, *Transformation of Intellectual Life*, 62, 75).

24 *GB*, 15 April 1877, 171.

25 In her diary, she wrote, "I enjoyed the grand dinner parties in which I was in great demand" (see 20 April 1877, 98; and also see 12 May 1877, 105). In contrast, her green book lamented over her parents' reservations about

the venture and Fanny Campbell's view of her as subservient to Lumsden (see 15 April 1877, 171; 13 April 1877, 170; and 25 April 1877, 180).

26 For Dora's comment, see *GB*, 19 February 1877, 158. For Lumsden's issues with Beale, see 25 March 1877, 173. Beale had quarrelled with and subsequently fired a fellow teacher. For problems between Maynard and Lumsden see, for example, 20 April 1877, 78; and 13 May 1877, 189.

27 Firth, *Constance Louisa Maynard*, 150.

28 *GB*, 10 June 1877, 190. It is unclear as to whether their new lodgings only had one bedroom, or whether Lumsden simply wanted them to sleep together. However, the fact that Lumsden and Maynard shared a bed was not unusual for Victorians and was not unusual for Maynard. She slept with Dora until she left for Girton, and friends staying at Oakfield always shared a bed with either Maynard or her sisters.

29 *GB*, 15 June 1877, 199–200. For more on such medical conditions as neurasthenia and hysteria see Brumberg, *Fasting Girls*, 5; Marc Micale, *Approaching Hysteria: Disease and Its Interpretations* (Princeton: Princeton University Press, 1995), 72, 247, 299; and Janet Oppenheim, *Shattered Nerves: Doctors, Patients, and Depression in Victorian England* (New York: Oxford University Press, 1991).

30 *GB*, 3 June 1877, 195.

31 *GB*, 31 December 1877, 217.

32 *GB*, 3 May 1887, 70. As noted above, Maynard did not consider her marriage to Lumsden to be anti-normative. Nonetheless, her questioning of her emotions or possibly sexual acts with Lumsden suggests Maynard's sense of transgressing the boundaries of female-female intimacy. In this, Maynard's concerns contrasted with the comments quoted by Marcus from Victorian obituaries, letters, and newspaper articles, which indicated to Marcus that female marriage included a sexual component that was "conducted openly and discussed neutrally in respectable society" (*Between Women*, 201).

33 When Maynard re-evaluated this incident in 1934, she dismissed "psychoanalytical" interpretation by assuring the reader that her struggle was spiritual.

34 *A*, IV, 30, "Cheltenham 1876," 181, written in March 1918.

35 See, for example, *A*, IV, 30, "Cheltenham 1876," 225–6, written in March 1918, and *GB*, 8 May 1887, 73. For sexological classification, see Ellis, *Psychology of Sex*, 157–9. In her *The Practice of Love: Lesbian Sexuality and Perverse Desire* (London: Bloomington, 1994), 308, Teresa de Lauretis interestingly explains how individuals can absorb "external representations" and then "rework the fantasy in their internal world" of the self.

36 *D*, 8 July 1877, 189. Lumsden apparently left because "she felt grumpy thinking about nothing except examinations."

37 St. Leonards was originally called St. Andrews School for Girls until it moved from the town of St. Andrews to what was formally St. Leonards College, a property that was closer to and had originally belonged to the University of St. Andrews. The exact year and date is not known, but it was likely during 1883 ("Historical Notes," 10, *St. Leonards School Register*, Special Collections, courtesy of St. Leonards Archives, St. Andrews, Scotland, hereafter cited as *St. Leonards School Register* plus page numbers). Since Maynard simply referenced St. Andrews School for Girls as "The Schoolhouse" in her diaries, and St. Leonards in her autobiography, the name St. Leonards shall be used here.

38 In Maynard's view, religious school books had "no real approach to the Bible." Her fellow teachers were Madame Bondet, Miss Comyns, Fraulein Frieda, Miss Young, and Kate Kinnear. None are mentioned at length (*GB*, 7 October 1877, 235).

39 *D*, 12 October 1887, 99.

40 See *GB*, 25 May 1877, 260; and for a similar comment, see 9 January 1878, 7–10.

41 For more on the rivalry between all three women see, for example, *D*, 30 October 1877, 189; 21 June 1877, 67; *GB*, 1 November 1879, 148; and 15 December 1879, 157–9. In terms of Maynard's sense of being Lumsden's ornament, I am reminded of Marcus' chapter on "the Feminine Plaything" (*Between Women*, 147–9), which posits that consumer culture encouraged women (as well as men) to dominate other women. Marcus' proposal that "Dolls were to girls what, in fashion press, girls were to women: beautifully dressed objects to admire or humiliate" (150, 166), does reflect Lumsden's ongoing objectification and denigration of Maynard, both professionally and personally.

42 Maynard transcribed most of Robertson's letters in her green book. Based upon this evidence, Robertson does appear to have concentrated on his own needs rather than hers. He expected her to take care of his manse, entertain his friends, and oversee the "aging neighbourhood" (see *GB*, 23 April 1877, 178–9; and 28 May 1877, 192). For more on the norms of Victorian marriage see Barbara Caine, *Destined To Be Wives* (Oxford: Clarendon Press, 1986).

43 Her father's comment, "a man like that is rare indeed," was echoed by Gazy: "He is the one man I have heard of more than anyone else. It could be years before you meet someone like him again." Maynard continued to write to Robertson on a fairly regular basis (see, for example, *GB*,

6 May 1877, 188; 27 May 1877, 194–5; and Firth, *Constance Louisa Maynard*, 155–6).

44 *GB*, 10 February 1878, 32.

45 *GB*, 2 March 1878, 48.

46 *GB*, 29 February 1878, 45.

47 See *GB*, 19 March 1878, 55–6; and 20 March 1878, 57.

48 *GB*, 21 April 1878, 75. The fact that they shared the same bed at Glenbogie once again suggests that it was culturally acceptable in the 1870s, even though there were spare bedrooms. Perhaps the economies of lighting fewer fires also played a part since each room in Victorian mansions had to be separately heated.

49 *GB*, 22 April 1878, 78. Lumsden did not mention this aspect of her personality in *Yellow Leaves*, but was frank in stating that "friendships were an extremely important thing in [her] life" (74). For Victorian views on female friendship see, for example, Rounsville Alger, *Friendships of Women*.

50 In *The Transformation of Intimacy* (Cambridge: Polity Press, 1992), 99, Anthony Giddens provides some useful insight into "queering" human relationships. In his view, individuals "have a strong tendency towards relationships based upon emotional communication rather than institutionally given roles - in relations between men and women [or] between same sex partners."

51 See *A*, V, 33, "St. Leonards School 1878," 294–7, written in October 1918. In her *GB*, 22 April 1878, 7–10, Maynard took comfort in a conversation with Fanny Campbell after attending her mother's funeral: "We all really missed you [Maynard]. You must know that there is no-one that could take your place, however good a teacher we could find."

52 For St. Leonards, see Julia M. Grant, Katherine H. McCutcheon, and Ethel F. Sanders eds., *St. Leonards School, 1877–1927* (London: Oxford University Press, 1927), 38–40. For first-hand accounts on the development of middle-class female education see, for example, Sara Burstall, *Retrospect and Prospect*, 161; and Zimmern, *Renaissance of Girls' Education*, 156.

53 *D*, 30 March 1878, 99. Other information about St. Leonards development derived from Lumsden, *Yellow Leaves*, 76–81; and Grant, McCutcheon, and Saunders, eds., *St. Leonards School*, 37–54.

54 See *D*, 19 July 1878, 134; 7 October 1878, 167; and 9 June 1879, 269. It is important to note Maynard's establishment of sport and art as an important aspect of St. Leonards. The school did excel in these fields, yet little credit is given to Maynard's early efforts in such primary texts as Lumsden's, *Yellow Leaves*; *S.L.S. Gazette*; and Grant, McCutcheon, and Saunders, eds., *St. Leonards School*. Sport remains an important element at St. Leonards.

It was the first girls' school to establish lacrosse matches in 1890, and in recent years, Lacrosse Scotland has relied on schools to produce future Scottish Internationalists (see Jane Clayden, *St. Leonards Cradle of Lacrosse*, (Fife: West Port Print, 2008), 10, 103.

55 See *D*, 10 May 1877, 78; and 12 October 1877, 89. Setting up still life classes involved "persuad[ing] local people to donate flowers from the Conservatory." For the end-of-term exhibition, see 29 July 1879, 149.

56 Arch Forbes was the war correspondent of the *Daily News* (*GB*, 18 March 1879, 98). For Maynard's rethinking of worldly activities see, for example, *D*, 27 March 1879, 100; and 1 February 1879, 99. Here Maynard exclaimed, "Acting opens our eyes to a whole new world; an openness that could rid me of this miserable self-consciousness!"

57 For Lumsden's harsh behaviour towards Maynard, see *GB*, 6 May 1878, 56; 5 October 1879, 155; and *A*, V, 35, "St. Leonards School 1880," 294–7, written in October 1918. For Lumsden's behaviour during the diphtheria outbreak, see *D*, 23 March 1879, 55.

58 *GB*, 31 December 1878, 67–9. Dora met missionary Frank Moilliet in the summer of 1878 when nursing his mother through typhoid fever at the McAll Mission in Paris.

59 Compare *GB*, 27 October 1878, 145; 30 November 1878, 33; and 3 March 1879, 47, with *A*, V, 34, "St. Leonards School 1878," 329, written in June 1919. Besides Fanny Campbell, it is unclear with whom Lumsden socialized at this time.

60 See Anna Clark, "Twilight Moments," 141, 156; and Clark, *History of European Sexuality* (London: Routledge, 2008), which adopts the "twilight metaphor" to describe the sexual practices that were neither celebrated (like marriage) nor utterly forbidden (like incest) during some periods.

61 See *GB*, 30 October 1879, 170–2; 6 February 1880, 21; and *A*, V, 34, "St. Leonards School 1878–79," 354–5, 376, written in June 1919. Mary Tait was the daughter of Peter Guthrie Tait. Tait was an esteemed Professor of Philosophy at Edinburgh, the author of the well-known *The Unseen Universe*, and the Chair of St. Leonards.

62 See *GB*, 30 October 1879, 170–2; and 6 February 1880, 21. Tait apparently claimed that reading about eternal damnation in *Daily Light* disturbed her so much that she must see Maynard alone in order to be "calmed down." For more on individuals' refute of atonement theology at this time see, for example, Hilton, *Age of Atonement*, 298–320.

63 See *GB*, 6 February 1880, 21; and 8 March 1880, 32. There is no mention of how Tait's family reacted to any of this. However, the fact that Maynard

worried over Tait's threat to write "a rude letter home" is telling. For Maynard's hindsight observations see *A*, V, 33, 34, "St. Leonards School 1879," 380, written in July 1921.

64 Compare Maynard's account in her *A*, V, 33, "St. Leonards School 1879, 376, 380, written in July 1919, with her *GB*, 20 July 1880, 127. Tait remained at St. Leonards until 1881, and appeared to do well. She was made a "Captain of Games," and was "the winner of the 1st Latin prize for the Cambridge Senior Local" (girls' examinations). Even after her marriage Tait maintained her interest in St. Leonards, becoming one of the founders of St. Leonards School Library (*St. Leonards School Register*, 23).

65 See *GB*, 27 March 1879, 67. Ironically, this is likely what Louisa Maynard would have disapproved of too. In Constance's view, having students record their spiritual feelings through poetry made sense because this was what she had done herself at Belstead. However, one wonders if she encouraged writings about damnation, given Tait's experiences. For more on Maynard's discussions with Lumsden about Scripture class, see for example, 8 March 1879, 169; and 23 June 1879, 173.

66 *A*, V, 35, "St. Leonards School 1880," 356–65, written in July 1919.

67 See *GB*, 12 May 1879, 78; and 18 May 1879, 84. For Maynard's later thoughts on Lumsden and leadership, see *A*, V, 35, "St. Leonards School 1880," 367–70, written in July 1919.

68 For Lumsden and Scripture see *GB*, 1 November 1879, 148; and 31 December 1879, 187. For Robertson see *GB*, 18 December 1879, 120. She refused to see Robertson again. When he recorded his anger at being turned down she used it as an excuse to criticize his lack of sensitivity over her feelings or her aims (11 January 1880, 122).

69 See *GB*, 6 June 1880, 7; and 1 August 1880, 39–40.

70 *A*, V, 35, "St. Leonards School 1880," 462, written in May 1924.

71 *A*, V, 35, "St. Leonards School 1880," 463, written in May 1924. In her *Yellow Leaves*, 66, Lumsden presented a different picture. She wrote, "After five years hard work, and worry about mother, I resigned my post and recommended Frances as my successor." A similar account can be found in the *S.L.S. Gazette*, and in Grant, McCutcheon, and Saunders, eds., *St. Leonards School*. By the time Dove left St. Leonards in 1896, over two hundred students were enrolled. November 20 was "a school holiday in honour" of Dove's younger sister who "was the first student from the school to gain a Medical degree in 1890" ("Historical Notes," *St. Leonards School Register*, 13).

72 See *GB*, 12 May 1911, 89; 7 May 1912, 109; 9 July 1923, 287; and 23 March 1925, 78; and *A*, V, 35, "St. Leonards School 1880," 463, written in May 1924.

73 Compare her *GB*, 21 June 1880, 29, and 3 July 1880, 34, with her *A*, V, 35, "St. Leonards School 1880," 463, written in May 1924. At the time, Maynard was considering running a women's college in London under the directorship of a Major Charles Malan. When the scheme fell through, due to a lack of funds, Maynard felt "relieved" because Malan's focus was on missionary work and domestic training rather than women's rights to higher education.

Chapter 5

1 See *GB*, 16 May 1879, 17–18, transcribed from 16 May 1872, 77–8; and 16 May 1879, 18, transcribed from 7 October, 1876, 44. Victorian concepts of the Magdalene suggest a more sexually- and spiritually-wise woman than the Madonna. Besides direct references to prostitution, Victorians noted Christ's "forgiveness" of Mary Magdalene who must repent for her sins (see Maynard, *Victorian Discourses on Sexuality and Religion*, 135, 249, 298; and Linda Mahood, *The Magdalene's: Prostitution in the Nineteenth Century* [London: Routledge, 1990]). Perhaps Maynard, similarly to novelist Susan Warner, blurred the lines between Madonna/Magdalene and eroticism/faith in her subversion of gender and sex (for Warner see Argersinger, "Unholy Kiss," 269–74).

2 *GB*, 16 May, 1876, 17.

3 Maynard added here, "I do *so* want a 'Come! *we* will share it *all*!' from a voice I can trust" (*GB*, 16 July, 1880, 17).

4 For more on the tenuous relationship between scripts about sexuality and individual performance, see Butler, *Gender Trouble*, vii. For queer history on Victorian female sexuality see, for example, Clark, "Twilight Moments," 141, 156; and Roden, *Same-Sex Desire*, 43–81; and for queerness-as-being see, for example, Jankowski, *Queer Virginity*.

5 Compare *A*, VI, 38, "Tour in Italy, Slade School 1880," 39, written in June 1924, with *GB*, 17 May 1879, 81; 18 January 1878, 7; and 6 March 1879, 90. Similarly to Part's IV and V, Maynard began Part VI of her autobiography at page one, although pages 15–21 are missing.

6 See, for example, *GB*, 8 August 1880, 39; and 14 August 1889, 45.

7 See *GB*, 20 August 1880, 50; and 6 October 1880, 69–70. Upon their return, Campbell lured her into an empty room at Oakfield, and "in a moment, gathered [her] to him...till [she] felt as if [her] very soul would slip away."

8 Carter, "On Mother-Love," 128, taken from Smith-Rosenberg, "The Female World." For more on the nuances of Victorian female friendship see Hall, *Outspoken Women*. As Hall notes, even although lesbian-like acts did

feature, for example, in Victorian pornography, we cannot extrapolate that intense emotional bonds between Victorian women of the middle-class were defined as sexual in their nature.

9 *GB*, 7 October 1880, 77.

10 *GB*, 9 October 1880, 80. For more on sexual mores see Walkowitz, *Prostitution and Victorian Society: Women, Class, and the State* (Cambridge: Cambridge University Press, 1980) and *Dreadful Delight*, 90–3; and Tosh, *Man's Place*, 66–90.

11 For Maynard's comments regarding Lumsden and Campbell, see *GB*, 14 December 1881, 1; and 28 October 1880, 92. I attempt to queer or dismantle power, in order to better understand how Maynard visualized power, or was at least intrigued by the idea of it. Of course, as Doan notes, queerness can only ever disturb an identity, not define it (Doan, *Disturbing Practices*, viii).

12 For her experiences in art studies see, for example, *A*, VI, 39, "Slade School 1880," 29–33, 55–64, written in June 1924; *D*, 1 November 1880, 122; and 29 November 1880, 126. Maynard became disillusioned with art after her fear of welding resulted in low marks. Unfortunately, the Slade deemed (male) students who could weld "the most talented and promising artists."

13 See *D*, 6 January 1881, 78; 12 February 1881, 85; and 13 November 1880, 90. We might argue that these diary entries convey how rescue work allowed Maynard to revisit her feelings for Campbell, Lumsden, and Tait, much like her chance street encounters with former Belstead friend Virginia Dalrymple. For more on the idea of female vagrants as sex delinquents see Lynda Nead, *Myths of Sexuality: Representations of Women in Victorian Britain* (Oxford: Blackwell, 1988).

14 For Maynard's views on rescue work and "Bad reputation" see *GB*, 12 December 1880, 126. Although many Victorians viewed prostitutes as "sewers" (quote taken from Victorian social critic, Dr. G. Richolet, cited in Nead, *Myths of Sexuality:*, 121), Koven, Walkowitz, and others argue that those engaged in philanthropy did not consider it immoral. In fact, social reformer Josephine Butler sought to elevate the status of prostitutes by emphasizing that their suffering ennobled them in comparison to the outcasts of the workhouses (see Walkowitz, *Dreadful Delight*, 41, 88–92; and Seth Koven, *Slumming: Sexual and Social Politics in Victorian London* [Princeton: Princeton University Press, 2004]).

15 The G.P.M. Ring echoed those used in Methodist meetings. Letters were placed in a little pouch, circulated around, and then replaced by a new letter. Maynard's addition of Ring's II, III, and IV facilitated her initiation

of a Divinity program at Westfield in 1901 through both advertising and financial support (see *GB*, 27 April 1880, 54; 9 May 1879, 34; and *A*, VI, 40, "A New Start 1881," 70–8, written in October 1924). For more on the S.A. movement see R. Sandall, *History of the Salvation Army*, vols. 1–3 (London: Salvation Army, 1964).

16 See *A*, III, 11, "My first term at Hitchin, 1872," 374, written in December 1915, and for more on Victorian women's erotic sense of self as a "Divine female" see, for example, Roden, *Same-Sex Desire in Victorian Religious Culture* 35–68; and Vicinus, *Intimate Friends*, 98–101. In her *Aims for Higher Education* (London: Simmons and Botten, 1881), 7–13, Cavendish outlines her foundation of the C.W.E.U. For more on the conference see *GB*, 8 February 1881, 21; and 23 February 1881, 283.

17 Maynard, *Cultivation of the Intellect*, 7, 18, 26. Another reason for the neglect of women's education, she argued, was the middle and upper-middle classes' focus on social reform of the poor.

18 *A*, VI, 42, "Dawn of Westfield 1882," 106, written in May 1926. Mary Petrie was among the first women taking the B.A. degree at University College. Petrie's family were friends of Dudin-Brown, who knew of Cavendish's foundation of the C.W.E.U.

19 *GB*, 12 February 1882, 41. Col. Petrie was Mary's father; Vicar Fleming presided over St. Michael's parish in Chester Square; Boultbee was the Principal of St. John's, a training ministry in Highbury; and Barlow was the Principal of a C.M.S. institution in Clapham. Boultbee proposed a form of "trenching" or writing of promissory notes to each on a bank loan (4 March 1882, 3, 18–19).

20 See *GB*, 12 April 1882, 76; 5 March 1882, 61; and *Minutes of Council*, 4 March 1882, 3. Denny was a staunch Evangelical who donated thousands towards the S.A. Shaftsbury, was a well renowned social reformer who sought change in education and working conditions in factories.

21 For more on attitudes towards female education see Zimmern's *Renaissance of Girls' Education*; and Senders Pederson, "Schoolmistresses and Headmistresses." For more on how Victorian's classified women's physiological bodies see Henry Maudsley, "Sex in Mind and in Education," *Fortnightly Review* 15 (1874), 466–8; and Edward Clarke, *Sex in Education* (Boston: James Osgood, 1873). See Elaine Showalter, *The Female Malady: Women, Madness, and English Culture, 1830–1980* (New York: Pantheon Books, 1985), for a good account of the history of the female body.

22 *GB*, 16 April 1882, 82. Interestingly, according to Janet Sondheimer in *Castle Adamant: A History of Westfield College 1882–1982* (London: Westfield

College, 1983), 26, there is no evidence beyond Maynard's diaries to suggest Shaftesbury's condemnation of her venture. See also Edwin Hodder, *The Seventh Earl of Shaftesbury, K. G., as Social Reformer* (Chicago: Fleming H. Revell, 1886), 176, which traces Shaftesbury's support of women's education for over sixty years.

23 She assured the Council that religious teaching would be in accordance with the Protestant Church of England to deflect Fanny Metcalfe's open accusation, which continued throughout her tenure at Westfield (*GB*, 17 May 1882, 91–3; and see also *Minutes*, 30 June 1882, 41–9).

24 *GB*, 18 June 1882, 112.

25 For more on Victorian views of female piety see Brown, *Death of Christian Britain*, 211, 58–87. For discussion on how faith gave women access to the public sphere and the means to fight for women's rights see, for example, Dixon, *Divine Feminism*, 1–17, and Suzanne Rickard, "Victorian Women with Causes: Writing, Religion and Action," in Morgan ed., *Women Religion and Feminism*, 141–7.

26 See *GB*, 30 June 1882, 41–9; and *Minutes*, 2 July 1882, 128. Kate Tristram's age and lack of Matriculation was a disadvantage, but Maynard persuaded Tristram from accepting an offer from Frances Dove, who was now Mistress at St. Leonards.

27 See "My Life's Work, 1882," 4, written in May 1925. Maynard began Part VII, the final part of her autobiography, at page one again. For more on the designs for women's colleges see, for example, McWilliams-Tullberg, *Women at Cambridge*.

28 *D*, 10 September 1882, 61–2. Although all five candidates, who were clergyman's daughters, passed the Entrance Examination, they were admitted before Maynard and Petrie had actually corrected the exam. For the Entrance Examination, see "Proposed College For Women," 41, Special Collections, Courtesy of Queen Mary University of London Archives/Westfield College/WFD.

29 See *GB*, 1 October 1882, 167; and *D*, 22 October 1882, 78. She perhaps rightly complained about living in a damp, smoke-filled room, and about the limitations of getting each cheque from the treasurer. However, her elitist, perhaps unsympathetic attitude was clear in her stereotyping of "lazy domestics" who, she claimed, were "the biggest problem in institutions."

30 Details of The Matriculation requirements are given in the *University of London Calendar*. See also *Minutes*, 10 May 1899, 294.

31 According to Maynard, Frances Synge and Margaret Brooke struggled the most as Belstead graduates. Meanwhile, Bleby was so far advanced that she "left college twice until they caught up to her." Kate Tristram was "keen to read for the B.A. degree," and joined Bleby and Thompson for Physics, Chemistry, Latin, and German (*A*, VII, 44, "My Life's Work, 1882," 38–46, written in May 1925).

32 See *A*, VII, 45, "44, "Westfield 1883," 57–60, written in May 1926; and Sondheimer, *Castle Adamant*, 30–32. See also Sara Burstall, *Sixty Years of Women's Education*, for a good account of the changes in women's education at this time.

33 *A*, VII, 44, "My Life's Work 1882," 46–50, written in June 1925.

34 See, for example, *GB*, 31 August 1869, 99; 26 June 1870, 210; and 8 October 1882, 149. The Church was called Divinity and the minister was Henry Sharpe. For more on women's interactions with the Church Missionary Society see Brown, *Death of Christian Britain*, 68.

35 For more on Maynard's discussion of her motto, see *GB*, 21 December 1884, 56; 16 October 1891, 88; 1 November 1899, 99; and 20 October 1904, 3. For the honeysuckle emblem see, *A*, I, 1, "Childhood 1849–1860," 47, written in June 1925,

36 *GB*, 12 November 1882, 12–15. Brooke instituted the name "Pie," which meant that they could discuss anything with "Miss." See also Carus-Wilson, ed., *Westfield College*, 13–25.

37 See *GB*, 16 October 1882, 4. Maynard had made a similar comment at Girton (see 20 April 1874, 171). However, even at Girton, she assumed that seeking a career meant that she would probably be with a woman. This is not to suggest that her desire was female-focused, but rather culture-forced.

38 See *GB*, 28 October 1882, 5; and 5 November 1882, 10.

39 *GB*, 5 November 1882, 11.

40 *GB*, 7 November, 1882, 12.

41 *GB*, 22 March 1883, 69. She noted here, "at 19, she [MGB] seems to have a more passionate past than most women of her age, but has been satisfied with nothing."

42 *GB*, 11 February 1883, 59.

43 See *GB*, 22 March 1883, 69, 71; 7 May 1883, 84; and 19 August 1883, 117, for other examples of their husband and wife role playing. Brooke did eventually marry after leaving Westfield.

44 *GB*, 12 January 1883, 46.

45 See *GB*, 12 January 1883, 46; and 17 December 1883, 69. In other words, the researcher's *feeling* the erotic or what Doan calls "queerness-as being" through the past subject's words. This noted, a queer-method approach

to past sexual experiences is perhaps more useful (*Disturbing Practices* 44, 90–1). For more on Butler's depiction of gendered sexual norms see Walkowitz, *Dreadful Delight*, 21, 88–92.

46 See *GB*, 5 November 1882, 8; and 3 May 1883, 71–3.

47 "I spoke to her [Tristram] wisely," Maynard simply noted of this incident on 19 November 1882, 14. "I said, 'God's hands can bring joy, but you must do His work in the dark.'"

48 *GB*, 18 January 1883, 45.

49 Victorians adopted Aristotle's view of women as weak vessels who lacked coherence of thought, thus Maunder's behaviour must have been stressful for Maynard. Apparently, Maunder climbed into Maynard's bed each night and "cl[u]ng to [her] for hours" (*GB*, 14 January 1883, 44). For more on Jules Falret's and others views on deranged, hysterical women, see Micale, *Approaching Hysteria*, 247.

50 *GB*, 13 May 1883. Colville was the first to study mathematics. She appears to have used the Bible to discredit Maynard. See description of the whiten sepulchre in Matt. xxiii. 27.

51 See for example, *D*, 24 May 1883, 46; and *GB*, 10 June 1883, 90. She also resented MGB's comment about her "shabby" attire, and was further "irritated" to be told that she was "too opinionated" (19 August 1883, 114). See also *A*, VII, 44, "My Life's Work 1882," 42, written in June 1925.

52 *GB*, 8 June 1882, 122. Firth suggested that Richardson's governess had attended the Liverpool C.W.E.U. conference and had sent Richardson a copy of Maynard's paper (*Constance Louisa Maynard*, 176).

53 See *A*, VI, 44, "My Life's Work 1882," 128, written in August 1925; and *GB*, 6 January 1883, 209; 12 March 1883, 256; and 16 June 1883, 302.

54 *GB*, 24 May 1883, 85. Gray passed the Cambridge Higher Local with distinctions in both English and Divinity.

55 See *GB*, 17 June 1883, 91; and *A*, VII, 45, "My Life's Work 1882," 38, written in May 1925.

56 If we adopt a queer approach to Maynard's view of Pie, and of Westfield as a family, we could argue that a power-based familial relationship – in this case Mistress and student – was constructed by Maynard as a part of a shared femininity, as opposed to what we may call lesbian or incestuous-like behaviour.

57 See *GB*, 16 September 1883, 123.

Chapter 6

1 *A*, VII, 44, "My Life Work 1883," 3, written in May 1926.

2 *GB*, 31 December 1884, 199.

3 Vicinus, *Intimate Friends*, xix. For more on the fluidity of past experiences see, for example, Rupp, "Global History of Same-Sex Sexuality," 287–302; and Estelle B. Freedman, "'The Burning of letters Continues': Elusive Identities and the Historical Construction," *Journal of Women's History* 9 (1998), 181–99.

4 Roden, *Same-Sex Desire*. See also Vanita, *Sappho and the Virgin Mary*; and Prins, "Greek Maenads, Victorian Spinsters."

5 Audre Lorde, "Uses of the Erotic: The Erotic as Power," in *Sister Outsider*, (California: Crossing Press, 1984), 54; and Roland Barthes, *Sadel/Fourier/Loyala*, trans. Richard Miller, (New York: Hill & Wang, 1976), 3–6, 64. For more on the erotic as a set of dynamics see, for example, the work of such cultural psychologists as Griffiths, *What Emotions Really Are*; and Victor S. Johnson, *Why We Feel: The science of Human Emotions* (Reading: Perseus Books, 1999), 46.

6 For Davies see Davies, "Instruction Relating to Girls," in *Thoughts*, 60–3; and McWilliams-Tullberg, *Women at Cambridge*, 68. For Anne Jemima Clough see Vicinus, *Independent Women*, 125–62. Compare these accounts with Heyck's discussion on men's college rules in *Transformation of Intellectual Life*, 166–86.

7 See Firth, *Constance Louisa Maynard*, 251–2. Maynard sat at "the High" and a lecturer sat at each small table. It was "law that no student went twice consecutively to the same table." The same rule applied at night when students joined one another for "tea, cakes and jam" (letter to Janet Sondheimer, 25 March 1976, from F. Lyle in reply to her letter 16 March 1976, Ms. 317, Special Collections, Courtesy of Queen Mary University of London Archives/Westfield College/WFD.

8 In her *GB*, 12 January 1884, 204, Maynard explained that the student Marie Pechinet adored Gray and so could "not tolerate 'professional'" criticism of her work. She never forgave Gray who refused to carry on as Pechinet's tutor. See more on Agnes Maitland's insights see "The Student Life of Women in Halls of Residence," in *National Union of Women Worker's Report for 1894* (London: National Union of Women Workers, 1894), 100. See also Vicinus, *Independent Women*, 143–52.

9 Firth, *Constance Louisa Maynard*, 323. For more on ideas of holiness and cultural changes in late-nineteenth-century Britain see M.E. Dieter, *The Holiness Revival of the Nineteenth Century* (New Jersey: Metuchen, 1980), 81–6.

10 Anne Richardson, "History of Westfield College up to 1913," 19, Special Collections, Courtesy of Queen Mary, University of London Archives/Westfield College/WFD. See also Sondheimer, *Castle Adamant*, 12. For

secularist discourse and a culture that was becoming increasingly (male) capitalist see Heyck, *Transformation of Intellectual Life.*

11 Dixon, *Divine Feminism*, 2–9; and Jacqueline deVries, "Feminism, History and Religious Cultures," in *Women, Gender and Religious Culture*, 198. Interestingly, the *Women's Penny Paper* began publication in 1888 under the direction of Henrietta Muller, who as noted in chapter 3, was Maynard's "arch enemy" at Girton. For Function see *GB*, 29 October 1885, 3; Firth, *Constance Louisa Maynard*, 296–7; and Carus-Wilson, ed., *Westfield College*, 13–25.

12 *D*, 2 May 1909, 99.

13 See Constance Louisa Maynard, *We Women: A Golden Hope* (London: Morgan and Scott, 1913), 130–132. Maynard had taken aspects of this quote from the New English Bible. See Gal. III: 28, 657.

14 See *Minutes*, 8 July 1887, 26; and *A*, VII, 49, "October Term 1887," 177, written in May 1927. Not surprisingly, many students were ill prepared for these exams. In 1885, for example, ten out of an enrolment of sixteen students did not intend to take the B.A. degree (*Minutes*, 12 October 1885, 142).

15 See *Minutes*, 6 June 1894, 12; *D*, 2 May 1913, 199; and Sondheimer, *Castle Adamant*, 44. For more on the changes in girls' education in general in the late 1880s see Zimmern, *Renaissance of Girls' Education*, 103–22; and Burstall, *High Schools for Girls*, and *Retrospect and Prospect*.

16 See *Report*, October Term, 1883, 88–91. Gray taught elementary Classics while Tristram taught elementary science. Tuition expenses had been reduced by £50 as a result of having a second resident lecturer and a chemistry lab for introductory work.

17 Compare, for example, Maynard's lament, "Ralph is so sweet, but there is a hard part to her that is so cruel," in her *GB*, 20 December 1884, 93–4, with Maynard's outpourings about her physical encounters with Brooke in her *GB*, 4 November 1883, 48: "I try to dismiss my 'thrills' of excitement ... I feel have reached such a height, that it can only go downwards after such happiness!"

18 *GB*, 31 December 1883, 305. For other accounts of close college friendships see, for example, Alice Stronach, *A Newnham Friendship* (London: Blackie and Son, 1901); and Rosamond Lehmann, *Dusty Answer* (New York: Grosset & Dunlap, 1927).

19 See Vicinus, "'One Life,'" 625; and *Independent Women*, 158–65. Maynard recalled that Katherine Porter and Maria Parry "bought a cottage together and lived as man and wife." Their physical relationship in unknown, but "Katherine worked and Maria kept house" (Constance Maynard, *Sundial*

Diary, 19 February 1915, 78, Special Collections, courtesy of Queen Mary University of London Archives/Constance Maynard/PP7/3 (hereafter cited as *Sundial*).

20 See Marcus, *Between Women*, 109–49. While fashion magazines featured women who gazed suggestively at each other's body parts, advice manuals included discussion on mothers' birching of daughters. For Tristram see *GB*, 27 April 1884, 201. Maynard persuaded Tristram to stay and successfully gain her B.Sc. in 1887, but Tristram left Westfield shortly after to pursue life-long missionary work in India.

21 See *GB*, 10 December 1884, 78; and 10 May 1884, 210. As noted earlier, Firth did not discuss Maynard's emotional life. This is a serious deficiency in Firth's biography because Maynard's love for Gray is core to understanding Maynard's experiences during these potent years of her life.

22 See *Report*, 20 January 1884, 163, for Maynard's lament over Gray's focus on Westfield's course work over faith. Maynard's diary meanwhile voiced concern over Gray's challenge of the banning of college dances, plays, and singing (see, for example, *D*, 20 February, 1884, 9; and 26 March 1884, 19).

23 See *GB*, 12 December 1884, 296. For Maynard's emphasis on the "Parable of the Sower" see *GB*, 21 December 1884, 56; 16 October 1891, 88; 1 November 1899, 99; and 20 October 1904, 3. See Maynard *Cultivation*, 21, for more on Maynard's views on science versus faith.

24 See *GB*, 2 October 1884, 265; 17 June 1883, 91; and *A*, VII, 44, "October Term 1884," 270–3, written in December 1926.

25 *A*, VII, 44, *A*, VII, 44, "October Term 1884," 273–6, written in December 1926. See also Vicinus, "One Life," 615–66, and *Independent Women*, 158–65.

26 *GB*, 6 March 1884, 64.

27 *GB*, 12 August 1884, 110. As noted earlier, Maynard likely crossed the line with Emma Maunders and Minna Colville. Her toying with Mary Tait's emotions at St. Leonards seemed even more evident.

28 *GB*, 17 June 1884, 160.

29 *A*, VII, 43, "Autumn Term 1883," 60, written in June 1927. No evidence of this interaction exists beyond Maynard's autobiography. However, before Westfield was founded, Metcalfe advised Maynard to "offer [her]self without pay for the Principal-ship" of Holloway college in London, and so perhaps Westfield Council had similar expectations of Maynard as Mistress. We glean more about the Council's attitude towards Maynard from their negativity towards "getting a housekeeper" who was willing to work for only room and board (*A*, VI, 41, "A New Start 1881," 90–2, written in October 1924).

30 See *GB*, 31 December 1884, 302–4. Maynard accepted their position since anger was considered deviant feminine behaviour until the 1920s. In hindsight, she wished she had "expressed [her] opinions more" (see *A*, VII, 46, "Autumn Term 1883," 61–9, written in June 1927). For more on negative views about female anger see Stearns, "Girls, Boys, and Emotions," 36–73.

31 See *A*, VII, 49, "Autumn Term 1885," 133–9, written in December 1926; *D*, 3 June 1885, 120; and *Minutes*, 3 June 1885, 156. The Council initially decided that Tristram and Willoughby (Natural Sciences Tripos) could share a salary of £80 per term, but then, for some reason, recanted.

32 See *D*, 12 May 1885, 99; and 6 March 1886, 122, for Maynard's perspective. For the Council's, see *Minutes*, 4 May 1885, 74; and 6 April 1886, 120.

33 In her *GB*, 20 December 1885, 94, Maynard explained, "For Ralph, it was the old, old story of Troy, besieged yet content as long as Helen was within its walls." The Gray family was moving to London so that Sara Gray could pursue medicine.

34 See Roden *Same-Sex Desire*, 48, 67, 83; and Yopie Prins, "Greek Maenads, Victorian Spinsters," 43–81. Although Harrison (1850–1928) thought religiosity could be "dogmatic," she believed it a necessity. Faith, similarly to desire, had "be felt and lived" rather than "intellectually analyzed." For more on women's link of Hellenism and Christianity to challenge heteronormativity see, Vanita, *Sappho and the Virgin Mary*; and Vicinus, *Intimate Friends*, 178, 81, 222.

35 Such green book entries as 20 January 1886, 66; 15 May 1886, 99; 4 January 1886, 58; and 20 March 1886, 88, reflect Barthes' observations about "intensified emotional states" like idolization and self-torture in *Sadel/Fourier/Loyala*, 3–6, as well as Fuss' analysis of the gender neutral erotic in *Identification Papers*.

36 See *GB*, 15 April 1884, 197. Richardson's views, similarly to Lumsden's hopes for St. Leonards, seemed to reflect those of Thomas Arnold, who spoke at length on such masculine qualities as strong, non-emotive leadership and integrity (see Heyck, *Transformation of Intellectual Life*, 130–78). In 1886, however, Richardson's caution to Maynard suggested that Richardson sensed of a form of sexual dissidence on Maynard's part: "She [Gray] says, 'there are two sides to you: one devoted to the College, but she always seems to be in contact with the *other* something wrong'" (30 April 1886, 138).

37 See *A*, VII, 59, "May Term 1896," 402, written in February 1928. For Lumsden see *GB*, 3 May 1885, 73; and for Maynard's remarks about the Council, see 12 December 1885, 199. In her *A*, written in 1928 about the year

1896, Maynard explained, "I had read *Phoedo* and realized a powerful kind of unity ran through the world." She later called this unity "inner decadence."

38 *GB*, 12 December 1885, 199. Maynard's discussions with both Richardson and Gray about her "something wrong" suggests that Maynard's link of her wrongdoing with "Christian" same-sex desire was a safer discourse than the Hellenist-Christian model she wrote about in her autobiography (see note 37 above).

39 See *GB*, 31 December 1886, 142. Her green book entries had clearly changed in tone since May 1886, and continued to do so (see, for example, 2 January 1887, 14; and 12 May 1887, 2, which read more like her diary entries). For examples of Maynard's threat to destroy parts of her green book, see *A*, VII, 49, "May Term 1886," 160, written in May 1927; *GB*, 6 September 1886, 150; and 19 February 1910, 347.

40 Firth, *Constance Louisa Maynard*, 250.

41 See *A*, VII, 49, "October Term 1886," 177, written in May 1927; and also VII, 50, "May Term 1887," 182, written in June 1927. For more on women's description of their "self-flagellation" to cope with emotional/sexual loss see, for example, Roden's, *Same-Sex Desire in Victorian Religious Culture*, 38–43, 78–80, which depicts Christina Rossetti's and Eliza Keary's symbolic "death of the world" for same-sex love. According to Foucault, our "obligation to confess" is so powerful that it '"demands' only to surface" as liberation (*History of Sexuality*, 60). Surely Maynard's *A* was not simply a manipulative plea for absolution?

42 *D*, 2 November 1890, 100. Maynard's sense of purpose was fuelled by Westfield's representation at "Capping Day" for the first time that May.

43 Cornford's father was an engineer (see *Westfield Register*, 16, Special Collections, courtesy of Queen Mary University of London Archives/Westfield College/WFD, hereafter cited as *Westfield Register* plus page numbers).

44 See *Minutes*, 7 April 1886, 208; *Report*, Lent Term and May Term, 1888, 78, 118; and *D*, 30 November 1887, 66. This was largely thanks to Brown's donation of £500 and such G.P.M. friends as Amy Mantle. As Maynard explained, "Some members have offered scholarships as tokens of appreciation and financial aid for their sisters."

45 See, for example, *A*, VII, 49, "May Term 1887," 188, written in June 1927; and VII, 55, "Autumn Term 1892," 300, written in December 1927. Richardson's night visits happened about once every two terms. For Barthes see *Sadel/Fourier/Loyala*, 3–6, 64.

46 See *A*, VII, 49, "May Term 1888," 232, written in July 1927; and *D*, 7 June 1995, 45, for her views on Dante. For more on links between faith, same-sex desire, and Dante, see Maynard, *Victorian Discourses on Sexuality and Religion*, 204–5. See Stachniecoski, *Prosecutory Imagination*, 67–80, for the levels of penance that Evangelicals inculcated to atone for sin.

47 The W.S.S. was established by Florence Booth, daughter-in-law of General Booth of the S.A. A fallen woman was generally forced to become an underpaid live-in domestic. She could not raise her child in her employer's home even though English law before 1927 made no provision for legal adoption of a child whose mother was still alive (F.K. Prochaska, *Women and Philanthropy in Nineteenth-Century England* [Oxford: Oxford University Press, 1980], 98–123).

48 In her *A*, VII, 50, "October Term 1888," 230–3, written in June 1927, Maynard assured the reader that she had kept her promise to "do nothing unless a child 'was thrown at [her] head.'" Yet it seems unlikely that Pash suddenly offered Maynard a child, as Maynard claimed, because they had not kept in contact after Girton. Maynard perhaps felt some level of guilt about her commitment as a mother when writing her autobiography.

49 *A*, VII, 50, "October Term 1888," 233–4, written in June 1927. Effie's mother became pregnant by the family pastor and left in disgrace to live with distant relatives until giving birth. She then begged on the streets until rescued by an S.A. officer, who took Effie to a Paris orphanage. Effie was given her mother's first name as her surname, as this was the usual practice with illegitimate children.

50 See *A*, VII, 50, "October Term 1888," 247, written in June 1927; *D*, 7 November 1888, 57; and 3 February 1889, 66. Firth devoted an entire chapter on Effie. She explained, "I chose to treat [events around Effie] at disproportionate length, as a study within a study" (*Constance Louisa Maynard*, 56). I would counter that while Effie was important to Maynard, she seemed less so than Gray or the running of Westfield due, in part, to Maynard's discomfort over Effie's race, class, and illegitimacy. Here we see the fluidity and interconnection between class, race, faith, and female-female dominance.

51 See *A*, VII, 50, "October Term 1891," 264–6, written in June 1927; and Firth, *Constance Louisa Maynard*, 226–9. For more on Maynard's changing opinion of Effie, compare *D*, 3 February 1889, 66, with D, 6 January 1892, 104.

52 See *A*, VII, 50, "October Term 1891," 317–20, written in June 1927; and Firth, *Constance Louisa Maynard*, 228–9. For more on social attitudes

about illegitimate children see, for example, Ann R. Higginbotham, "Respectable Sinners: Salvation Army Rescue Work with Unmarried Mothers, 1884–1914," in *Religion in the Lives of English Women*, ed. Malmgreen, 216–33.

53 See *A*, VII, 50, "October Term 1891," 320–2, written in June 1927; and *D*, 12 December 1888, 97. See also Maynard's notebooks on Effie (*Stephanë 1888–1915*, vols. I–VI); and Pamela J. Walker, *Pulling the Devil's Kingdom Down: The Salvation Army in Victorian Britain* (Berkeley: University of California Press, 2001), 149–63, for more on this mother-daughter relationship.

54 See *D*, 7 April 1889, 59–60, for Maynard's observations on Richardson and changes in the relationship between Richardson and Gray. It was at this time that Richardson received an offer to become Mistress of the Mount School in York in 1889, but then turned it down.

55 See *D*, 12 January 1890, 56; 2 March 1890, 73; and 19 May 1890, 4.

56 *A*, VII, 53, "May Term 1891," 286, written in October 1927, quote taken from *GB*, 14 April 1891, 66.

57 For Lumsden see *GB*, 31 December 1877, 217; and 3 May 1887, 70. For Brooke see *GB*, 12 January 1883, 46; 12 January 1883, 46; and 17 December 1883, 69. There is not enough evidence in Maynard's records to suggest that she achieved orgasm with other women or adopted a code for sex acts. For women who were more explicit see, for example, Lister, in *I Know My Own Heart*, ed. Whitbread; and Donohue, *Passions between Women*. Yet we cannot assume Maynard's naivety about sex, the clitoris, and orgasm. Although Victorians classified women as passionless or asexual, many wrote about female lust and desire (see, for example, excerpts collected in Patricia Jalland and John Hooper, eds., *Women from Birth to Death: The Female Life Cycle in Britain 1830–1914* [Brighton: Harvester Press, 1986], 232–4). In terms of sex acts, which Maynard and Gray possibly subverted, we could examine Alfred Kinsey, W.B. Pomeroy, C.E. Martin, and Paul H. Gebhard, *Sexual Behaviour in the Human Female* (New York: Harper and Brothers, 1951), which lists scratching and biting as a part of precoital male-female sex. A queer approach to Maynard's and Gray's intimacy discloses the ways that raves afforded some college women same-sex self-explorations apart from larger society. We might also argue that, similar to Maynard's "marriage" to Lumsden, Maynard's and Gray's same-sex eroticism was a variation of the passion between Victorian women.

58 See *D*, 20 November 1890, 67, for her concerns about Gray. Perhaps Maynard was rightly ambivalent about the move. In her *A*, VII, 53, "May Term 1891," 263, written in October 1927, she explained that the Council

gave her no say in the decision-making process even though she had asked repeatedly to join in the selection of a new college site.

59 *Ring*, 23 January 1891. There was tension around the "cut off" following a petition from students requesting that they all eat their evening meal at Kidderpore.

60 See *D*, 23 February 1891, 89; and *A*, VII, 53, "May Term 1891," 283, written in October 1927.

61 *A*, VII, 53, "May Term 1891," 287, written in October 1927.

62 Compare *A*, VII, 53, "May Term 1891," 288–9, written in October 1927, with *D*, 14 February, 1892, 112; and 8 April 1892, 89.

63 See *GB*, 5 June 1903, 199; *D*, 6 April 1890, 99; and 20 September 1890, 122. Each time Maynard punished Effie for her bad behaviour, Effie retaliated with temper tantrums and more rude behaviour. This would have likely countered Maynard's own upbringing.

64 *A*, VII, 55, "October Term 1892," 360, written in December 1927. Sadly, although Effie's biological mother could still claim custody rights she did not do so because she had married.

65 Compare *D*, 8 May 1895, 99; and 6 April 1896, 12, with Walker, *Devil's Kingdom*, 163. At age thirteen Effie could not have legally consented to sexual relations because the Criminal Law Amendment Act rose the age of consent to sixteen. Yet according to Maynard, and the S.A., the guilt was firmly Effie's and she must seek forgiveness from society and from God (See Prochaska, *Women and Philanthropy*, 98–123, on the S.A.'s work with fallen women). Given these powerful cultural-religious mores, it is perhaps understandable that Firth downplays Maynard's questionable behaviour as a mother (see *Constance Louisa Maynar*d, 232–9). Maynard did financially support Effie until her death of consumption at age thirty in 1915.

66 See *D*, 27 February 1894, 67, and compare with *A*, VII, 57, "Lent Term 1894," 312–17, written in November 1927. One setback for Gray, in regards to St. Andrews, was her Methodist background. Maynard expected this would deter Gray, and so she was furious about Richardson's encouraging Gray to convert to Anglicanism in order to qualify for the post.

67 Firth, *Constance Louisa Maynard*, 337. Beyond this sentence, Firth's account of Maynard's long reign as Mistress of Westfield only hinted at this struggle. Firth culled her few references to Gray from Gray's biography, *Gladly, Gladly* (London: Hodder, 1923), which traced Gray's work at Westfield to the running of St. Paul's School for Girls. Gray herself wrote kindly of Maynard in *Gladly, Gladly*, but she never mentioned their personal relationship.

68 As noted earlier, sexologists classified sexual practices through scientific discourses around normal and deviant sex. Freud's subsequent theories on childhood psychosexual development further instituted the idea of "normal" heterosexual development. This noted, these ideas did not permeate British society until after the 1920s. Although some scholars argue that sexology was known in Europe and beyond by the mid-1800s, Crozier is among those who point out that Ellis knew how to "sell" sexology to the British market because he was a part of it. His work was not published until the end of the century (see Crozier, "Havelock Ellis," 287–9; and also Porter and Hall, *Facts of Life*, 178–202; Bland and Doan, eds., *Sexology in Culture*; and for Freud see Christopher Badcock, *Essential Freud* [Cambridge: Blackwell, 1992]).

69 See *A*, VII, 57, "May Term and Long Vacation 1894," 362, 366–7, written in December 1927; and *D*, 8 June 1894, 124. As McCrone suggests, it can not be surprising that Victorian women sought mental and physical health through sport just as modern women do (*Playing the Game*, 286).

70 For Gray, see *D*, 20 April 1895, 88; 30 April 1896, 90; and 10 July 1895, 99. As Vicinus notes in "'One Life,'" 618, "we cannot know what Ralph lost by narrowing her personal life" in order to pursue a career. For Maynard's conversation with Frances Dove, see *GB*, 15 April 1892, 197. For Maynard's hindsight reflection on her feelings at this time see *A*, VII, 57, "May Term and Long Vacation 1894," 346, written in December 1927.

Chapter 7

1 These lines, transcribed from Maynard's sonnet, are taken from *A*, VII, 48, "October Term 1885," 122, written in October 1926.

2 See *GB*, 8 August 1905, 59.

3 *A*, VII, 60, "October Term 1899," 435, written in May 1928. For more on the challenges and changes to Evangelicalism at the fin de siècle see, Bebbington, *Evangelicalism in Modern Britain*, 191; and Maynard, *Victorian Discourses on Sexuality and Religion*, 201–2.

4 See deVries, "Feminism, History and Religious Cultures," in *Women, Gender and Religious Culture*, ed. Morgan and deVries, 198; and Jane Rendall, *The Origins of Modern Feminism: Women in Britain, France and the United States, 1780–1860*, (Chicago: Lyceum Books, 1985). For more on female piety see, for example, Brown, *Death of Christian Britain*, 211, 58–87.

5 See *GB*, 20 August 1901, 46; and 16 April 1904, 308. Adrienne Rich and Teresa de Lauretis are amongst those scholars who observe the significance of love between mothers and daughters to a modern lesbian

experience, but they do not fully address the implications of past mother-love as an actual erotic bond (see Rich, "Compulsory Heterosexuality," 143–145; and de Lauretis, *The Practice of Love: Lesbian Sexuality and Perverse Desire* [Indiana: Bloomington Press, 1994], 58–65).

6 Vicinus, *Intimate Friends*, 113–43. For more on the mother-daughter bond see, for example, Norma Clarke, *Ambitious Heights: Writing, Friendship, Love – the Jewsbury Sisters, Felicia Hemens and Jane Welsh Carlyle* (London: Routledge, 1990); and Rosemarie Bodenheimer, *The Real Life of Mary Jane Evans: George Eliot, Her Letters, and Fiction* (Ithaca: Cornel University Press, 1994).

7 See, for example, *GB*, 20 August 1901, 46, and compare Maynard's account of eroticism with Barthes, *Sadel/Fourier/Loyala*, 3–6, 64; Wurmster, *Mask of Shame*, 45–6; and Jaco Hamman, "The Rod of Discipline: Masochism, Sadism, and the Judeo-Christian Religion," *Journal of Religion and Health* 39, 4 (2000), 319–27.

8 Carter, "Mother-Love," 129.

9 *A*, VII, 60, "October Term 1897," 400, written in March 1928. In 1895, out of the twelve B.A. candidates, only two failed. Seven of these achieved a First Class. Lillian Whitby was to be a temporary replacement for Tristram, but her talents gained her a permanent position in 1896 (*Minutes*, 2 May 1894, 77; and 4 December 1895, 99).

10 *Ring*, 19 October 1896.

11 *A*, VII, 60, "October Term 1897," 403–12, written in March 1928. For changes in attitudes towards emotions, see Micale, *Approaching Hysteria*, 3–19; and Badcock, *Essential Freud*. By the early 1900s, the idea that anorexia or depression could also be related to repressed sexuality was starting to be discussed.

12 *D*, 20 November 1897, 89. For the lists of minimum and maximum salaries at the time, see "Girls Schools with Special Regard to Salaries of Head Mistresses as Recommended by the Endowed Schools Commission," *Journal of the Women's Education Union* IV (1876), 96.

13 See *D*, 13 March 1898, 190; and 13 October 1898, 230.

14 Compare *D*, 31 October 1897, 66, with 13 November 1897, 66, and 6 October 1898, 78. Southwark was founded in the hopes of improving workers' lives, but fell into bankruptcy when workers failed to pay their rent (*Ring*, 28 May 1898). Not all workers were paupers. By 1891, educated workers, including women, were a vital and large part of the British work force in such occupations as banking and nursing (see Clara Collet, *Educated Working Women: Essays on the Economic Position of Women Workers* [London: P.S. King] 1902).

15 Firth, *Constance Louisa Maynard*, 261. See also, Carus-Wilson ed., *Westfield*, 22; and Westfield graduate Mary Butts' account of Maynard's special qualities in *The Crystal Cabinet* (London: Hodder, 1937), 252.

16 As noted in chapter 3, "The Church that [was] Girton" was Maynard's room at Girton, where the Girton Prayer Meeting was formulated. For more on Maynard's development of the S.C.M., the S.V.M.U., and the B.C.C.U. see *D*, 6 January 1900, 54; 4 May 1902, 99; 9 October 1904, 231; and Sondheimer, *Castle Adamant*, 66–8. In her *A*, VII, 61, "Lent Term 1898," 389, written in May 1929, Maynard noted, "In attendance [at the inaugural meeting of the S.C.M.] were Christian Union Students from Bedford, the Slade, University College, School of Medicine, Bushey, and 50 Mistresses from various Schools."

17 See *D*, 31 December 1904, 365; and Firth, *Constance Louisa Maynard*, 324. For more on Biblical Criticism see, for example, R.A. Riesen, *Criticism and Faith in Late Victorian England* (Lanham: George Adam Smith, 1985). Biblicism tended to focus on a broad analysis of the text rather than the meaning of words in the Bible.

18 See *A*, VII, 59, "May Term 1896," 338, 359, written in February 1928; Firth, *Constance Louisa Maynard*, 337; and Vicinus, "'One Life,'" 615.

19 *A*, VII, 59, "Lent Term 1896," 360, written in February 1928.

20 *A*, VII, 59, "Lent Term 1896," 377, written in February 1928. Westfield's Trust Deed thus firmly tied the hands of its successors (Sondheimer, *Castle Adamant*, 21).

21 In her *A*, VII, 59, "May Term 1896," 406, written in April 1928, Maynard lamented over their friendship: "We never touch on our personal relation. I sigh for it now and then, but *she* likes this better."

22 *A*, VII, 59, "May Term 1897," 407, written in April 1928.

23 See *A*, VII, 59, "May Term 1897," 411, written in April 1928. Firth did not mention Wakefield at all within the otherwise corresponding text in her biography. This absence does not surprise in light of her avoidance of discussion about Campbell, Lumsden, Gray, and even Richardson. However, as Firth wrote at the end of her work, Wakefield "was one of the four women who at different times had caused [Maynard] pain by withdrawing from an emotional relationship that she eagerly desired."

24 Helen of Troy was a character from Greek Mythology over who a ten-year war was fought (*GB*, 20 December 1885, 94). The ferocious Minotaur was an unnatural offspring of man and beast who devoured man because he had no other natural source of nourishment. For Rossetti, Dickinson and Keary, see Roden, *Same-Sex Desire in Victorian Religious Culture*, 48,

67; and Maynard, *Victorian Discourses on Sexuality and Religion*, 272–3. For Harrison, see Prins, "Greek Maenads, Victorian Spinsters," 43–81.

25 See *A*, VII, 59, "Lent Term 1896," 338, written in February 1928; and VII, 61, "October Term 1898," 430–6, written in May/June 1929. It was only in later years, Maynard claimed, that she learned the depths of Richardson's disapproval of her relationship with Wakefield.

26 *A*, VII, 63, "May Term 1899," 440–2, written in June 1929.

27 See *A*, VII, 63, "May Term 1899," 443, written in June 1929; and Barthes, *Sadel/Fourier/Loyala*. For more on the intensity and variation of the erotic see Johnson, *Why We Feel*; Fuss, *Identification Papers*; and Sedgwick, *Epistemology of Closet*, 62.

28 See *A*, VII, 63, "May Term 1899," 444, written in June 1929. Maynard had not used floral imagery to connote passion/resistance in her records before this time, or at least before her green books went missing. For more on "bloom" as female genitalia, and "fire" as Holy Spirit, see Roden, *Same-Sex Desire*, 43, 207–17; Vicinus, *Intimate Friends*, xx, 98–108; and Donoghue, *Passions Between Women*; and *We Are Michael Field* (Bath: Absolute Press, 1998). Based upon my analysis of Maynard's archives, I would challenge these authors proposition that women could better articulate their same-sex desires by the end of the century. Maynard had creatively voiced her same-sex longings through various religious and secular discourses since the early 1870s.

29 *A*, VII, 61, "October Term 1898," 430, written in June 1929.

30 See Maynard, "Postscript" (1888), 32, in *Cultivation of Intellect*. See also *D*, 20 October 1897, 226; and 10 November 1897, 237. Apparently, twenty-one institutions were preparing students for London degrees at this time. The University of London Act of 1898 stated that all schools of the University must work with established standards set by the Royal Commissions.

31 Compare *Minutes*, 8 November 1897, 265, with *D*, 13 October 1897, 77.

32 See *Minutes*, 7 June 1898, 285; and *Minutes*, 19 September 1900, 42. Italics mine.

33 See *Minutes*, 7 June 1899, 312; 12 August 1899, 322; and see also *D*, 11 June 1899, 78. "Recognized Teachers" stemmed from the formation of an Association for promoting a Teaching University for London in 1884, which sought to standardize education by better preparing students for the London degree (see Fitch, "Women," 342).

34 See *D*, 7 May 1897, 78; 7 August 1900, 99; and 10 May 1903, 200. See also Beatrice Boeke nee Cadbury to Janet Sondheimer, April 1974, Ms. 213 Special Collections, courtesy of Queen Mary University of London

Archives/Westfield College/WFD; Biss, *Reminiscences*, 12; and Firth, *Constance Louisa Maynard*, 251–2.

35 For Maynard's view of the proposed change see *GB*, 16 October 1891, 88; 1 November 1899, 99; and 20 October 1904, 3. For Cobbe see Peacock, *Writings of Frances Power Cobbe*, 264. Quote for suffrage taken from Elizabeth Robbins, *In Defence of the Militants* (London: Women's Social and Political Union, 1912). Maynard remained sceptical of some aspects of suffrage, but her ambivalence at this time likely stemmed from the Council, who disapproved of student participation, but "did not forbid it" (Sondheimer, *Castle Adamant*, 66).

36 See *D*, 23 February 1902, 43; 9 November 1907, 55; and Biss, *Reminiscences*, 1–18. The Imperial Federation League (1884) aimed at imperial political consolidation to ensure British power. Maynard, it seems, supported this view, which suggests that she had not shed her familial ties to imperialism or her classist values.

37 In *Constance Louisa Maynard*, 255, Firth noted, "She sharpened our wits and trained our manners socially … The effort was so great that to this day I know the spot where I first stood to speak 'in public'" For sports, see Biss, *Reminiscences*, 12.

38 As Sondheimer notes in *Castle Adamant*, 66–8, the later Student Christian Movement (converged S.V.M.U. and B.C.C.U.) tended to interconnect higher criticism with a broad doctrine of theology. In contrast, Maynard's views on the Atonement in *GB*, 29 December 1901, 117; and 17 April 1904, 210, seemed similar to that of Irving. For example, in *Life of Irving*, 12, 20, Fleming emphasizes Irving's intense devotion to Jesus and his unquestioning acceptance of the authority of the Bible.

39 *GB*, 1 Jan 1901, 1. As noted earlier, one wonders if this was a coincidence or if Maynard began at page 1 after destroying the earlier records.

40 *A*, VII, 64, "Switzerland, Egypt and the Holy Land, 1900," 454, written in January 1930. See also *GB*, 1 Jan 1902, 90.

41 *A*, VII, 64, "Egypt and the Holy Land, 1900," 455, written in January 1930. The esteemed Reverend Fawkes published regularly in such scholarly journals as the *Spectator* and *North British Review*. For the quote, see Firth, *Constance Louisa Maynard*, 32.

42 See *GB*, 25 March 1875, 47; 27 April 1880, 54; and *A*, VII, 64, "Egypt and the Holy Land, 1900," 456, written in January 1930. For more on the idea of the prophet see Swindburne, *Existence of God*, 40–7; and Andre Godin, *The Psychological Dynamics of Religious Experience* (Birmingham, Ala.: Religious Education Press, 1996), 10, 50.

43 See Bebbington, *Evangelicalism in Modern Britain*, 190–2; and *GB*, 31 December 1901, 3.
44 See *GB*, 31 December 1901, 3; and Firth, *Constance Louisa Maynard*, 326.
45 See deVries, "Feminism, History and Religious Cultures," in *Women, Gender and Religious Culture*, ed. Morgan and deVries, 198; and Rendall, *Origins of Modern Feminism*. See also Brown, *Death of Christian Britain*, 211, 58–87.
46 Compare *A*, VII, 64, "Switzerland, Egypt and the Holy Land, 1900," 454, written in January 1930, with Warner, *Wide, Wide World*, 568. Peter Gardella's study of American faith offers helpful parallels to the English situation. He examines various Evangelical thinkers, from those who brought sex-like ecstasy into conversion to those who explicitly read sex as a positive act in Christian marriage (*Innocent Ecstasy: How Christianity Gave America an Ethic of Sexual Pleasure* [Oxford: Oxford University Press], 1985).
47 Compare *GB*, 11 May 1901, 25–6, with *Minutes*, 12 May 1901, 74. While Maynard wrote at length about funding for Divinity, the *Minutes* reveal that the Council focussed instead on upgrading Westfield in order to get it recognized as a School of the University.
48 *GB*, 12 October 1901, 67.
49 *A*, VII, 66, "October Term 1901," 478–80, written in March 1930. Maynard aimed to train genteel Christian women at both Westfield and the London School of Medicine for Women to become medical missionaries and notable Evangelicals overseas. Meanwhile, Caroline Skeel was hired for her "expertise in History," while Marion Delf and Eleanor McDougal were deemed "assets to the science department" at Westfield (see *Minutes*, 9 July 1897, 288; 12 June 1901, 680; and 12 May 1906, 330).
50 See *GB*, 31 December 1901, 98 (she had noted something similar on 6 May 1886, 146; and 29 December 1901, 117). For more on women's particular engagement in forms of compensatory suffering due to faith see Stachniecoski, *Prosecutory Imagination*, 64.
51 See *GB*, 3 January 1902, 68; 22 January 1902, 89; and 30 January 1902, 100, for more on Maynard's concerns about trying to cease her passionate encounters with Wakefield.
52 See *GB*, 13 February 1902, 98; and 24 February 1902, 113. Odd as this may seem, some ascetic Victorians viewed sexual self-expression as a failure of character (see Maynard, *Discourses on Sexuality and Religion*, 110–11). For more on other mixed-age couple's atonement-like struggle with same-sex desire, see Vicinus' account of the aunt-niece couple Kathryn Bradley and Edith Cooper in *Intimate Friends*, 102–9.

53 *GB*, 19 February 1902, 110–12.

54 See, *GB*, 20 February 1902, 117; and for more on Maynard's thoughts on the matter see *A*, VII, 67, "Lent Term 1902," 446, written in May 1929. For Victorian views of female conditions, such as neurasthenia and hysteria, see Brumberg, *Fasting Girls*, 5; and Janet Oppenheim, *Shattered Nerves: Doctors, Patients, and Depression in Victorian England* (New York: Oxford University Press, 1991).

55 *D*, 7 May 1902, 89. The physician's task was to "add flesh to the emaciated frame of the food refuser." For more on this treatment see Sander L. Gilman, Helen King, Roy Porter, George Rousseau and Elaine Showalter, eds., *Hysteria beyond Freud* (Berkeley: University of California Press, 1993).

56 *D*, 8 July 1902, 102. Apparently, another bad symptom of neurasthenia was temperature loss (Brumberg, *Fasting Girls*, 5).

57 See *GB*, 20 February 1902, 117; 10 May 1903, 90; and *A*, VII, 67, "Lent Term 1902," 446, written in May 1929. For Ellis' views on religious-sexual impulses see Joy Dixon, "The Transformation of Religious Cultures," in *Women, Gender and Religious Cultures in Britain*, ed. Morgan and deVries, 223.

58 In "Rethinking Gendered Perversion," 139, Moore argues that sexologists rarely discussed but nonetheless classified the "female sadist" implied by the masochist scenario, which was a pathology that has been less commonly observed by present-day scholars. Yet according to Diedrick, poet Mathilde Blind was "fearless" in her praise of female sexual aggression through her depiction of women who liked giving pain to men ("My Love is a Force," 363).

59 See *GB*, 12 April 1901, 9; 17 April 1902, 12; 20 May 1902, 116; and 6 June 1902, 133.

60 *A*, VII, 67, "Lent Term 1902," 445, written in May 1929. Although Maynard was referencing a "'devil-like' curse" here, she may have known that psychiatrists after Freud suggested links between psychosexual dysfunction and conditions like anorexia nervosa and hysteria.

61 See *A*, VII, 67, "Lent Term 1902," 445, written in May 1929. Maynard was likely once again referencing psychoanalytical language here, since her thoughts echoed Freud's and others' ideas of repression. She would also mull over psychoanalysts calling her longing for Gray "a thwarted sex instinct."

62 Vicinus, "'One Life,'" 620.

63 *GB*, 20 August 1901, 46.

64 *GB*, 20 May 1902, 116.

65 *GB*, 16 April 1904, 308.

66 See Marcus, *Between Women*, 196. It makes sense that Maynard would view her relationship with Wakefield in this light, given her faith and imperialist values.

67 *GB*, 22 October 1904, 267. Mary Armitage was the granddaughter of Canon Gibbon. It seems that she was constantly by Wakefield's side until they parted in 1907.

68 *GB*, 29 September 1906, 126.

69 See *GB*, 25 March 1908, 10; and 30 December 1910, 364. Maynard summed her thoughts in a letter to Wakefield, who replied, "Your reprimand is a milestone which opens up a new life before me" (14 December 1907, 172). According to the Archives of Royal Holloway, University of London, London, Wakefield enrolled at Bedford College as a student in 1911, and then re-entered in 1914 and 1918 (Vicky Holmes, College Archivist, to Pauline Phipps, 17 December, 2010).

70 In her *A*, VII, 66, "October Term 1901," 481, written in March 1930, Maynard noted, "They [Council] wished for good solid Bible study" or, as Bebbington would explain, the broader theological approach popular at the time (*Evangelicalism in Modern Britain*, 181–90). According to the *GB*, Fawkes no longer taught Divinity due to Maynard's "severe faith" (4 October 1902, 98; and 4 January 1902, 113). Meanwhile, her diary conveyed her struggle at large: "Wrote 75 letters: Mildmay, CMS, the BCCU, and Matlock ... Very disappointing. Only got 6, and then no one came" (*D*, 18 June 1902, 78; and 12 January 1903, 88). In contrast, American Evangelicals advocated an erotic-like surrender to God (see Kathryn Lofton, "Queering Fundamentalism," 446).

71 *A*, II, 4, 8, "Young Womanhood 1871," 158, written in April 1915. Maynard aimed to place women's missionary work and roles in Evangelical conversion in the public sphere, as did some other women of the time (see deVries, "Feminism, History and Religious Cultures," 198; and Leslie Howsam, *Cheap Bibles: Nineteenth-Century Publishing and the British and Foreign Bible Society* [Cambridge: Cambridge University Press, 1991], 171–8).

72 See *GB*, 31 October 1908, 168; 31 December 1908, 253; 28 July 1908, 33; and *Minutes*, 8 October 1908, 68. For more on how intellectuals viewed the change in religious climate see Hugh McLeod, *Religion and Society in England, 1850–1914* (New York: St. Martin's Press, 1996).

73 For more on the extension of Westfield and new scholarship support see *D*, 11 May 1904, 89; 26 June 1905, 79; and Firth, *Constance Louisa Maynard*,

259–265. Maynard's contribution lay in raising staff salaries to bring them in line with Bedford, Holloway, and East London (*Minutes*, 8 March 1909, 182–184). By the 1900s, Westfield was largely comprised of the daughters of middle-class professionals, and at least one student per year received an M.A. This signified for Maynard the loss of her cozy Christian genteel family (see *College Register*, 1–73; *D*, 2 May 1912, 8; and *GB*, 3 May 1913).

74 *GB*, 6 February 1911, 142. Maynard found a piece of land the size of a field at Little Bookham in Surrey and had a good-sized cottage, which she would name "The Sundial," built on the land.

75 In her *GB*, 8 May 1913, 73, Maynard noted that her friend and Council member Lady Chapman had bluntly said, "Yes, the time is right to seek a new Mistress." For more on Maynard's resignation see *GB*, 10 October 1912, 109–12; and *Minutes*, 9 October 1912, 186.

76 *GB*, 21 May 1912, 118. After graduating in the Classics, De Selincourt worked in India and had then returned to England to take a senior position in the S.C.M. Unfortunately, De Selincourt died shortly after becoming Westfield's new Mistress (Sondheimer, *Castle Adamant*, 69).

77 See *GB*, 24 May 1913, 151. On 22 June 1913, 159, Maynard rather nastily noted, "It is sad to see her [Richardson's] power of judgment gone, and yet 'the judgments of the Lord are true and righteous altogether.'"

78 In *Constance Louisa Maynard*, 259–67, Firth correctly argues that Westfield was wronged by being described as "all pi and cant" given graduates' pursuits in many academic fields. See also Sondheimer, *Castle Adamant*, 68.

79 *GB*, 31 December 1913, 202. Apparently, Tissington Tatlow, secretary of the Student Christian Missionary, was one of the first professional theologians to deliver a Divinity lecture at Westfield on broad theological/higher criticism. The policy for the S.C.M. reflected the changing theological climate (Sondheimer, in *Castle Adamant*, 76–7, 81).

80 For Maynard's final thoughts on her "mistakes" as Mistress, see *GB*, 31 December 1913, 202.

Conclusion

1 Sonnet written in *GB*, 31 December 1927, 56.

2 *GB*, 20 December 1920, 45. Maynard spoke regularly at Belstead, Girton, and Westfield after her retirement. She assumed that everyone expected her to address faith and science.

3 An example can be seen in her *GB*, 12 July 1917, 96. Here she noted, "If we believe that God is governing the world, we must accept the Zeitgeist, for

the seed comes from Him." She maintained this sort of position until her death on 26 March 1935.

4 "Woman Waited 53 Years for Her M.A.," *Daily Mirror* (London), 16 October 1933, 4.

5 In her *GB*, 31 December 1923, 112, Maynard noted, "The result so far is seven publications and two more in the press." For more on her publication successes, see *GB*, 25 December 1925, 76. For Victorians' imagined role of prophet, see Maynard, *Victorian Discourses on Sexuality and Religion*, 201–2; Swindburne, *Existence of God*, 50; and Godin, *Dynamics of Religious Experience*, 10, 50.

6 See Constance Louisa Maynard, "Perfect Law of Liberty," which was published in religious periodicals; and Constance Louisa Maynard, *The Prophet Daniel & Other Essays* (London: Morgan and Scott, 1914). Most scholars posit that Biblicism remained core to Evangelical faith into the mid-1900s. Cheap bibles, published by the British and Foreign Bible society, were read in millions of homes (see Bebbington, *Evangelicalism in Modern Britain*, 75–105; and Howsam, *Cheap Bibles*, xiii).

7 *GB*, 31 December 1925, 23. For Maynard's recorded conversation with Campbell, see *GB*, 27 March 1872, 124; and 18 February 1872, 122. As noted in chapter 2, Campbell's incarnational-based views starkly contrasted that of Maynard's belief in the Atonement, which she still claimed to uphold in 1925 and until her death in 1935.

8 See, Bebbington, *Evangelicalism in Modern Britain*, 181–190; Heyck, *Transformation of Intellectual Life*; and Newsome, *Victorian World Picture.*

9 *A*, II, 4, 8, "Young Womanhood 1871," 158, written in April 1915; and Firth, *Constance Louisa Maynard*, 67–8.

10 For more, see for example, Hempton, *Religion and Political Culture*. For Maynard, see Firth, *Constance Louisa Maynard*, 324–5.

11 Maynard, *We Women*, 6–8.

12 In *We Women*, 130–2, Maynard explained that her quote was taken (although modified) from Gal. III: 28, 657. It is notable that Maynard was not alone in adopting this quote to challenge patriarchal, heteronormative culture. See, for example, Roden's analysis of Christina Rossetti in *Same-Sex Desire*, 48.

13 Maynard, *We Women*, 109. For more on "The Parable of the Sower," see *GB*, 8 October 1890, 214; 8 October 1923, 163; and *Cultivation of the Intellect*, 29. In *Death of Christian Britain*, 211, 58–87, Brown argues that counter to popular belief, women continued to forge Victorian-based self-identities through "patterns of religiosity" into the 1950s.

14 See *We Women*, 139. For her earlier views on suffrage see, for example, *D*, 11 June 1911, 45, where she remarked, "I like it [suffrage], but I see no hurry for it."

15 *GB*, 9 December 1923, 251. As noted in chapter 1, her father's values seemed shaped by Malthusian and Darwinist theories. For feminist Fabians see Ray Strachey, *'The Cause': A Short History of the Woman's Movement in Great Britain.* London: H.R. Allenson, 1928. Reprint, Port Washington: Kennikat Press, 1969.

16 Constance Louisa Maynard, *The Life of Dora Greenwell* (London: H.R. Allenson, 1926), 34, 66.

17 See Maynard, *We Women*, 130–2; *Greenwell*, 212; and *GB*, 19 February 1927, 104. Firth argued that these "conflicting spirits" were actually "clearer to Maynard than to Greenwell," which may be true (see *Constance Louisa Maynard*, 303). For a queer approach to the Cloister see O'Malley, "Epistemology of the Cloister," 553. O'Malley posits that some male Victorians adopted the term "Cloister" to symbolize their retreat from same-sex worldliness. Maynard linked the Cloister to her "recklessness" with college loves. Her fluid understanding of the Cloister reflects her own complex negotiation between embracing and resisting human desire. For sexology, see Bland and Doan eds., *Sexology in Culture*; and Weeks *Sexuality and Discontents*.

18 For Maynard's ongoing views on the changes at Westfield, see for example, *GB*, 25 December 1921, 154; and 25 April 1924, 21. See also *Minutes*, 28 October 1920, 23; and Sondheimer, *Castle Adamant*, 95–111.

19 See *GB*, 25 April 1924, 21; and 12 March 1926, 91. For more on Maynard's views about the impact of secularism on society and on women's higher education, see Maynard, *Then Shall We Know* (London: Society for Christian Knowledge, 1926). Maynard was not alone in her thinking as an intellectual woman. Writing a decade earlier, Frances Power Cobbe chided herself for wanting "to travel the scientific road to reach a spiritual destination" (Peacock, *Writings of Frances Power Cobbe*, 264).

20 See *GB*, 25 April 1924, 21; and 12 March 1926, 91.

21 *GB*, 17 June 1922, 187.

22 See *GB*, 8 February 1924, 123. For more of Richardson's contributions by individuals of the time see, for example, Biss, *Reminiscences*, 32; Moy-Evans to Janet Sondheimer, 3 February 1976; *Westfield Register*, 66; and Carus-Wilson ed., *Westfield College*, 43.

23 *GB*, 10 January 1926, 79. She was apparently accepting an award on behalf of Frances Dove, and had been asked to speak about her college experiences in the 1870s.

24 *GB*, 6 May 1934, 265–6.
25 See *Ring*, 6 June 1899, in which she wrote, "I feel a lack of Christianity from your letters. Here is a little sermon from Heb.11; 1, choice that others may think strange; 2, difference in what is really valuable." The Ring letter ceased shortly after this. For her ongoing lament over Divinity see *D*, 12 November 1915, 102; *GB*, 6 May 1927, 45; and 12 October 1932, 162.
26 Educational pioneers of Maynard's generation paved the way for the next generation of pioneers, who exposed existences of such social wrongs as the double standard of sexual morality, poor working conditions, and disenfranchisement (see Vicinus, *Independent Women*, 121–162; and also Patrick Scott and Pauline Fletcher, *Culture and Education in Victorian England* [Cranbury: Association University Press, 1990]).
27 See *GB*, 19 February 1919, 203; 8 June 1925, 98; and for Jim Gillet see 24 April 1920, 112–13.
28 Compare *GB*, 12 September 1920, 77, with her "little quiet outlet" at St. Leonards mentioned in *A*, V, 34, "St. Leonards School 1878," 329, written in June 1919.
29 See *GB*, 23 April 1921, 114; and 4 December 1920, 85. As noted in chapter 7, Maynard's later thoughts on evangelizing were shaped by her connection to American Evangelicals who, as Kathryn Lofton explains, "established manliness as an advertising scheme" to call on male sinners to "surrender to God" ("Queering Fundamentalism," 446). For more on women's subversion of the manly Evangelical see, for example, Douglas, *Feminization of American Culture*, 18; and Kelley, *Private Woman, Public Stage*, 285–315.
30 *GB*, 12 September 1920, 78.
31 See *GB*, 30 July 1923, 228–31; 14 April 1924, 18; and 15 July 1926, 92. These green book entries describe Gillett as sullen, angry, and finally, offhand with her. He seemed to tire of what may have been bullying on Maynard's part, and slowly disappeared from her life after completing his degree.
32 In her *GB*, 9 March 1914, 217, Maynard wrote, "There lay the sonnet he [Campbell] had sent to me on the table between us, undisguised … Had she [Fanny Campbell] just discovered it? Or did she know of it over 40 years ago?" See also *A*, VI, 35, "Summer 1880," 24, written in July 1919.
33 See *A*, I, 5, "Adolescence 1863–64," 67, written in March 1915; II, 10, "Year of Crisis, Restraint and Liberty 1872," 286, written in June 1915; VI, 35, "St. Leonards School 1880," 340, written in July 1919; VI, 47, "Lent Term 1884," 92, written in October 1926; VII, 50, "October Term 1888," 232, 236, written in June 1927; and VII, 70, "Lent Term 1902," 486, written in May 1929.

34 For Amy Mantle, compare *A*, III, 25, "My Last Term, 1875," 763, written in July 1919, with *A*, III, VII, 52, "Westfield 1886," 172–3, written in July 1926. For Mary Tait see *A*, V, 34, "St. Leonards School 1878–79," 354–5, 376, written in June 1919.

35 Although Ellis' monumental study influenced other scientists, he faced skepticism from society and had to publish subsequent volumes of *Psychology of Sex* outside of Britain (Porter and Hall, *Facts of Life*, 164–9; and John D'Emilio and Estelle Freedman, *Intimate Matters*, 302–14). For more on Stopes see, for example, Lesley Hall, "Feminist Reconfigurations of Heterosexuality in the 1920s," in *Sexology in Culture*, ed. Bland and Doan, 142–3). For debate on Maud Allen see, for example, Deborah Cohler's "Sapphism and Sedition: Producing Female Homosexuality in Great War Britain," *Journal of the History of Sexuality* 16, 1 (2007), 68–94.

36 D.H. Lawrence, *The Rainbow* (London Marshall Bros., 1915, reprint, New York: Random House), 2002. For more on the attempts to illegalize homosexual acts between women see Sheila Jeffreys, *The Spinster and Her enemies, Feminism and Sexuality 1880–1930* (London: Pandora, 1985); and Faderman, *Surpassing Love of Men*, 249.

37 *A*, VII, 44, "Westfield 1882," 3, written in August 1926. For Freud's ideas on the thwarted sex instinct see *The Standard Edition of the Complete Psychological Works of Sigmund Freud*, trans. James Strachey (New York: Hogarth Press, 1955), 45.

38 *A*, VII, 52, "Lent Term 1887," 172, written in June 1926.

39 *A*, VII, 52, "4th College Session, 1886," 174, written in May 1927.

40 *A*, III, 23, "My Years at Girton 1874," 280, written in July 1915. For debate on sexology versus psychology see Porter and Hall, *Facts of Life*, 189; Hall, *Sex, Gender and Social Change*, 108–9; Kingsley Kent, *Making Peace*, 102–3; Willis, *No More Nice Girls*, 12–14; and Teresa de Lauretis, "Freud, Sexuality, and Perversion," in *Discourses on Sexuality: From Aristotle to AIDS*, ed. Donna C. Stanton (Ann Arbor: University of Michigan Press, 1992), 216–34. Most scholars argue that psychoanalytical discourses on homosexuality had made considerable headway into Britain by the 1930s, when Ellis' work began to be dismissed.

41 *A*, VII, 53, "May Term 1892," 320, written in December 1927. Sex reformer Edward Carpenter was strongly influenced by Ellis, but he argued for a new evolutionary type, the bisexual (Weeks, *Sexuality and Its Discontents*, 123–32).

42 See *GB*, 31 December, 1901, 3; and Dixon, *Divine Feminism*, 114–15.

43 In *Sex, Gender and Social Change*, 135–7, Hall points to the example of

Virginia Woolf, whose relationship with Vita Sackville-West and vision of the third sex was celebrated in the whimsical androgyny of *Orlando*. Perhaps Maynard sympathized with some modern women's claims that life circumstances – loss of men to the Great War – led them to seek alternative life styles (see Cohler, *Citizen, Invert, Queer,* on this). After all, Maynard had sought freedom(s) during an era as distinct for its patriarchal imperialism and gender mores.

44 *A*, VII, 53, "May Term 1892," 320, written in December 1927. Maynard's particular struggle to understand her past same-sex desire as a late-Victorian can be compared to such writing as Stronach's *Newnham Friendship*; Townsend's *Memories for Friends*; and Lehmann's *Dusty Answer*. It is notable that none of these authors discussed their past intimacy with college women within the context of the new theories on sex.

45 See *GB*, 24 December 1912, 99; and 16 October 1913, 161. After 1910, Lumsden was a regular speaker at Westfield until Maynard retired in 1913. She visited Maynard perhaps twice in the 1920s, thus Maynard's comment at age eighty-five, "L is still alive at 92, but I know almost nothing of her this past 45 years," seems correct (8 February 1935, 271). Despite Maynard's criticism of Lumsden's capability at St. Leonards, such primary sources as *S.L.S. Gazette*, and Grant, McCutcheon, and Saunders, eds., *St. Leonards School*, provide glowing reports of Lumsden's leadership while Maynard is barely mentioned. One wonders if Maynard was aware of this in later life and felt justifiably wronged.

46 Maynard's green book emphasized that while Gray was "always friendly, she remained remote, almost unapproachable" (see 4 November 1901, 98; 30 December 1923, 260–1; and 15 July 1924, 92). For Maynard's later thought on Gray see 30 January 1934, 255; and *D*, 4 February 1935, 123. For changes in the churches medical-based views of homosexuality see, for example, Morgan "The Word Made Flesh," 178.

47 Maynard's feelings for Effie, while clearly class- and race-based, were also grounded in shame. For example, in her *GB*, 29 October 1912, 115, she noted, "Seeing her [Effie] dressed as a servant-maid raises a guilty storm of feeling." For more on Effie see *GB*, 12 February 1910, 76; *D*, 7 March 1913, 109; and 12 June 1914, 32. See also Firth, *Constance Louisa Maynard*, 243–5; and Walker, *Devil's Kingdom*, 145–53.

48 *GB*, 30 December 1923, 260.

49 See *GB*, 31 December 1915, 24. Quote and translation on Nietzsche taken from Leon Wurmster, "Nietzsche's War against Shame and Resentment," in Lansky and Morrison eds., *Scope of Shame*, 181 (italics mine). Wakefield had enrolled at Bedford to study Philosophy, Psychology, and History,

and according to Maynard, bragged about "loving" psychology. Vicinus notes Wakefield's interest in Nietzsche in "One Life," 620, but she does not really address the sexual aspect that seemed so important to Wakefield's denial of Maynard's faith.

50 *GB*, 18 September 1917, 80. There is no evidence in any of Maynard's records to suggest whether she read psychoanalysis herself or discussed it with anyone other than Marion Wakefield. For more on Maynard's discussions on psychoanalysis with Wakefield see, for example, *GB*, 12 December 1918, 364; and 30 December 1920, 20.

51 *A*, VII, 59 "Long Vacation 1895," 367, written in March 1928.

52 See *A*, VII, 64, "Egypt and the Holy Land 1900," 453, written in January 1930.

53 See, for example, *GB*, 24 January 1935, 55. This entry was written shortly before Maynard's death.

54 GB, 8 June 1931, 88. For more on Radclyffe Hall's novel see, for example, Lesley Hall, *Sex, Gender and Change*, 113–15. Most scholars contend that Hall's plea for homosexual tolerance was a shocking revelation to women who knew themselves different.

55 *GB*, 24 May 1934, 261.

56 *GB*, 27 May 1934, 264.

57 *GB*, 30 January 1934, 255.

58 *GB*, 8 February 1934, 256.

59 See *GB*, 1 April 1884, 98. As argued in the Introduction, my queer interpretation of Maynard differs from that of Martha Vicinus' early work. I propose that Maynard's struggle as a late-Victorian woman did not prevent her from expressing her feelings or from exploiting her position of power.

60 See A, III, 12, "My Girton Years 1874," 345, written in October 1915. Here, one can see the influence of her upbringing. She asked, "What determines the Will? It *cannot* start off without the reasonable basis of faith. Yet if we force out Feeling and Intellect, can we hope that both may yet again become present and personal and living."

61 See, for example, Willis, *No Nice Girls*, 12; Teresa Brennan, *The Interpretation of the Flesh: Freud and Femininity* (London: Routledge, 1992); and Louise Kaplan, *Female Perversions* (New York: Doubleday Dell Publishing, 1991).

62 *D*, 4 February 1935, 123. Even so, it seems curious that Maynard did not view her relationship with Gray in quite the same way that she did Wakefield. If Maynard had, one presumes she would not have offered Gray her love poems.

63 *A*, I, 3, "Adolescence 1863–64," 41, written in February 1915. For more on Freud see Badcock, *Essential Freud*, 74–6; and for female masochism see

Freud, *Complete Psychological Works*, 19, 159–70. Later psychoanalytic writers, such as Helene Deutsch, elaborated on Freud's assumption about the naturalness of female masochism (Deutsch, "'Feminine' Masochism and Frigidity," 48–61).

64 In her *GB*, 22 May 1905, 92, for example, Maynard confessed, "Often I have talked about self-denial ... It is not voluntary, I would break it if I could." For more on sexologists' interconnection of masochism, sadism, gender, and perversion in the late 1800s see Moore, "Rethinking Gendered Perversion," 138. For discussion on suffering as part of the history of Western Christian culture in general see, for example, Foucault, *History of Sexuality*; Maynard, *Victorian Discourses on Sexuality and Religion*, 34–7; and Bullough et al., "Sadism, Masochism and History," 49, 63–82.

65 *GB*, 1 January 1905, 1.

66 See Butler, *Gender Trouble*, vii; and for other examples see, for example, Doan, *Disturbing Practices*; and Morgan and deVries eds., *Women, Gender and Religious Cultures*.

67 For discussion on life writing see, for example, Ware, "Writing Women's Lives"; Brodzki and Schenck, *Life/Lines*; and Bell and Yalom, eds., *Revealing Lives*. As noted earlier, bringing an obscure woman to wider attention is one goal of feminist biography and of women's history in general. Writing about Maynard's life revealed to this researcher that an analysis of a past life is always open to multiple interpretations.

68 For more on Maynard's struggle see Phipps, "An Atonement," and "Faith, Desire, and Sexual Identity," 265–86.

Selected Bibliography

Unpublished Primary Sources

Boeke, Beatrice nee Cadbury to Janet Sondheimer, April 1974, Ms. 213 Special Collections, Queen Mary University of London Archives, London.

Girton Review, 1875–1881. Special Collections, Girton College Archives, Cambridge.

Maynard, Constance Louisa. Green Books, 1866–1935. Special Collections, Queen Mary University of London Archives, London. Copies of Maynard's unpublished personal documents are also available on microfilm at Wayne State University, Detroit, Michigan and the University of Toronto, Toronto, Ontario. In May, 2012, Maynard's green book and autobiography were digitized at Queen Mary, University of London Archives. For access, visit, http://www.library.qmul.ac.uk/archives/digital/constance_maynard.

– Diary, 1886–1935. Special Collections, Queen Mary University of London Archives, London.

– Unpublished Autobiography, 1915–1927. Special Collections, Queen Mary University of London Archives, London.

– Life of Stephanë: 1888–1915, vols. 1–6. Special Collections, Queen Mary University of London Archives, London.

– "The Inception of Westfield College," 1881. Special Collections, Queen Mary University of London Archives, London.

– Budget Letters, 1887–1899. Special Collections, Queen Mary University of London Archives, London.

Minutes of Council. Special Collections, Queen Mary University of London Archives, London.

Richardson, Anne W. "Notes on the history of Westfield College up to 1913." Special Collections, Queen Mary University of London Archives, London: 1–23.

St. Leonards School Gazette. Special Collections, St. Leonards School Archives, St. Andrews.

St. Leonards School Register. Special Collections, St. Leonards School Archives, St. Andrews.

Westfield College Register. Special Collections, Queen Mary University of London Archives, London.

Westfield College Alumnae, Reminiscences and Memorabilia. Special Collections, Queen Mary University of London Archives, London.

Primary Sources

Alger, William Rounsville. *The Friendships of Women*, 10th ed. Boston: Roberts Brothers, 1882.

Biss, Irene. *Reminiscences 1907–1911*. London: Hodder, 1921.

Burstall, Sara. *Retrospect and Prospect: Sixty Years of Women's Education*. London: Longmans Green, 1933.

Butts, Mary. *The Crystal Cabinet*. London: Hodder, 1937.

Clarke, Edward. *Sex in Education*. Boston: James Osgood, 1873.

Cavendish, Caroline. *Aims for Higher Education*. London: Simmons and Botten, 1881.

Davies, Emily. *Thoughts on Some Questions Relating to Women, 1860–1908*. Cambridge: Bowes and Bowes, 1910. Reprint, New York: Kraus, 1971.

Dove, Jane Frances. *Work and Play in Girls' Schools*. London: Hodder, 1901.

Ellis, Havelock. *Sexual Inversion, Studies in the Psychology of Sex Volume* II, 3rd ed. Philadelphia: F.A. Davies, 1915.

Faithfull, Lillian. *You And I: Saturday Talks At Cheltenham*. London: Chatto and Windus, 1927.

Fitch, J.G. "Women and the Universities." *Contemporary Review* 58 (1890): 333–354.

Fleming, James. *The Life and Writings of the Rev. Edward Irving*. London: Marshall, 1823.

Gibson, Emily. *Some Memories for her Friends*. London: Hodder, 1903.

Girton College Register, 1869–1946. Cambridge: Privately Published for Girton College, 1948.

Grant, Julia M., Katherine H. McCutcheon, and Ethel F. Sanders. *St. Leonards School, 1877–1927*. London: Oxford University Press, 1927.

Gray, Frances Ralph. *Gladly, Gladly*. London: Hodder, 1923.

Irving, Edward. "On the Humanity of Christ." *The Morning Watch*, 1 (1829): 400–421.

Layard, George Somes. *Mrs Lynn Linton: Her Life, Letters, and Opinions.* London: Methuen, 1901.
Lister, Anne. *I Know My Own Heart: The Diaries of Anne Lister, 1791–1840*, ed. Helena Whitbread. London: Routlege, 1988.
Lumsden, Louisa Innes. *Yellow Leaves: Memories of a Long Life*. Edinburgh: William Blackwood, 1933.
Maitland, Agnes. "The Student Life of Women in Halls of Residence." *National Union of Women Workers* (1894): 100–102.
Maudsley, Henry. "Sex in Mind and Education." *Fortnightly Review* 21 (1874): 466–483.
Maynard, Constance Louisa. *Between College Terms*. London: James Nisbet, 1910.
– *The Cultivation of the Intellect*. London: Westfield College, 1888.
– "From Early Victorian Schoolroom to University: Some Personal Experiences." *Nineteenth Century* 76 (1914): 1060–1073.
– *The Life of Dora Greenwell*. London: H.R. Allenson, 1926.
– *We Women: A Golden Hope*. London: Morgan and Scott, 1913.
Mulock Craik, Dinah. *A Woman's Thoughts about Women*. London: Hurst and Blackett, 1858.
Saunders, Frederick. *About Women, Love and Marriage*. London: Hodder, 1868.
Simcox Edith. "The Capacity of Women." *Nineteenth Century* 22 (1887): 391–402.
Stronach, Alice. *A Newnham Friendship*. London: Blackie and Son, 1901.

Secondary Sources: Books and Chapters of Books

Barthes, Roland. *Sadel/Fourier/Loyala*. Translated by Richard Miller. New York: Hill & Wang, 1976.
Bebbington, D.W. *Evangelicalism in Modern Britain: A History from the 1730s to the 1980s*. Grand Rapids: Baker Books, 1989.
Bell, Rudolf. *Holy Anorexia*. Chicago: University of Chicago Press, 1985.
Bell, Susan Groag, and Marilyn Yalom. *Revealing Lives: Autobiography, Biography and Gender*. Albany: New York Press, 1990.
Bland, Lucy, and Laura Doan, eds. *Sexology in Culture: Labelling Bodies and Desires*. Chicago: University of Chicago Press, 1998.
Bradbrook, M.C. *That Infidel Place*. London: Chatto and Windus, 1969.
Brennan, Teresa. *The Interpretation of the Flesh: Freud and Femininity*. London: Routledge, 1992.
Brodozki, Bella, and Celeste Schenck. *Life/Lines Theorizing Women's Autobiography*. Ithaca: Cornell University Press, 1988.

Brumberg, Joan Jacobs. *Fasting Girls: The Emergence of Anorexia Nervosa as a Modern Disease*. Cambridge: Harvard University Press, 1988.

Brown, Callum. *The Death of Christian Britain*. London: Routledge, 2001.

Bullough, Vern, Dwight Dixon, and Joan Dixon. "Sadism, Masochism and History, or when is Behaviour Sado-Masochistic?" In *Sexual Knowledge, Sexual Science*, ed. Roy Porter and Mikulas (Cambridge: Cambridge University Press, 1994): 63–82.

Butler, A. *Butler's Lives of the Saints*, new rev. ed. Herbert Thurston and Donald Attwater, 4 Vols. Reprint, New York: R.J. Kennedy and Sons, 1962.

Butler, Judith. *Gender Trouble*. New York: Routledge, Chapman and Hall, 1990.

Bynum, Caroline Walker. *Holy Feast and Holy Fast: The Religious Significance of Food to Medieval Women*. Berkeley: University of California Press, 1988.

Carus-Wilson, Eleanor, ed. *Westfield College, University of London, 1882–1932*. London: Favil Press, 1932.

D'Emilio, John and Estelle Freedman. *Intimate Matters*. New York: Harper and Row Publishers, 1988.

Davidoff, Leonore and Catharine Hall. *Family Fortunes: Men and Women of the English Middle Class, 1780–1850*. Chicago: The University of Chicago Press, 1991.

De Lauretis, Teresa. "Freud, Sexuality, and Perversion." In *Discourses on Sexuality: From Aristotle to AIDS*, ed. Donna C. Stanton (Ann Arbor: University of Michigan Press, 1992): 216–34.

– *The Practice of Love: Lesbian Sexuality and Perverse Desire*. London: Macmillan, 1994.

deVries, Jacqueline. "More Than Paradoxes To Offer." In *Women, Religion and Sexual Cultures*, ed. Morgan and deVries (New York; Routledge, 2010): 189–210.

Dixon, Joy. *Divine Feminism: Theosophy and Feminism in England*. Baltimore: John Hopkins University Press, 2001.

– "The Transformation of Religious Cultures." In *Women, Religion and Sexual Cultures*, ed. Morgan and deVries (New York; Routledge, 2010): 211–30.

Doan, Laura. "'Acts of Female Indecency': Sexology's Intervention in Legislating Lesbianism." In *Sexology in Culture*, ed. Lucy and Laura Doan (Chicago: University of Chicago Press, 1998): 199–213.

– *Disturbing Practices: History, Sexuality, and Women's Experiences of Modern War*. Chicago: University of Chicago Press, 2013.

Donohue, Emma. *Passions Between Women*. London: Harper Collins, 1993.

Faderman, Lillian. *Surpassing the Love of Men: Romantic Friendship and Love between Women from the Renaissance to the Present*. New York: William Morrow, 1981.

Firth, Catherine B. *Constance Louisa Maynard: Mistress of Westfield College*. London: George Allen and Unwin, 1949.

Foucault, Michel. *The History of Sexuality, Volume 1: An Introduction*. Translated by Robert Hurley. New York: Pantheon Books, 1985.

Franklin, Stephen T. *Speaking from the Depths*. Grand Rapids, Michigan: William B. Erdman, 1990.

Freud, Sigmund. *Works of Freud*. Translated by James Strachey. London: Hogarth Press, 1978.

– *The Standard Edition of the Complete Psychological Works of Sigmund Freud*. Translated by Alan Tyson. London: Hogarth Press, 1955.

– *Three Essays on the Theory of Sexuality*. Translated by James Strachey. New York: Basic Books, 1962.

Fuss, Diana. *Identification Papers*. New York: Routledge, 1995.

Gallop, Jane. *Feminist Accused of Sexual Harassment*. Durham: Public Planet Books, 1997.

Giddens, Anthony. *The Transformation of Intimacy*. Cambridge: Polity Press, 1992.

Glasgow, Joanne. "What's a Nice Lesbian like You Doing in the Church of Torquemada? Radclyffe Hall and Other Catholic Converts." In *Lesbian Texts and Contexts: Radical Revisions*, ed. Karla Jay and Joanne Glasgow (New York: New York University Press, 1990): 241–54.

Gorham, Deborah. *The Victorian Girl and the Feminine Ideal*. Bloomington: Indiana University Press, 1982.

– *Vera Brittain: A Feminist Life*. Cambridge: Blackwell Publishing, 1996.

Godin, Andre. *The Psychological Dynamics of Religious Experience*. Birmingham, Alabama: Religious Education Press, 1996.

Griffiths, Paul. *What Emotions Really Are*. Chicago: University of Chicago Press, 1997.

Hall, Lesley. "Feminist Reconfigurations of Heterosexuality in the 1920s." In *Sexology in Culture*, ed. Lucy Bland and Laura Doan (Chicago: University of Chicago Press, 1998): 135–49.

Hempton, David. *Religion and Political Culture in Britain and Ireland*. Cambridge: Cambridge University Press, 1996.

Heyck, T.W. *Transformation of Intellectual Life in Victorian England*. Chicago: Lyceum Books, 1982.

Higginbotham, Ann R. "Respectable Sinners: Salvation Army Rescue Work with Unmarried Mothers." In *Religion in the Lives of English Women*, ed. Gail Malmgreen (Indianapolis: Indiana University Press, 1986): 216–33.

Hilton, Boyd. *The Age of Atonement: The Influence of Evangelicalism on Social and Economic Thought, 1785–1865*. Oxford: Clarendon Press, 1988.

Howsam, Leslie. *Cheap Bibles: Nineteenth-Century Publishing and the British and Foreign Bible Society*. Cambridge: Cambridge University Press, 1991.

Jankowski, Theodora. *Pure Resistance: Queer Virginity in Early Modern English Drama.* Philadelphia: University of Pennsylvania Press, 2000.

Jones, Gareth Stedman. *Outcast London: A Study in the Relationship Between Classes in Victorian Society.* London: Penguin Books, 1971.

Kanner, Penny. *Women in English Social History 1800–1914: A Guide to Research, Vol. II.* London: Garland Publishing, 1988.

Kaplan, Louise. *Female Perversions.* New York: Doubleday Dell Publishing, 1991.

Lansky, Melvin R. and Andrew P. Morrison, eds. *The Widening Scope of Shame.* Hillsdale: The Analytic Press, 1997.

Macaulay, Julia S. A., ed. *St. Leonards School 1877–1977.* Glasgow: Blackie and Son, 1979.

Malmgreen, Gail, ed. *Religion in the Lives of English Women, 1760–1930.* Indianapolis: Indiana University Press, 1986.

Marcus, Sharon. *Between Women: Friendship, Desire, and Marriage in Victorian England.* Princeton: Princeton University Press, 2007.

Marcus, Steven. *The Other Victorians: A Study of Sex and Pornography in Mid-nineteenth-Century England.* New York: Basic Books, 1966.

Maynard, John. *Victorian Discourses on Sexuality and Religion.* Cambridge: Cambridge University Press, 1993.

McCrone, Kathleen E. *Playing the Game: Sport and the Physical Emancipation of English Women, 1870–1914.* Lexington: University Press of Kentucky, 1988.

McWilliams-Tullberg, Rita. *Women at Cambridge: A Men's University-Though of a Mixed Type.* London: Victor Gollancz, 1975.

Melnyk, Julie, ed. *Women's Theology in Nineteenth-Century Britain: Transfiguring the Faith of Their Fathers.* New York: Garland, 1998.

Micale, Mark, *Approaching Hysteria: Disease and its Interpretations.* Princeton: Princeton University Press, 1995.

Morgan, Sue. "The Word Made Flesh." In *Women, Religion and Sexual Cultures*, ed. Morgan and deVries (New York: Routledge, 2010): 159–87.

Newsome, David. *The Victorian World Picture: Perceptions and Introspection in an Age of Change.* New Brunswick: Rutgers University Press, 1997.

Oppenheim, Janet. *Shattered Nerves: Doctors, Patients, and Depression in Victorian England.* New York: Oxford University Press, 1991.

Peacock, Sandra. *The Theological and Ethical Writings of Frances Power Cobbe, 1822–1904.* New York: Edwin Mellen Press, 2002.

Phipps, Pauline. "The Symbolic Body of the Historical Subject." In *Literary Texts and the Arts*, ed. Corrado Federici and Esther Raventos-Pons (New York: Peter Lang, 2003): 163–74.

Porter, Roy and Lesley Hall. *The Facts of Life: The Creation of Sexual Knowledge in Victorian Britain, 1650–1950.* New Haven: Yale University Press, 1995.

Prins, Yopie. "Greek Maenads, Victorian Spinsters." In *Victorian Sexual Dissidence*, ed. Richard Dellamora (Chicago: The University of Chicago Press 1999): 43–81.

Roden, Frederick S. *Same-Sex Desire in Victorian Religious Culture*. Basingstoke: Palgrave MacMillan, 2002.

Sedgwick, Eve Kosofsky. *Epistemology of the Closet*. Berkeley and Los Angeles: University of California Press, 1990.

Showalter, Elaine. *The Female Malady: Women, Madness, and English Culture, 1830–1980.* New York: Pantheon Books, 1985.

Sondheimer, Janet. *Castle Adamant in Hampstead: A History of Westfield College 1882–1982.* London: Westfield College, 1983.

Stachniewski, John. *The Prosecutory Imagination: English Puritanism and the Literature of Religious Despair*. Oxford: Oxford University Press, 1991.

Strachey, Ray. *'The Cause': A Short History of the Woman's Movement in Great Britain.* London: H.R. Allenson, 1928. Reprint, Port Washington: Kennikat Press, 1969.

Swindburne, Richard. *The Existence of God*. Oxford: Clarendon Press, 1979.

Tosh, John. *A Man's Place: Masculinity and the Middle-Class Home in Victorian England*. New Haven: Yale University Press, 1999.

Traub, Valerie. *The Renaissance of Lesbianism in Early Modern England.* Cambridge: Cambridge University Press, 2002.

Vanita, Ruth. *Sappho and the Virgin Mary: Same-Sex Love and the English Literary Imagination*. New York: Columbia University Press, 1996.

Vicinus, Martha. *Independent Women: Work and Community for Single Women 1850–1920.* London: Virago Press, 1985.

– *Intimate Friends: Women Who Loved Women, 1778–1928*. Chicago: University of Chicago Press, 2004.

Walker, Pamela J. *Pulling the Devil's Kingdom Down: the Salvation Army in Victorian Britain*. Berkeley: University of California Press, 2001.

Walkowitz, Judith. *City of Dreadful Delight: Narratives of Sexual Danger in Late-Victorian Britain*. Chicago: University of Chicago Press, 1991.

Weeks, Jeffrey. *Sex, Politics and Society*. New York: Longman Group, 1981.

– *Sexuality and its Discontents: Meanings, Myths and Modern Sexualities*. New York: Routledge, 1985.

Willis, Ellen. *No More Nice Girls.* Hanover: Wesleyan University Press, 1992.

Wurmster, Leon. "Nietzsche's War against Shame and Resentment." In *The Widening Scope of Shame*, ed. Melvin R. Lansky and P. Morrisson (Hillsdale: The Analytic Press, 1997): 181–203.

Secondary Sources: Articles

Argersinger, Jana L. "Family Embraces: The Unholy Kiss and Authorial Relations in *The Wide, Wide World." American Literature* 74, 2 (2002): 251–85.

Diggs, Marlene. "'Romantic Friends or a Different Race of Creatures'? The Representation Of Lesbian Pathology In Nineteenth-Century America." *Feminist Studies* 21, 2 (1995): 317–40.

Duggan, Lisa. "The Trials of Alice Mitchel: Sensationalism, Sexology and the Lesbian Subject in Turn-of-the-Century America." *Signs* 18, 4 (1993): 791–813.

Carter, Julian. "On Mother-Love: History, Queer Theory, and Nonlesbian Identity." *Journal of the History of Sexuality* 14, 1/2 (2005): 107–38.

Clark, Anna. "Twilight Moments." *Journal of the History of Sexuality,* 14 1/2 (2005): 139–60.

Cohler, Deborah. "Sapphism and Sedition: Producing Female Homosexuality in Great War Britain." *Journal of the History of Sexuality* 16, 1 (2007): 68–94.

Crozier, Ivan. "Philosophy in the English Boudoir: Havelock Ellis, Love and Pain, and Sexological Discourse in Algophobia." *Journal of the History of Sexuality* 13, 3 (2004): 275–305.

Diedrick, James. '"My Love is a Force that will Force you to Care': Subversive Sexuality in Mathilde Blind's Dramatic Monologues." *Victorian Poetry* 40, 4 (2002): 359–86.

Duggan, Lisa. "The Trials of Alice Mitchel: Sensationalism, Sexology and the Lesbian Subject in Turn-of-Century America." *Feminist Studies* 21, 4 (1995): 791–813.

Flint, Kate. "The 'hour of pink twilight': Lesbian Poetics and Queer Encounters on the Fin-de-siècle Street." *Victorian Studies* 51, 4 (2009): 687–712.

Freedman, Estelle B. "'The Burning of letters Continues': Elusive Identities and the Historical Construction." *Journal of Women's History* 9, 4 (1998): 181–99.

Hamman, Jaco. "The Rod of Discipline: Masochism, Sadism, and the Judeo-Christian Religion," *Journal of Religion and Health* 39, 4 (2000): 319–27.

Hilliard, David. "Unenglish and Unmanly: Anglo-Catholicism and Homosexuality." *Victorian Studies* 25, 2 (1982): 181–210.

Lofton, Kathryn. "Queering Fundamentalism: John Balcom Shaw and the Sexuality of a Protestant Orthodoxy." *Journal of the History of Sexuality* 17, 3 (2008): 439–68.

Marcus, Sharon. "Queer Theory for Everyone: A Review Essay." *Signs: Journal of Women in Culture and Society* 31, 1 (2005): 191–218.

Mayhall, Laura. "Did the Victorians Accept Female Marriage?" *Victorian Studies* 50, 1 (2007): 75–80.

Moore, Lisa. "'Something More Tender Still Than Friendship': Romantic Friendship in Early-Nineteenth-Century England." *Feminist Studies* 18, 3 (1992): 499–521.

Moore, Alison. "Rethinking Gendered Perversion and Degeneration in Visions of Sadism and Masochism, 1886-1930." *Journal of the History of Sexuality* 18, 1 (2009): 139–63.

O'Malley, Patrick R. "Epistemology of the Cloister: Victorian England's Queer Catholicism." *GLQ: A Journal of Lesbian and Gay Studies* 15, 4 (2009): 532–64.

Partner, Nancy. "No Sex, No Gender." *Speculum* 68, 2 (1993): 436–42.

Pederson, Joyce Senders. "Schoolmistresses and Headmistresses: Elites and Education in Nineteenth-Century England." *Journal of British Studies* 15 (1975): 135–62.

Phipps, Pauline. "Faith, Desire, and Sexual Identity: Constance Maynard's Atonement for Passion." *Journal of the History of Sexuality* 18, 2 (2009): 265–86.

Rich, Adrienne. "Compulsory Heterosexuality and Lesbian Existence." *Signs* 5, 4 (1980): 631–790.

Rupp, Leila J. "Imagine My Surprise: Women's Relationships in Historical Perspective." *Frontiers* 5 (1980): 61–70.

– "Toward a Global History of Same-Sex Sexuality." *Journal of the History of Sexuality* 10, 2 (2001): 287–302.

Smith-Rosenberg, Carroll. "The Female World of Love and Ritual: Relations between Women in Nineteenth Century America." *Signs* 1, 1 (1975): 1–29.

Stearns, Peter. "Girls, Boys, and Emotions: Redefinitions and Historical Change." *Journal of American History* 22 (1993): 36–73.

Vicinus, Martha. "'One Life to Stand Beside Me': Emotional Conflicts in First-Generation College Women in England." *Feminist Studies* 8, 3 (1982): 603–27.

– "Distance and Desire: English Boarding-School Friendships." *Signs* 9, 4 (1984): 600–22.

– "'They Wonder To Which Sex I Belong:' The Historical Roots of the Modern Lesbian Identity." *Feminist Studies* 18, 3 (1992): 467–99.

– "The Gift of Love: Nineteenth-Century Religion and Lesbian Passion." *Nineteenth-Century Contexts* 23, 2 (2001): 241–64.

Vickery, Amanda. "Golden Age to Separate Spheres?: A Review of the Categories and Chronologies of English Women's History." *Historical Journal* 36, 2(1993): 383–414.

Wald, Lillian. "Smashing: Women's Relationships Before the Fall." *Chrysalis* 8 (1979): 17–27.

Index

STUDIES IN GENDER AND HISTORY

General editors: Franca Iacovetta and Karen Dubinsky

1 Suzanne Morton, *Ideal Surroundings: Domestic Life in a Working-Class Suburb in the 1920s*
2 Joan Sangster, *Earning Respect: The Lives of Working Women in Small-Town Ontario, 1920–1960*
3 Carolyn Strange, *Toronto's Girl Problem: The Perils and Pleasures of the City, 1880–1930*
4 Sara Z. Burke, *Seeking the Highest Good: Social Service and Gender at the University of Toronto, 1888–1937*
5 Lynne Marks, *Revivals and Roller Rinks: Religion, Leisure, and Identity in Late- Nineteenth-Century Small-Town Ontario*
6 Cecilia Morgan, *Public Men and Virtuous Women: The Gendered Languages of Religion and Politics in Upper Canada, 1791–1850*
7 Mary Louise Adams, *The Trouble with Normal: Postwar Youth and the Making of Heterosexuality*
8 Linda Kealey, *Enlisting Women for the Cause: Women, Labour, and the Left in Canada, 1890–1920*
9 Christina Burr, *Spreading the Light: Work and Labour Reform in Late-Nineteenth-Century Toronto*
10 Mona Gleason, *Normalizing the Ideal: Psychology, Schooling, and the Family in Postwar Canada*
11 Deborah Gorham, *Vera Brittain: A Feminist Life*
12 Marlene Epp, *Women without Men: Mennonite Refugees of the Second World War*
13 Shirley Tillotson, *The Public at Play: Gender and the Politics of Recreation in Postwar Ontario*
14 Veronica Strong-Boag and Carole Gerson, *Paddling Her Own Canoe: The Times and Texts of E. Pauline Johnson (Tekahionwake)*
15 Stephen Heathorn, *For Home, Country, and Race: Constructing Gender, Class, and Englishness in the Elementary School, 1880–1914*
16 Valerie J. Korinek, *Roughing It in the Suburbs: Reading* Chatelaine *Magazine in the Fifties and Sixties*
17 Adele Perry, *On the Edge of Empire: Gender, Race, and the Making of British Columbia, 1849–1871*
18 Robert A. Campbell, *Sit Down and Drink Your Beer: Regulating Vancouver's Beer Parlours, 1925–1954*
19 Wendy Mitchinson, *Giving Birth in Canada, 1900–1950*

20 Roberta Hamilton, *Setting the Agenda: Jean Royce and the Shaping of Queen's University*
21 Donna Gabaccia and Franca Iacovetta, eds, *Women, Gender, and Transnational Lives: Italian Workers of the World*
22 Linda Reeder, *Widows in White: Migration and the Transformation of Rural Women, Sicily, 1880–1920*
23 Terry Crowley, *Marriage of Minds: Isabel and Oscar Skelton Reinventing Canada*
24 Marlene Epp, Franca Iacovetta, and Frances Swyripa, eds, *Sisters or Strangers? Immigrant, Ethnic, and Racialized Women in Canadian History*
25 John G. Reid, *Viola Florence Barnes, 1885–1979: A Historian's Biography*
26 Catherine Carstairs, *Jailed for Possession: Illegal Drug Use Regulation and Power in Canada, 1920–1961*
27 Magda Fahrni, *Household Politics: Montreal Families and Postwar Reconstruction*
28 Tamara Myers, *Caught: Montreal Girls and the Law, 1869–1945*
29 Jennifer A. Stephen, *Pick One Intelligent Girl: Employability, Domesticity, and the Gendering of Canada's Welfare State, 1939–1947*
30 Lisa Chilton, *Agents of Empire: British Female Migration to Canada and Australia, 1860s–1930*
31 Esyllt W. Jones, *Influenza 1918: Disease, Death, and Struggle in Winnipeg*
32 Elise Chenier, *Strangers in Our Midst: Sexual Deviancy in Postwar Ontario*
33 Lara Campbell, *Respectable Citizens: Gender, Family, and Unemployment in the Great Depression, Ontario, 1929–1939*
34 Katrina Srigley, *Breadwinning Daughters: Young Working Women in a Depression-era city, 1929–1939*
35 Maureen Moynagh with Nancy Forestell, eds., *Documenting First Wave Feminisms, Volume 1: Transnational Collaborations and Crosscurrents*
36 Mona Oikawa, *Cartographies of Violence: Women, Memory, and the Subject(s) of the "Internment"*
37 Karen Flynn, *Moving beyond Borders: A History of Black Canadian and Caribbean Women in the Diaspora*
38 Karen Balcom, *The Traffic in Babies: Cross Border Adoption and Baby-Selling Between the United States and Canada, 1930–1972*

39 Nancy M. Forestell with Maureen Moynagh, eds., *Documenting First Wave Feminisms, Volume II: Canada – National and Transnational Contexts*
40 Patrizia Gentile and Jane Nicholas, eds., *Contesting Bodies and Nation in Canadian History*
41 Suzanne Morton, *Wisdom, Justice and Charity: Canadian Social Welfare through the life of Jane B. Wisdom, 1884–1975*
42 Jane Nicholas, *The Modern Girl: Feminine Modernities, the Body, and Commodities in the 1920s*
43 Pauline A. Phipps, *Constance Maynard's Passions: Religion, Sexuality, and an English Educational Pioneer, 1849–1935*

www.ingramcontent.com/pod-product-compliance
Lightning Source LLC
LaVergne TN
LVHW040151080826
844660LV00014B/923/J

* 9 7 8 1 4 4 2 6 5 0 3 3 6 *